Papaji

∽

Interviews

Sri Ramana Maharshi

Papaji

~

Interviews

EDITED BY

DAVID GODMAN

AVADHUTA FOUNDATION

Cover photo: *Bhakti* (taken during *Summa Iru* interview)
Cover design: The Design Network, Makawao, HI
Interior design: Sara Patton, Wailuku, HI
Photo p. 66 © James Lemkin Architectural Photography

ISBN 0-9638022-0-8

Library of Congress Catalog Card #93-072707

Contents

Preface

A few months ago the first edition of *Papaji* was brought out. Its five sections contained interviews and articles on various aspects of Papaji's life and teachings. Because it was produced rather hurriedly to meet a deadline, it contained an unacceptably large amount of printing mistakes. Soon after its publication a decision was taken to bring out a new version which would be more professionally produced.

Papaji himself decided to eliminate some of the material which had been included in the first edition, and he also asked that several new interviews and one new article be included. He chose these interviews himself, decided in which order they should be printed, and went through the final draft very carefully, making corrections in several places.

British spelling and punctuation have been used throughout the book since Poonjaji was brought up in a part of the world where these are the norm. There is a Glossary at the end of the book which gives explanations of all the undefined technical terms and little-known names which appear in the text.

Papaji wanted this new version to be brought out as quickly as possible. To conform to his wishes, many people have put in long hours to ensure that the work was done quickly and efficiently. I would like to thank all of the following for their assistance in editing, transcribing, typing and proof-reading: Gabi, Richa, Gurupad, Kerry, Nadhia, Chandi Devi, and Rama.

– DAVID GODMAN
LUCKNOW, INDIA
1 JUNE, 1993

About the Interviewers

David Godman has been living and working in India at the ashram of Sri Ramana Maharshi for the last seventeen years. He is the compiler and editor of *Be As You Are*, one of the most widely-read books on Sri Ramana's teachings. He is also the author of *No Mind – I am the Self: The Lives and Teachings of Sri Lakshmana Swamy and Mathru Sri Sarada*.

Catherine Ingram is the author of *In the Footsteps of Gandhi* and a forthcoming book entitled *The Journey Home*. Ms. Ingram began vipassana meditation practice in 1974 and co-founded the Insight Meditation Society in Barre, Massachusetts in 1976. She met Poonjaji in Lucknow in January, 1992 and conducted this interview over the following six weeks. It originally appeared in a slightly different form in the September/October 1992 issue of *Yoga Journal*.

Wes Nisker is a renowned radio news journalist based in the San Francisco Bay area. He leads workshops in 'crazy wisdom' and is the author of the book, *Crazy Wisdom*. His forthcoming book, *The Millenium and Me*, is a semi-autobiographical story of his life in the subcultures of America. Wes is co-editor of the Buddhist journal, *The Inquiring Mind*, which featured a longer version of this interview in its Fall 1992 issue. He has been a vipassana practitioner since 1970. This interview was conducted in Lucknow in February 1992.

Shanti Devi was born in France. After travelling extensively in Africa she ended up in its southernmost tip and stayed there for ten years. She now resides in Lucknow.

Henner Ritter is a medical doctor and psychotherapist. He leads the 'Padma' centre in Stuttgart, Germany, and conducts groups and seminars on a wide variety of subjects.

Jeff Greenwald is the author of *Mr. Raja's Neighborhood – Letters from Nepal* (John Daniel, publisher) and *Shopping For Buddhas* (Harper San Francisco). His work has appeared in the *New Age Journal*, *Whole Earth Review*, *Washington Post*, and many other magazines and newspapers. He lives in Oakland, California.

Ron Stark and **Henry Baer** are both vipassana meditators who practise dentistry in California. They travelled to India in March, 1990 and conducted this interview with Poonjaji in New Delhi.

Chokyi Nyima Rimpoche teaches Westerners Tibetan Buddhism in Kathmandu. He is recognised as a *tulku*, that is, he is the incarnation of a Lama who has taught the *Dharma* through several successive births. He is the author of *Union of Mahamudra and Dzogchen* and *The Bardo Guide Book*. The conversation took place at the Ka-Nying Shedrup Ling Monastery in Nepal.

Rama Crowell was educated at Syracuse and Columbia Universities in New York, U.S.A. After graduating with an M.A. in Classical Philology he came on a pilgrimage to India. From 1974 to 1978 he lived as a *sadhu*, studying Sanskrit and Indian philosophy. During this period he visited many saints and holy places. He returned to India in 1990 and now lives in Lucknow with his wife, Bhakti. They both study at Lucknow University and attend satsangs at the feet of the Master.

Papaji

~

Interviews

(l-r) Papaji, Madhukar, and David Godman

The following chapter is from *The Power of the Presence*, one of David Godman's forthcoming books. Though it is a first-person account, it was not actually written by Papaji himself. It was put together by David. Papaji later checked it to satisfy himself that it was a reliable account of his life.

H. W. L. Poonja

by David Godman

y earliest memory is of a striking experience which occurred when I was about eight years old. The year was 1919. The British, having recently triumphed in the First World War, had given all schoolchildren a one month holiday so that they could join in the victory celebrations. They even gave us a little badge to wear to commemorate the victory. We were living in Faisalabad at the time, in a part of the Punjab that is now in Pakistan. My mother decided that this unscheduled vacation would be an ideal time to go and visit some of our relatives who lived in Lahore. The visit must have taken place in the summer of that year because I distinctly remember that mangoes were in season at the time.

One evening, while we were all sitting in my relative's house in Lahore, someone started to prepare a mango, milk and almond drink for everyone. It should have been a mouth-watering treat for a boy of my age, but when a glassful of it was offered to me, I made no attempt to stretch out my hand to receive it. It was not that I didn't want to drink it. The truth was, I had just been consumed and engulfed by an experience that made me so peaceful and happy, I was unable to respond to the offered glass. My mother and the other women present were both astonished and alarmed by my sudden inactivity. They all gath-

3

ered around me, trying to decide what had happened and what to do. By this time my eyes were closed. Though I was unable to respond to their queries, I could hear the discussion going on around me, and I was fully aware of all their attempts to bring me back to my usual state. They shook me, they gently slapped my face, they pinched my cheeks. Someone even lifted me up in the air, but nothing elicited any kind of physical response from me. I was not being stubborn. The experience was so overwhelming it had effectively paralysed my ability to respond to any external stimuli. For about an hour they tried everything they could think of to bring me back to a normal state of consciousness, but all their attempts failed.

I had not been sick, this had not happened to me before and, just prior to its commencement, I had not been exhibiting any strange symptoms. Because of the suddenness of the event, because it had never happened before, and because no amount of shaking could wake me, my family came to the conclusion that I had suddenly and mysteriously been possessed by a malevolent spirit. In those days there were no doctors or psychiatrists to run to. When something like this happened, the standard response was to take the victim to the local mosque so that the *mulla* could perform an exorcism. We even used to take our buffaloes to him when they got sick or failed to give milk in the hope that his exorcisms and mantras would somehow remove the affliction.

So, even though I came from a Hindu family, I was carried to the local mosque and shown to the *mulla*. He chanted some words while simultaneously running some metal tongs over my body. That was the standard way of performing an exorcism. The *mulla*, with his usual optimism, said that I would soon recover, but his efforts, like those of my family before him, failed to bring me out of the state I was in. Still paralysed, I was carried home and put to bed. For two full days, I stayed in this peaceful, blissful, happy state, unable to communicate with anyone, but still fully aware of the various things that were going on around me.

At the end of this two-day period I opened my eyes again. My mother, who was an ardent Krishna *bhakta*, came up to me and asked, 'Did you see Krishna?' Seeing how happy I was, she had abandoned her initial idea that I had been possessed and had substituted for it a theory that I had had some kind of mystical experience involving her own favourite deity.

'No,' I replied, 'all I can say about it is that I was very happy.'

As far as first causes were concerned, I was as much in ignorance as my family. I did not know what I had been experiencing or what had precipitated this sudden immersion into intense and paralysing happiness.

I told my mother when she pressed me further, 'There was tremendous happiness, tremendous peace, tremendous beauty. More than that I cannot say.' It had been, in fact, a direct experience of the Self, but I did not understand this at the time. It was to be many years before I fully appreciated what had happened to me.

My mother would not give up her theory. She went and fetched a picture which portrayed Krishna as a child, showed it to me and asked, 'Did you see anyone like this?'

Again I told her, 'No, I didn't'.

My mother used to sing Krishna *bhajans* in our house. She had married when she was sixteen and given birth to me when she was eighteen. So, when all this happened, she was still a young woman. Since both her face and her voice were extremely beautiful, her *bhajans* attracted many people to our house.

Although it did not tally with my own direct experience, my mother somehow convinced my that the happiness had been caused by coming into contact with Krishna. She encouraged me to become a devotee of Krishna, saying that, if I meditated on Krishna and repeated His name, the experience I had had of Him would sooner or later return. This was a powerful argument for me. Ever since I had opened my eyes, I had felt a great longing to have that experience again. Since I could think of no other way of getting it back, I followed my mother's advice and began to worship Krishna. My mother herself taught me how to perform all the various rituals and practices associated with the Krishna cult. Once I began, it did not take me long to develop an intense and passionate love for the form of Krishna. I soon forgot that the purpose of my devotion was to get back to that state which I had experienced for two days. I became so fascinated with Krishna, so enamoured of His form, the love I felt for Him soon displaced my desire to get back to that original experience of happiness.

I was particularly attracted to one picture of the child Krishna, the same one that my mother had shown me on the last day of my experience. To me, the face was so indescribably beautiful, so magnetically attractive, I had little difficulty in pouring all my love and devotion into it. As a result of this intense *bhakti*, Krishna began to appear before me, taking the same form as the picture. He would regularly appear to me at night, play with me, and even try to sleep in my bed. I was very innocent at the time. I didn't realise that this manifestation was one of the great deities of Hinduism, and that some of His devotees spent whole lifetimes striving to get a single glimpse of Him. Naively, I thought that it was quite natural for Him to appear in my bedroom and play with me.

His physical form was as real as my own—I could feel

it and touch it—but He could also appear to me in a more subtle form. If I put a blanket over my head, I could still see Him. Even when I closed my eyes, the image of Him was still there in front of me. This Krishna was full of playful energy. He always appeared after I had gone to bed and His childish and enthusiastic playing kept me awake and prevented me from going to sleep. When the novelty of His initial visits had worn off, I started to feel that His appearances were becoming a bit of a nuisance because He was preventing me from sleeping, even when I was very tired. As I was trying to think up some way of making Him go away, it occurred to me that it would be a good idea if I sent Him off to see my mother. I knew that, as an ardent Krishna *bhakta*, she would be delighted to see Him too.

'Why don't you go and sleep with my mother?' I asked Him one night. 'You are not allowing me to go to sleep. Go to my mother instead.' Krishna seemed to have no interest in my mother's company. He never went to see her, preferring instead to spend all His time with me.

One night my mother overheard us talking and asked, 'Who are you talking to?'

'I am speaking with your Krishna,' I replied, ingenuously. 'He disturbs me at night and doesn't let me sleep. If I close my eyes I still see Him, sometimes more clearly than when they are open. Sometimes I put a blanket over my head, but I still see Him. He always wants to sleep with me, but I cannot sleep while He is here.'

She came into the room to investigate, but she didn't see Him. In all the times that Krishna came to our house, she never saw Him once.

When He wasn't there I always felt a desire to see Him. I really did want to see Him and play with Him. The only problem was that I was often so tired when He came I felt that He should, after a decent interval, leave me in peace so that I could lie down and get some sleep.

He didn't come every night. Sometimes I would see Him and sometimes I wouldn't. I never doubted His reality; I never had the idea it was some kind of vision. I even wrote a postcard to Him once, telling Him how much I loved Him. I posted it and wasn't at all surprised when I got a reply from Him, properly stamped and franked and delivered by the postman. He was so real to me, it seemed quite natural to correspond with Him by post.

From the moment that Krishna first came into my life, I lost interest in my schoolwork. I would sit in class, apparently paying attention, but my mind and heart would be on the form of Krishna. Sometimes, when waves of bliss would surge up inside me, I would abandon myself to the experience and lose contact with the outside world.

From the time of my first experience a desire to search for God and a hunger in me for Him were always present. I was always, unconsciously, looking for an outlet for these feelings. When I was about eleven, for example, a group of *sadhus* passed by our house. I was immediately attracted to them and tried to join their group. 'My parents are dead,' I told them. 'Will you look after me?' They agreed and we walked off together to a place about twenty kilometres away from the town. I didn't tell my parents, so they, of course, spent several days frantically looking for me. Then, following up a rumour that I had been seen with these *sadhus*, they tracked me down to our camp.

I remember my father exclaiming, after he had finally found me, 'I thought you were lost! I thought you were lost!'

I wasn't the least bit repentant about my adventures. I retorted, 'How can I be lost? Am I a buffalo that I can get lost and not know where I am? I always knew where I was.' I didn't have any appreciation of the worry and the concern I had caused my parents. By joining the *sadhus* I had merely expressed my yearning and hunger for God. I even went so far as to tell my father, 'Why have you come to look for me instead of leaving me with God?' My father, naturally, would not allow me to stay there. He lectured the *sadhus* on what he thought was their irresponsible behaviour and then took me back to town.

During my childhood other boys would act out their fantasies by playing soldiers or pretending they were famous sportsmen or rulers. I, on the contrary, had an urge to imitate *sadhus*. I knew nothing of the inner life of such people, but I was quite content merely to mimic the externals. I particularly remember one day when I decided to play at being a naked *sadhu* and persuaded my sister to join in the game. We stripped off, smeared our bodies with wood ash to imitate *vibhuti* and sat cross-legged in front of a fire which we made in our garden. That was as far as we could go because we didn't know anything about meditation or yoga. One of our neighbours who happened to look over the common garden wall was understandably shocked to see a naked girl there, covered with ash. We were so innocent it didn't occur to us that it wasn't proper for young girls to sit outside with no clothes on. The neighbour summoned our mother and the game came to an abrupt end.

My next major spiritual adventure occurred when I was about thirteen. It started when I saw a picture of the Buddha in a history book at school. This picture illustrated the period of his life when he tried to live on only one grain of rice a day. The face was very beautiful but the body was skeleton-like, all skin and bone. I immediately felt a great attraction to him, even though I didn't then know anything about his teachings. I simply fell in love with his beautiful face and decided that I should try to emulate him. In the picture he was meditating under a tree. I didn't know that at the time, in fact I didn't even know what meditation was. Undeterred, I thought, 'I can do that. I can sit cross-legged under a tree. I can be like him.' So I began to sit in a cross-legged position in our garden under some rose bushes that grew there, happy and content that I was harmonising my lifestyle with this person I had fallen in love with.

Then, to increase the similarity even more, I decided that I should try to make my body resemble his skeleton-like frame. At that time in our house we would collect our food from our mother before going off to eat it separately. This made it easy for me to throw my meals away. When no one was looking I would go outside and give all my food to the dogs in the street. After some time I managed to stop eating completely. I became so weak and thin, eventually my bones began to stick out, just like the Buddha's. That made me very happy and I became very proud of my new state. My classmates at school made my day by nick-naming me 'the Buddha' because they could see how thin I was getting.

My father worked for the railways. At this particular period of his life he was working in Baluchistan as a stationmaster. Because his job was a long way away, we only ever saw him when he came home on leave. About a month after my fasting began he came home on one of his regular visits and was shocked at how thin I had got during his absence. He took me off to see various doctors and had them examine me in order to find out what was wrong. None of them suspected that I was deliberately fasting. One of them told my father, 'He is growing tall very quickly, that is why he is getting so thin. Give him good food, lots of milk and dry fruits.'

My mother followed the advice, adding a bit of her

own: every day she would say, 'Eat more butter, eat more butter'. The dogs on the street got very fat and happy because the new diet went the same way as the old one.

The school history book which contained Buddha's picture was a simple guide for children. The main biographical facts were there, but the concepts of meditation and enlightenment were not adequately explained. Presumably the author did not think that these very essential points would be of interest to children. So, I remained ignorant of what he was really doing under that tree and why his final accomplishment was so great. Nevertheless, I still felt attracted to him and still felt an urge to imitate him as closely as possible.

I learnt from this book that the Buddha wore orange robes and that he begged for his food, going from house to house with a begging bowl. This was something I could, with a little ingenuity, copy.

My mother had a white sari which seemed to me to be the ideal raw material for a robe. I took it when she wasn't looking and dyed it ochre, the colour of the Buddha's robes. I draped it around myself in what I took to be the correct way and began to play at being a mendicant monk. I got hold of a bowl to beg with and walked up and down the streets of Faisalabad, asking for alms. Before I went home I would change into my ordinary clothes and wrap up the orange sari in a paper parcel. I kept the parcel among my school books, a place I thought no one would bother to look.

One of my friends found out what I was doing and told me, 'You can't get away with this. Somebody will recognise you and tell your family what you are doing.'

Feeling very confident about my ability to do it secretly, I told him, 'Your parents know me. I will come to your house in my robes and ask for food. If I can fool them

I can fool anybody.'

I put on my sari, smeared ashes all over my face to further my disguise, put a cap on my head and went off to their house with my begging bowl. It was about 8 p.m. so the darkness also helped my disguise. I called out 'Bhiksha! Bhiksha!' [Alms! Alms!] because I had seen *sadhus* beg for food by calling in this way. Since it did not occur to me that anyone might recognise my voice, I made no attempt to disguise it. My friend's mother came to the door, showed no sign of recognition, and invited me in to eat.

'Swamiji, Babaji, come in and eat something,' she said, taking me in and offering me food.

I went with her, acting out the role I had assigned myself. 'My child,' I said to her, even though she must have been about thirty years older than I, 'you will have children and get lots of money.' I had heard swamis bless women like this. Since most women wanted to get rich and have several sons, itinerant swamis would give these fantasies their blessings in the hope of getting a better reception and something good to eat.

Then, laughing, she removed my cap and told me that she had always known who I really was. 'Your appearance is quite good,' she said, 'but I recognised you from your voice.' Then her husband came and she explained to him what was going on.

Scornfully he said, 'Who will not recognise you if you go out begging like that? You will soon be detected.'

Now it was my turn to laugh because earlier that day I had begged at his shop and got a one paisa copper coin from him. I showed him the coin.

He had to revise his opinion a little. 'I must have been busy with my customers,' he said. 'I must have given it to you without looking.'

'No, that's not true,' I responded truthfully. 'You saw

me very clearly. I walked past your shop, begging. You saw me, called me back and handed me this coin. My disguise is good enough and I can get away with it so long as I don't talk to people who might recognise my voice.'

These people were amused by my antics, not knowing that I was doing this sort of thing regularly in a stolen dyed sari. They didn't tell my mother, so I was able to carry on with my impersonation.

My mother only had three saris. One day, fairly soon after I had taken the white one, she washed the other two and started looking for the third because she needed to wear it. Of course, she couldn't find it anywhere. She never asked me about it because, since I was not a girl, it did not occur to her that I might have had any possible use for it. She eventually decided that she must have given it to the *dhobi*, and that he had lost it or forgotten to return it.

The final phase of my Buddha impersonations came when I discovered that he used to preach sermons in public places. This excited me because it was a new facet of his life that I could copy. I knew absolutely nothing about Buddhism, but the thought that this might be a handicap when I stood up to preach never occurred to me.

There was a clock-tower in the middle of our town and near it was a raised platform where all the local politicians used to give their speeches. It was very much the centre of Faisalabad because all the routes to other towns radiated out from it. I put on my usual disguise, strode confidently up the steps, and began to give my first public speech. I cannot recollect anything that I said—it couldn't have been anything about Buddhism because I knew absolutely nothing about it—but I do remember that I delivered my speech with great flair and panache. I harangued the passers-by with great gusto, occasionally raising my arm and wagging my finger to emphasise the points I was making. I had seen the politicians gesture like that when they made their speeches.

I felt I had made a successful start to my oratorical career and taken a step further towards my goal of imitating the Buddha in everything he did. I went back to the clock-tower on several occasions and preached many sermons there. Unfortunately, Faisalabad was not a big city and it was inevitable that sooner or later someone who knew me would recognise me. It was not surprising, therefore, that one day one of my neighbours spotted me and reported my antics to my mother.

At first she was very sceptical. 'How can it be he?' she asked. 'Where would he get an orange robe from?' Then, remembering her missing sari, she went to the cupboard where I kept my books and found the paper parcel. The game was over, for that discovery effectively ended my brief career as an imitation Buddha.

It was an absurd but very entertaining episode in my life which, in retrospect, I can see as reflecting my state of mind at the time. I had this intense yearning for God but I had nothing to channel it into except the external forms of the deities. Something in me recognised the Buddha as divine and my childish and ignorant attempts to follow in his footsteps were merely a manifestation of that burning inner desire to find God. I wasn't being mischievous. I never regarded it as some kind of childhood prank. Some power was compelling me to do it. Some old *samskaras* were coming up and compelling me towards reality, towards the truth of the Self. It was a serious attempt on my part to find my way back to the state of happiness and peace that I had once experienced and known as my own inner reality.

My mother did not get very angry with me. We had always had a good relationship and she could see the humour of the situation. Because she had been so young when I was born, we behaved with each other as if we were brother and sister, rather than mother and son. We played, sang and danced together, and quite often we even slept in the same bed.

I have already mentioned that my mother was an ardent Krishna *bhakta*. I should also mention that she had a Guru who was a well-known teacher of *Vedanta*. He knew many vedantic works and could lecture on them all with great authority. His favourite was *Vichar Sagar* by the Hindi saint Nischaldas. My mother could recite large portions of it by heart. Many years later, when I became acquainted with Sri Ramana Maharshi, I found that he too liked it and that he had even made a Tamil abridged rendering of it under the title *Vichara Mani Mala*.

My mother's Guru had made her memorise many vedantic *slokas* which she used to chant at various times during the day. Traditional vedantic *sadhana* is done by affirmation and negation. Either one repeats or contemplates one of the *mahavakyas* such as 'I am *Brahman*' or one tries to reject identification with the body by saying and feeling, 'I am not the body, I am not the skin, I am not the blood,' etc. The aim is to get into a mental frame of mind in which one convinces oneself that one's real nature is the Self and that identification with the body is erroneous.

My mother used to chant all these 'I am not...' verses and I used to find them all very funny. I was, at heart, a *bhakta*. I could appreciate any *sadhana* which generated love and devotion towards God, but I couldn't see the point of these practices which merely listed, in endlessly trivial ways, what one was not. When my mother had a bath she would chant, 'I am not the urine, I am not the excrement, I am not the bile,' and so on. This was too much for me. I would call out, 'What are you doing in there? Having a bath or cleaning the toilet?' I ridiculed her so much that eventually she stopped singing these verses out loud.[1]

My mother's Guru encouraged me to join a local lending library which had a good selection of spiritual books. I started to read books on *Vedanta* and Hindu saints. It was this library which introduced me to *Yoga Vasishta*, a book I have always enjoyed. One day I tried to borrow a book about Swami Ram Tirtha, a Hindu saint who went into seclusion in the Himalayas in his twenties and who died there when he was only thirty-four. I had a special reason for borrowing this book: he was my mother's elder brother, so I naturally wanted to find out more about him.

The librarian had watched me borrow all these books with an increasing sense of alarm. In middle-class Hindu society it is quite acceptable to show a little interest in spiritual matters, but when the interest starts to become an obsession, the alarm bells go off. This well-meaning librarian probably thought that I was taking my religion too seriously, and that I might end up like my uncle. Most families would be very unhappy if one of their members dropped out at an early age to become a wandering *sadhu* in the Himalayas. The librarian, feeling that he was acting for the best, refused to let me borrow this book about my uncle. Later, he went to my mother and warned her that I was showing what was, for him, an unhealthy interest in mysticism. My mother paid no attention. Because her own life revolved around her *sadhana*, she was delighted to have a son who seemed to be displaying a similar inclination.

My mother's Guru liked me very much. He suggested books for me to read and frequently gave me advice on spiritual matters. He owned a lot of land, had many cows, and spent half his time in teaching and the other half in managing his properties and possessions. One day he made my mother an astounding offer: 'Please give me your son. I will appoint him my heir and spiritual successor.

When I die everything I have will be his. I will look after his spiritual development, but to get all this he must agree to one condition. He must not marry and he must remain a *brahmachari*. If he agrees, and if you agree, I will take full responsibility for him.'

My mother had great love and respect for this man, but she was far too attached to me to consider handing me over to someone else. She turned down his offer. I too had great respect for him. If my mother had accepted his offer, I would happily have gone with him.

At around this time she announced that she was going to take me to a different swami because she wanted me to get some special spiritual instructions from him. I didn't like the idea and I didn't like the man she chose for me. I told her, 'If you take me to this man I will test him to see if he has really conquered his passions. As soon as I see him I shall slap him in the face. If he gets angry, I will know that he has no self-control. If he doesn't get angry, I will listen to him and accept whatever he has to teach me.' My mother knew that I was quite capable of carrying out the threat. Not wishing to be embarrassed by my disrespectful activities, she dropped her plans to take me to see him.

When I was about fifteen I went to a friend's house during the annual Holi celebrations. His mother offered me some *pakoras* which she had made for the festival. I happily ate two. As they were very tasty, I asked for some more. Surprisingly, she refused. I could see that she had been making them in large quantities, and that she planned to make a lot more, so I couldn't understand why she was restricting me to two. The answer, as I was to discover later, was that she was putting *bhang* [cannabis leaves] in them and didn't want me to ingest too large a dose. In those days it was quite common to put a little *bhang* in the food on festival days. At weddings, for example, the *bhang* would make the guests very happy and would also increase their appetites. Weddings were great occasions for overeating. With appetites stimulated by *bhang*, the guests would get ravenously hungry and would perform great feats of gluttony.

I went home and sat down to my evening meal. My mother was making chapatis. After consuming all the ones she had cooked I asked for some more because I still felt hungry. She made extra, but even they were not enough to satisfy my hunger. I ate them as fast as she could prepare them and kept on asking for more. It was not until I had eaten about twenty that she realised what had happened to me. She laughed and exclaimed, 'You've been eating *bhang*, haven't you? Who has been feeding you *bhang*?' I told her about the *pakoras* and she laughed again. I was now beginning to understand why my friend's mother had restricted me to two. In addition to being extremely hungry, I was also beginning to feel a little intoxicated.

That night we all slept in the same room. At about midnight I got out of bed, sat in the *padmasana* position, and called out in a loud voice, 'You are not my father! You are not my mother!' Then I went into a deep meditation. My parents woke up but they were not very alarmed by my behaviour. They just assumed that I was still suffering from the effects of the *bhang* I had eaten.

At 3 a.m. I was still sitting there with my eyes closed. My parents woke up because strange and unrecognisable sounds were coming out of my mouth. They tried to wake me up but I was in too deep a meditation to be roused. My mother, thinking that I was getting delirious, persuaded my father to go out and find a doctor. He had a hard time persuading one to come because it was the middle of the night and a festival day. Eventually, though, he found one and brought him back to the house.

This doctor gave me a thorough examination while my parents watched anxiously. I was aware of what he was doing and of my mother's worried comments, but I couldn't bring myself out of the state or behave in a normal way. The doctor finally announced his decision.

'Congratulations,' he said, addressing my parents. 'You have a very fine boy, a very good son. There is nothing physically wrong with him. He is just immersed in a very deep meditation. When it is over he will come out of it quite naturally and be perfectly normal.'

For all of that night and for the whole of the next day I was immersed in that state. During the day I continued to utter strange sounds which no one could understand until a local pandit passed by our house. He heard what I was saying, recognised it, came in and announced, 'This boy is chanting portions of the *Yajur Veda* in Sanskrit. Where and when did he learn to chant like this?'

The answer, most probably, is that I learned in some previous life. At the time I knew Punjabi, my native language, Urdu, the language of the local Muslims, and a little Persian. I knew no Sanskrit and had never even heard of the *Yajur Veda*. The *bhang* must have triggered some memories and knowledge left over from a previous life. As the doctor had predicted, I eventually returned to normal—with no knowledge of Sanskrit or the *Vedas*—and resumed my usual everyday life.

My next unusual experience occurred when I was about sixteen years of age. I was attending a school which was run by the Arya Samaj, a Hindu reform movement founded in the nineteenth century. The school was named after Swami Dayananda, the founder of the organisation. Because it was a residential school, I slept in a hostel with all the other boys.

Every morning we would assemble outside and sit in a

semicircle while a prayer was chanted. It always ended with the words 'Om shanti shanti' [Om, peace, peace]. At the conclusion of the prayer, a flag would be raised in the school grounds with an 'Om' printed on it. As the flag was being raised, we all had to jump up and shout, 'Victory to the *dharma*! Victory to Mother India! Victory to Swami Dayananda!'

One morning, at the conclusion of the prayer, the chanting of 'Om shanti shanti' caused my whole body to go numb. I became paralysed in much the same way that I had been when, as an eight-year-old boy, I had been offered the mango drink in Labore. I was aware of everything that was going on around me, there was a great feeling of peace and happiness inside, but I couldn't move any of my muscles or respond to what was going on around me. The other boys jumped up and saluted the flag, leaving me sitting on the floor in my paralysed state.

The teacher who was supervising the prayers saw me sitting on the floor and just assumed that I was being lazy or disobedient. He put my name on a list for punishment by the headmaster. This meant that I had to appear before him the next morning and be caned. The teacher left the scene without ascertaining the real cause of my immobility. The other boys, meanwhile, started to make fun of me. When they realised that I was not capable of responding to their taunts, they decided to stage a mock funeral. They picked up my body, stretched me out on their shoulders and then pretended that they were carrying me off to the cemetery to be cremated. I had to go along with their game because I was not capable of complaining or resisting. When they had had their fun, they carried me home and dumped me on my bed. I remained there for the rest of the day, paralysed, but absorbed in an inner state of peace and happiness.

The next morning, fully recovered, I reported to the headmaster for my punishment. He took out his cane, but before he had a chance to use it I asked him, 'Please sir, what am I supposed to have done? What mistake am I supposed to have committed?' The headmaster had no idea. The teachers had merely given him a list of boys to be caned because the teachers themselves were not allowed to administer corporal punishment. He checked with the teacher who had sent me to him and was told about my act of 'disobedience' the day before.

I told him, 'I didn't refuse to stand up. I suddenly went numb all over and couldn't move.' I told him about the experience, explaining that it had been triggered by hearing the words *'shanti shanti'* at the end of the morning prayer. This headmaster was a very good man. A supporter of Mahatma Gandhi, he did the job without taking any salary because he believed that Hindu boys should be brought up and educated in a Hindu environment. In those days, most schools were either secular institutions run by the government or Christian organisations operated by missionaries. Since he was supposed to be inculcating us with Hindu values and ideals, he recognised the absurdity of punishing me for having had a mystical experience as a consequence of listening to a Hindu prayer. He let me off and in later years we became quite good friends.

Because of my continuing interest in Krishna, I didn't do well enough in school to go to college. Instead, at the age of eighteen, I got a job as a travelling salesman. I enjoyed the work very much because it gave me the opportunity to travel all over India. Then, in 1930, when I was twenty years old, my father decided that it was time for me to get married. I didn't like the idea at all, but to avoid a big family argument I agreed to marry the woman my father selected for me. I became a householder and in due course fathered a daughter and a son.

During the next few years my interest in nationalist politics temporarily competed with my continuing interest in Krishna. To understand this part of my story it will be necessary to give a little background information about the conditions we were then living and working in.

The 1930's were a time of great political unrest. The British rule of India was being challenged in many ways. There was a feeling in the air that if we organised ourselves properly and put enough pressure on the government, we could put an end to the colonial occupation. Gandhi, the most well-known of the freedom fighters, was espousing a campaign of non-cooperation and non-violence, hoping that if enough Indians refused to obey the orders of the British, they would accept that the country was ungovernable and leave us to look after our own affairs. I didn't accept this theory at all. I was and am a great believer in direct action and I felt that we should confront the British with a show of force. 'If some people break into my house,' I reasoned, 'and take it over so completely that they have us running around obeying their orders, what should we do?' The Gandhian answer would be, 'Politely ask them to leave, and if they say "no", refuse to obey any of their orders'. I thought that this approach was being pusillanimous. In my experience, squatters who have appropriated someone else's property don't listen to polite requests. I, therefore, was in favour of picking up a stick and driving them out by force.

But how to do it? The British were very well organised and I knew that a direct physical assault would not make much of a dent in their power structure. I decided instead to gain some yogic *siddhis* and then use these *siddhis* to attack the British. I took to frequenting a graveyard at night, my idea being that if I could summon up spirits of the dead and gain control over them, I could then unleash these forces on the British. I succeeded in summoning up an assortment of spirits and even managed to control them enough for them to do my bidding, but I soon realised that these entities had very little power and that they would not be effective weapons against the British.

Undaunted, I joined a group of freedom fighters who had decided to take direct military action against the British. We were essentially a group of saboteurs whose aim was to conduct a guerrilla war against our rulers by attacking key military, economic and political targets. I was trained how to make bombs and looked forward to the day when I would see some direct military action.

Although I was not directly involved, our group was responsible for blowing up the Viceroy's train as he was travelling to Peshawar. Our equipment was a bit primitive, for we had to rely on a fuse rather than detonation by remote control. The timing was not quite right and we ended up blowing up the carriage that was adjacent to the one which the Viceroy was occupying. The Viceroy escaped unhurt.

This bold attack galvanised the British authorities. An extensive manhunt was organised which resulted in most of the leading members of our group being arrested. I escaped undetected. Our organisation was hit so badly by the arrests, it was effectively disbanded. A few of us then decided on a different approach. The Second World War was in progress and the British government was actively recruiting Indian soldiers for their army. We decided that we should join the army as infiltrators, learn about tactics, strategy and warfare, and then, when the time was right, we would stage a coup or simply turn our guns on the British. Some of us also thought that once we had learned the art of warfare, we could desert and join up with the Indian

National Army which was fighting with the Japanese against the British. I applied for an officer training course at the Indian Military Academy and was immediately accepted. The British, fortunately, seemed to have no record of my guerrilla activities.

I soon discovered that our plans were impractical. There were too few of us to form an effective nucleus for a coup, and the rigid, hierarchical structure of the army made it virtually impossible to organise any effective subversive activities. My interest in revolution declined in the face of the practical realities.

It may sound strange, but my obsession with Krishna, and my intense love for Him, never diminished during this militant period of my life. Waves of bliss would still surge up within me whenever I thought of Him, and I quite often found myself in ecstatic states in which I had no control over my body. Once, for example, I casually heard someone mention the name 'Krishna' as I was walking down a city street. The mere mention of the name sent me into a kind of rapture in which I had great difficulty in controlling myself. As a wave of *bhakti* swept over me, I nearly went into a trance in the middle of the road.

Life in the army meant keeping up an outer front of normality and military sobriety. Open exhibitions of love for a Hindu God would have been frowned on to such an extent that they would have jeopardised my career. This caused me to lead a dual life. By day I played the officer-sahib, complete with stiff upper lip. At night, behind locked doors, I would transform myself into a Krishna *gopi*. I would dismiss my orderly, telling him not to disturb me with the usual 5 a.m. cup of tea. That gave me the whole night with my beloved Krishna. I was not content with doing *japa* of His name, or with worshipping an inanimate picture or statue, I wanted Krishna Himself to appear before me, as He had frequently done when I was young, so that I could pour out my love to Him directly.

I pretended I was Radha, the consort of Krishna, because I thought that if I imitated her in every way, Krishna would come and appear before me. I dressed myself in a sari, decorated my body with bangles and women's jewellery, and even put make-up on my face. I got into the *bhava* that I really was Radha, pining away for her divine lover. It worked. Krishna would appear and I would pour out my heart to Him. On the mornings after Krishna had appeared to me my face would be lit up with the happiness of divine love. One of my superior officers mistook my state for drunkenness and gave orders to the barman in the mess that I should not be given more than three small drinks a day. He was told by the barman, quite correctly, that I never drank at all, but he didn't believe him. He simply couldn't understand how someone could look so radiantly happy without having had any alcoholic stimulants.

My nationalist ambitions withered and died during my brief spell in the army, but, on the contrary, my passion for Krishna increased to the point where I could think about little else. The army was not a congenial place for a *bhakta* who only wanted to indulge in his obsession for Krishna, so I resigned my commission. It was a difficult thing to do during wartime, but with the assistance of a sympathetic commanding officer, to whom I explained my predicament, I managed to free myself from my military obligations.

I returned home to face the wrath of my father. Having a wife and family to support, he found it inexcusable that I had given up a promising career without having anything else to fall back on. It was true—I could have had a glittering career in the army. All my classmates from the officer's training school who made the military their career went on to occupy all the senior positions in the army in the years that followed independence in 1947. I didn't care. Nothing mattered to me anymore except finding God and holding on to Him.

After leaving the army, I had no desire to get a job. I felt instead that I needed a spiritual Master who could help me to consummate my love affair with Krishna. I had been sporadically successful in getting Him to appear before me, but I wanted Him all the time. Since I was unable to summon up Krishna at will, I felt that I should find a Master who could help me to do it, or who could do it for me. There was, therefore, only one quality I was looking for in my prospective Master: he must have seen God himself, and he must have the ability to show Him to me. No other qualifications mattered.

With this criterion in mind I began a tour of India which took me to almost every famous ashram and guru in the country. I went to see such well-known people as Swami Sivananda, Tapovan Swami, Ananda Moyi Ma, Swami Ramdas, two of the Shankaracharyas and a host of lesser-known spiritual figures. At each place I stopped I asked the same question: 'Have you seen God? Can you show me God?' All of them responded in much the same way. They tried to give me a mantra, or they tried to make me meditate. All of them made a point of saying that God could not be produced like a rabbit out of a conjuror's hat, and that if I wanted to see Him I would have to undergo years of strenuous *sadhana*.

This was not what I wanted to hear. I told all these swamis and gurus, 'I am asking you if you can show me God. If you can, and if you can do it immediately, then say so. If there is a price to be paid, then tell me. Whatever the price is, I will pay it. I am not interested in sitting here, year after year, chanting one of your mantras. I want to see God now. If you can't show Him to me right now, I will look for someone else who can.' Since none of the people I met claimed they could show me God, I eventually had to return to my father's house, disillusioned and dispirited.

Shortly after my return a *sadhu* appeared at our door, asking for food. I invited him in, offered him some food and asked him the question that was uppermost in my mind. 'Can you show me God? If not, do you know of anyone who can?'

Much to my surprise, he gave me a positive answer. 'Yes, I know a person who can show you God. If you go and see that man, everything will be all right for you. His name is Ramana Maharshi.'

Not having heard of him before, I asked where he lived and was told, 'Sri Ramanasramam, Tiruvannamalai'. Since I had never heard of the place either, I asked him for directions to get there.

He gave me detailed instructions: 'Take a train to Madras. When you get to Madras, go to Egmore station. That is where the metre gauge trains leave from. Take a train from there to a place called Villupuram. You have to change trains there. Then catch a train from there to Tiruvannamalai.'

I wrote all these details down with mixed feelings. I was very happy to hear that there was at least one man in India who could show me God, but I also knew that I had no means of getting to see him. I had spent all the money I had saved from my spell in the army on my unsuccessful pilgrimage, and I knew that my father would not give me any assistance. He disapproved of my spiritual trips, feeling, with some justification, that I should be devoting my time instead to supporting my family.

When I told him that I wanted to go to the South to see yet one more swami, he exploded with anger. 'What about your wife and children?' he demanded. 'Was it not enough to leave the army that you must now rush to the other end of India, indulging in your mad search for spiritual adventures?' Obviously, no help would be forthcoming from that quarter.

Shortly afterwards, I went into town and happened to meet one of my old friends. He was running a tea-stall.

'I haven't seen you for a long time,' he remarked. 'I heard a story that you resigned your commission in the army.'

'Yes,' I replied, 'I have given it up for good.'

'So what are you doing now?' he enquired.

'Nothing,' I answered. 'I am looking for some sort of job.'

'Well sit down,' he said. 'I will give you some milk to drink. Since you are not employed at the moment, you don't need to pay.'

I sat down and began to glance through a newspaper that was lying on one of the tables. Having just been reminded of my unemployed state, I turned to the page which listed all the job advertisements. One vacancy seemed to be tailor-made for me: 'Ex-army officer required in Madras.' The British army was looking for an ex-officer to manage all the stores in a canteen which was being run for British servicemen. I looked for the address to apply to and found that the contractor who had placed the advertisement was based in Peshawar, a nearby city. I sent my application there, along with a photo of myself in army uniform, and was immediately engaged. Not only that, the contractor gave me money to get to Madras and told me that I need not report for duty for one month. I thus got money to go to the Maharshi and an opportunity to spend time in his presence before I reported for work.

It was 1944 and I was thirty-four years of age.

I followed the *sadhu's* advice and took a train to Tiruvannamalai. On disembarking there I discovered that the Maharshi's ashram was about three kilometres away, on the other side of the town, so I engaged a bullock cart to take me and my belongings there. As soon as we reached the ashram, I jumped out of the cart, put my bags in the men's dormitory, and went off to look for this man who could show me God. I peeped in through his window and saw, sitting on a sofa inside, the same man who had visited my house in the Punjab. I was disgusted. 'This man is a fraud,' I said to myself. 'He appears in my house in the Punjab, tells me to go to Tiruvannamalai, then hops on the train so that he can get there before me.' I was so annoyed with him I decided that I wouldn't even go into the hall where he was sitting. Mentally adding him to the long list of frauds I had met on my first pilgrimage round India, I turned on my heels and went off to collect my bags.

As I was preparing to leave on the same cart that had brought me to the ashram, one of the residents accosted me and asked, 'Aren't you from the North? You look like a North Indian.' I found out later that he was called Framji and that he owned a cinema in Madras.

'Yes I am,' I replied.

'Haven't you just arrived?' he asked, noting that I was making preparations to leave. 'Aren't you going to stay here for at least a couple of days?'

I told him the story of how I had come to be in Tiru-vannamalai, concluding by saying, 'This man has been travelling around the country, advertising himself. I don't want to see him. I came here because he said there was a man here who could show me God. If this man really does have the capacity to show me God, why did he not do it in my house in the Punjab when he came to see me? Why did he make me come all this way? I am not interested in seeing such a man.'

Framji said, 'No, no, you are mistaken. He has not moved out of this town in the last forty-eight years. It is either a case of mistaken identity or somehow, through his power, he managed to manifest himself in the Punjab while his physical body was still here. Some girl from America came here once and told a similar story. These things do happen occasionally. Are you sure that you have not made a mistake?'

'No,' I answered, absolutely sure of myself. 'I recognise the man. I have not made a mistake.'

'In that case,' he responded, 'please stay. I will introduce you to the manager and he will give you a place to stay.'

I went along with his suggestion merely because my curiosity had been aroused. Something strange had happened and I wanted to find out exactly what it was. It was my intention to confront the Maharshi in private and ask for an explanation of his strange behaviour.

I soon discovered, though, that he never gave private interviews, so I decided instead that I would try to see him when the big room in which he saw visitors was relatively empty.

I ate lunch in the ashram. At the conclusion of the meal the Maharshi went back to his room with his attendant. No one else followed him. I didn't know that there was an unofficial rule that visitors should not go to see him between 11.30 a.m. and 2.30 p.m. The manager had decided that the Maharshi needed to rest for a few hours after lunch, but since the Maharshi would not go along with a rule which prevented people from coming to see him, a compromise was reached. His doors would remain open but all visitors and devotees were actively discouraged from going to see him during these hours. Not knowing this, I followed the

Maharshi into his room, thinking that this was the best time to have a private interview.

The Maharshi's attendant, a man called Krishnaswami, tried to discourage me. 'Not now,' he said. 'Come back at 2.30.' The Maharshi overheard the exchange and told Krishnaswami that I could come in and see him.

I approached him in a belligerent way. 'Are you the man who came to see me at my house in the Punjab?' I demanded. The Maharshi remained silent.

I tried again. 'Did you come to my house and tell me to come here? Are you the man who sent me here?' Again the Maharshi made no comment.

Since he was unwilling to answer either of these questions, I moved on to the main purpose of my visit. 'Have you seen God?' I asked. 'And if you have, can you enable me to see Him? I am willing to pay any price, even my life, but your part of the bargain is that you must show me God.'

'No,' he answered, 'I cannot show you God or enable you to see God because God is not an object that can be seen. God is the subject. He is the seer. Don't concern yourself with objects that can be seen. Find out who the seer is.' He also added, 'You alone are God,'[2] as if to rebuke me for looking for a God who was outside and apart from me.

His words did not impress me. They seemed to me to be yet one more excuse to add to the long list of those I had heard from swamis all over the country. He had promised to show me God, yet now he was trying to tell me that not only could he not show me God, no one else could either. I would have dismissed him and his words without a second thought had it not been for an experience I had immediately after he had told me to find out who this 'I' was who wanted to see God. At the conclusion of his words he looked at me, and as he gazed into my eyes, my whole body began to tremble and shake. A thrill of nervous energy shot through my body. My nerve endings felt as if they were dancing and my hair stood on end. Within me I became aware of the spiritual Heart. This is not the physical heart, it is, instead, the source and support of all that exists. Within the Heart I saw or felt something like a closed bud. It was very shining and bluish. With the Maharshi looking at me, and with myself in a state of inner silence, I felt this bud open and bloom. I use the word 'bud', but this is not an exact description. It would be more correct to say that something that felt bud-like opened and bloomed within me in the Heart. And when I say 'Heart' I don't mean that the flowering was located in a particular place in the body. This Heart, this Heart of my Heart, was neither inside the body nor out of it. I can't give a more exact description of what happened. All I can say is that in the Maharshi's presence, and under his gaze, the Heart opened and bloomed. It was an extraordinary experience, one that I had never had before. I had not come looking for any kind of experience, so it totally surprised me when it happened.[3]

Though I had had an immensely powerful experience in the presence of the Maharshi, his statement 'You alone are God' and his advice to 'Find out who the seer is' did not have a strong appeal for me. My inclination to seek a God outside me was not dispelled either by his words or by the experience I had had with him.

I thought to myself, 'It is not good to be chocolate, I want to taste chocolate'. I wanted to remain separate from God so that I could enjoy the bliss of union with Him.

When the devotees came in that afternoon I viewed them all with the rather prejudiced eye of a fanatical Krishna *bhakta*. So far as I could see, they were just sitting quietly, doing nothing. I thought to myself, 'No one here seems to be chanting the name of God. Not a single person has a *mala* to do *japa* with. How can they consider themselves to be good devotees?' My views on religious practice were rather limited. All these people may have been meditating, but so far as I was concerned, they were wasting their time.

I transferred my critical gaze to the Maharshi and similar thoughts arose. 'This man should be setting a good example to his followers. He is sitting silently, not giving any talks about God. He doesn't appear to be chanting the name of God himself, or focusing his attention on Him in any way. These disciples are sitting around being lazy because the Master himself is sitting there doing nothing. How can this man show me God when he himself shows no interest in Him?'

With thoughts like these floating around my mind it was not long before I generated a feeling of disgust for both the Maharshi and the people who surrounded him. I still had some time before I had to report for duty in Madras, but I didn't want to spend it with all these spiritually lazy people in the ashram. I took off to the other side of Arunachala, a few kilometres away, found a nice quiet spot in the forest on the northern side of the hill, and settled down there to do my Krishna *japa*, alone and undisturbed.

I stayed there for about a week, immersed in my devotional practices. Krishna would often appear before me, and we spent a lot of time playing together. At the end of that period I felt that it was time to go back to Madras to make preparations for my new job. On my way out of town I paid another visit to the ashram, partly to say goodbye, and partly to tell the Maharshi that I didn't need his assistance for seeing God because I had been seeing Him every day through my own efforts.

When I appeared before him, the Maharshi asked,

'Where have you been? Where are you living?'

'On the other side of the mountain,' I replied.

'And what were you doing there?' he inquired.

He had given me my cue. 'I was playing with my Krishna,' I said, in a very smug tone of voice. I was very proud of my achievement and felt superior to the Maharshi because I was absolutely convinced that Krishna had not appeared to him during that period.

'Oh, is that so?' he commented, looking surprised and interested. 'Very good, very nice. Do you see Him now?'

'No sir, I do not,' I replied. 'I only see Him when I have visions.' I was still feeling very pleased with myself, feeling that I had been granted these visions, whereas the Maharshi had not.

'So Krishna comes and plays with you and then He disappears,' said the Maharshi. 'What is the use of a God who appears and disappears? If he is a real God, He must be with you all the time.'

The Maharshi's lack of interest in my visionary experiences deflated me a little, but not to the extent that I was willing to listen to his advice. He was telling me to give up my search for an external God and instead find the origin and identity of the one who wanted to see Him. This was too much for me to swallow. A lifetime of devotion to Krishna had left me incapable of conceiving the spiritual quest in any other terms than that of a quest for a personal God.

Though his advice did not appeal to me, there was still something about the Maharshi that inspired and attracted me. I asked him to give me a mantra, hoping thereby to get his sanction for my own form of spirituality. He refused, although later, when I was back in Madras, he did give me one in a dream. I then asked him if he would be willing to give me *sannyasa* since I was not very keen to take up my new job in Madras. I had only taken it because it had offered me a way of getting to see the Maharshi. He refused that request too. Having therefore got, in my own jaundiced opinion, nothing from the Maharshi except a good experience and some bad advice, I returned to Madras to take up my new job.

I found a nice house to live in, big enough to accommodate my family, and began my work. The job itself did not interest me much but I did it dutifully and to the best of my ability, because I had a wife and children to support. All my spare time and energy were devoted to communing with Krishna. I made a *puja* room in my house, informing my wife that when I was in it, I was never to be disturbed. At 2.30 each morning I would get up and begin my *sadhana*. Sometimes I would read the various Krishna stories or the *Upanishads* or the *Gita*, but mostly I would do *japa* of the name. I synchronised the *japa* with my breathing. Calculating that I breathed about 24,000 times a day, I decided that I should repeat the name of God at least once for every breath I took. I cultivated the idea that any breath I took that was not utilised in uttering the divine name was a wasted one. I found this a relatively easy target to meet.

Then the thought occurred to me: 'There have been years of my life when I did not chant the name at all. All those breaths were wasted. If I increase my recitations to 50,000 a day, I can make up for all those breaths I wasted when I was young.' I soon achieved this new target, managing all the time to synchronise the chanting with some part of the breath.

I would stay in my *puja* room, chanting the name, from 2.30 a.m. to 9.30 a.m., at which point I had to leave to go to the office. Work started there at 10 a.m. At the end of each working day I would return home, lock myself in my *puja* room again, and carry on chanting the name of Krishna until it was time for me to go to sleep. I also slept in the *puja* room, thus effectively cutting myself off from all interaction with my family. I even stopped speaking with them.

One morning, around 2.00 a.m., I heard voices outside my door. I knew it could not be my wife because I had given her strict instructions that I was not to be disturbed while I was inside my *puja* room. It then occurred to me that it might be some of my relatives from the Punjab who had come to visit us. The train from the Punjab usually arrived at Madras in the evening, but it seemed quite possible to me that the train had arrived several hours late and that the passengers had only just managed to reach our house. My curiosity piqued, I decided to open the door to find out who they were. Imagine my astonishment, on opening the door, when I saw not a group of relatives but the shining forms of Rama, Sita, Lakshmana and Hanuman standing outside. I couldn't understand what they were doing there. I had spent most of my life calling on Krishna, never feeling much attraction to Rama, or any interest in Him. Nevertheless, I prostrated to them all with great awe and reverence.

It was Sita who raised her hand and began to speak to me. 'We have come from Ayodhya to visit you because Hanuman told us that there was a very great Krishna *bhakta* here in Madras.' I looked at her raised hand, noting casually all the lines that were on the palm. That image must have imprinted itself permanently on my memory because every time I recall that vision, I clearly see all the lines on that hand just as they were on the day she appeared before me. Their bodies were not, so far as I could ascertain, normal human bodies because I could see through them and dimly take in what was behind them, but they were all exquisitely beautiful. After some time the vision changed into a landscape in which I saw a mountain and a great garuda flying in the sky, moving towards me, but never reaching me. There was no perception of time while all this was going on. The vision seemed only to last a short time, but I was eventually drawn out of it by my wife calling to me that if I didn't leave soon, I would be late for work. I suppose, therefore, that it must have lasted from about 2.30 in the morning till about 9.30 a.m. Because of the vision, this was the first day on which I failed to fulfil my self-assigned quota of 50,000 repetitions of Krishna's name. Though the vision had been awe-inspiring, I still felt guilty that I had neglected my *japa*. I did not mention the night's events to anyone in the office because I had got into the habit of keeping my conversation there to a minimum. I would speak when there was business to be transacted; otherwise I would keep quiet.

Later that day, when I tried to resume my chanting, I found that I could not repeat the name of Krishna any more. Somehow, my mind refused to cooperate. I couldn't read any of my spiritual books either. My mind, thought-free and quiet, refused to concentrate on or pay attention to any of the spiritual objects I tried to put in front of it. It was all very mystifying. For a quarter of a century the divine name had been flowing effortlessly through my mind; now I couldn't even utter it once.

I immediately went to see the head of the Ramakrishna Mission in Madras, a man called Swami Kailasananda, and told him that I was having problems with my *sadhana*. I explained that I had been chanting the name of God for years and that I had also been reading many spiritual books. Now, I told him, no matter how hard I try, my mind will not focus on anything to do with God.

Swami Kailasananda responded by telling me that this was what Christian mystics call 'the dark night of the soul'. It is a stage in *sadhana*, he said, in which the practitioner finds, after years of effort, that practice suddenly becomes very hard or unrewarding. After asking me not to give up trying, he told me to come and attend the regular satsangs which were being held at the Mission because he felt that in such an atmosphere I might find it easier to resume my thoughts of God. I didn't find his advice very satisfactory. I never went back, nor did I ever attend any meetings. I went to several other well-known swamis in Madras, but they all told me more or less the same thing: 'Don't give up trying, attend our satsangs, and we are sure that the problem will soon go away.'

I never attended any of these meetings, partly because I didn't think much of the advice, and partly because I didn't think that these people were qualified to advise me. Though I could see that they were quite good *sadhaks*, I also felt that they had not had a direct experience of God, an experience which would, in my opinion, have made them more qualified to pass judgement on my case.

My thoughts turned once more to the Maharshi in Tiruvannamalai. I had recently had a vision of him in my *puja* room in which he had stood smiling before me. He had not said anything to me and at the time I had not attributed much significance to the appearance. Now I began to revise my opinion.

'This man,' I thought, 'came all the way to the Punjab in some form, appeared at my door and directed me to come and see him at Tiruvannamalai. I went there and got a very good experience when I sat with him. This man must be qualified to advise me. Perhaps his appearance in my room here means that he wants me to go and see him again in Tiruvannamalai. Anyway, since there is no one else in Madras whose opinion I value, I may as well go to him and see what he has to say.' I still had no interest in his philosophy, but I did recollect that I had been quite attracted by his personality and presence.

The following weekend I was scheduled to have a half-day holiday on Saturday afternoon. Sunday, of course, was a holiday every week. I took the train on Saturday and made my way once more to the hall where the Maharshi sat. As on my first visit, I felt that my business was private, so I looked for another opportunity to talk to him when no one else was around. Resorting to the same ruse I had used on my previous visit, I went to see him after lunch. I knew the hall would be empty then. As on my previous trip, the attendant tried to persuade me to come back later, but again the Maharshi intervened and gave me permission to enter and speak to him.

I sat in front of the Maharshi and began to tell him my story. 'For twenty-five years I have been doing *sadhana*, mostly repeating the name of Krishna. Up till fairly recently I was managing 50,000 repetitions a day. I also used to read a lot of spiritual literature. Then Rama, Sita, Lakshmana and Hanuman appeared before me. After they left, I couldn't carry on with my practice. I can't repeat the name any more. I can't read my books. I can't meditate. I feel very quiet inside but there is no longer any desire in me to put my attention on God. In fact, I can't do it even if I try. My mind refuses to engage itself in thoughts of God. What has happened to me and what should I do?'

The Maharshi looked at me and asked, 'How did you come here from Madras?'

I didn't see the point of his question but I politely told him the answer: 'By train.'

'And what happened when you got to the station at Tiruvannamalai?' he inquired.

'Well, I got off the train, handed in my ticket and engaged a bullock cart to take me to the ashram.'

'And when you reached the ashram and paid off the

driver of the cart, what happened to the cart?'

'It went away, presumably back to town,' I said, still not clear as to where this line of questioning was leading.

The Maharshi then explained what he was driving at. 'The train brought you to your destination. You got off it because you didn't need it anymore. It had brought you to the place you wanted to reach. Likewise with the bullock cart. You got off it when it had brought you to Ramanasramam. You don't need either the train or the cart any more. They were the means for bringing you here. Now you are here, they are of no use to you.

'That is what has happened with your *sadhana*. Your *japa*, your reading and your meditation have brought you to your spiritual destination. You don't need them anymore. You yourself did not give up your practices, they left you of their own accord because they had served their purpose. You have arrived.'

Then he looked at me intently. I could feel that my whole body and mind were being washed with waves of purity. They were being purified by his silent gaze. I could feel him looking intently into my Heart. Under that spellbinding gaze I felt every atom of my body being purified. It was as if a new body were being created for me. A process of transformation was going on—the old body was dying, atom by atom, and a new body was being created in its place. Then, suddenly, I understood. I knew that this man who had spoken to me was, in reality, what I already was, what I had always been. There was a sudden impact of recognition as I became aware of the Self. I use the word 'recognition' deliberately, because as soon as the experience was revealed to me, I knew, unerringly, that this was the same state of peace and happiness that I had been immersed in as an eight-year-old boy in Lahore, on the occasion when I had refused to accept the mango drink. The silent gaze of the Maharshi re-established me in that primal state, but this time it was permanent. The 'I' which had for so long been looking for a God outside of itself, because it wanted to get back to that original childhood state, perished in the direct knowledge and experience of the Self which the Maharshi revealed to me. I cannot describe exactly what the experience was or is because the books are right when they say that words cannot convey it. I can only talk about peripheral things. I can say that every cell, every atom in my body leapt to attention as they all recognised and experienced the Self that animated and supported them, but the experience itself I cannot describe. I knew that my spiritual quest had definitely ended, but the source of that knowledge will always remain indescribable.

I got up and prostrated to the Maharshi in gratitude. I had finally understood what his teachings were and are. He had told me not to be attached to any personal God, because all forms are perishable. He could see that my chief impediments were God's beautiful form and the love I felt towards Him. He had advised me to ignore the appearances of these ephemeral Gods and to enquire instead into the nature and source of the one who wanted to see them. He had tried to point me towards what was real and permanent, but stupidly and arrogantly I had paid no attention to his advice.

With hindsight I could now see that the question 'Who am I?' was the one question which I should have asked myself years before. I had had a direct experience of the Self when I was eight and had spent the rest of my life trying to return to it. My mother had convinced me that devotion to Krishna would bring it back and had somehow brainwashed me into undertaking a quest for an external God whom she said could supply me with that one experience which I desired so much. In a lifetime of spiritual seeking I had met hundreds of *sadhus*, swamis and gurus, but none of them had told me the simple truth the way the Maharshi had done. None of them had said, 'God is within you. He is not apart from you. You alone are God. If you find the source of the mind by asking yourself "Who am I?" you will experience Him in your Heart as the Self.' If I had met the Maharshi earlier in my life, listened to his teachings and put them into practice, I could probably have saved myself years of fruitless external searching.

I must make one other comment about the greatness of the Maharshi. In the days that followed my vision of Rama I went all over Madras, looking for advice on how to start my *sadhana* again. The swamis I saw there gave me pious platitudes because they could not see into my Heart and mind the way the Maharshi could. Several days later, when I came and sat in front of the Maharshi, he didn't tell me to keep on trying because he could see that I had reached a state in which my *sadhana* could never be resumed again. 'You have arrived,' he said. He knew I was ready for realisation and through his divine look he established me in his own state. The real Master looks into your mind and Heart, sees what state you are in, and gives out advice which is always appropriate and relevant. Other people, who are not established in the Self, can only give out advice which is based on either their own limited experience or on what they have heard or read. This advice is often foolish. The true teacher will never mislead you with bad advice because he always knows what you need, and he always knows what state you are in.

Before I carry on with my story I should like to recapitulate some of the main events in my spiritual career because they illustrate, in a general way, how the process of realisation comes about. Firstly, there must be a desire for God, a love for Him, or a desire for liberation. Without that, nothing is possible. In my own case, the experience I had had when I was eight awakened such a great desire for God within me that I spent a quarter of a century in an obsessive search for Him. This desire for God or realisation is like an inner flame. One must kindle it and then fan it until it becomes a raging fire which consumes all one's other desires and interests. A single thought or a desire other than the thought 'I want God' or 'I want Self-realisation' is enough to prevent that realisation from taking place. If these thoughts arise, it means that the fire is not burning intensely enough. In the years I was an ecstatic Krishna *bhakta* I was fanning the flames of my desire for God, and in the process burning up all my other desires. If this inner fire rages for long enough, with sufficient intensity, it will finally consume that one, central, overwhelming desire for God or the Self. This is essential because realisation will not take place until even this last desire has gone.[4] After this final desire disappears, there will be the silence of no thoughts. This is not the end, it is just a mental state in which thoughts and desires no longer arise. That is what happened to me in Madras after Rama appeared before me. All my thoughts and desires left me, so much so, I couldn't take up any of my practices again.

Many people have had temporary glimpses of the Self. Sometimes it happens spontaneously, and it is not uncommon for it to happen in the presence of a realised Master. After these temporary glimpses, the experience goes away because there are still thoughts and latent desires which have not been extinguished. The Self will only accept, consume and totally destroy a mind that is completely free of *vasanas*. That was the state of my mind for the few days I was in Madras. But realisation did not happen in those few days because the final ingredient was not present. I needed the grace of my Master; I needed to sit before him; I needed to have him tell me, 'You have arrived,' and I needed to believe him; and I needed to have him transmit his power and grace via his divine look. When the Maharshi's gaze met my *vasana*-free mind, the Self reached out and destroyed it in such a way that it could never rise or function again. Only Self remained.

I mentioned earlier that it was my mother who turned me into a Krishna *bhakta*. I discovered after my realisation that she had merely been the instrumental cause, for the roots of that particular passion for Krishna could be traced back to my previous life as a yogi in South India. When knowledge of this previous life came to me, it went a long way to explaining the pattern of my current life. In my last life I was a great Krishna *bhakta* who had disciples of his own and who had built a temple dedicated to Krishna in which was installed a large, white, stone statue of the deity. During that particular life I had frequently reached the state of *nirvikalpa samadhi*, but I had not managed to realise the Self. One of my impediments then was that I still had a sexual desire for one of the workers in my ashram. She was a low-caste woman who used to do odd jobs there. I never made any advances to her and I tried hard to control my desire, but it never completely left me. When I was reborn as H.W.L. Poonja, this was the woman I ended up marrying. That one *vasana* had been enough to bring about a rebirth in which I had to marry her and raise a family with her. Such are the workings of karma.

My life as a Krishna yogi ended in an unusual and somewhat gruesome way. I had entered a state of *nirvikalpa samadhi* and remained in it for twenty days. My devotees thought that I had died because they could detect no signs of breathing or blood circulation. One man from a local village, who was supposed to be an expert in these matters, was brought in to see if the *prana* had left the body. He scrutinised my fontanelle before announcing that he was going to drill a hole there to see if there was any life still in the body. He borrowed a tool which was used to scrape out coconuts and gouged a hole in the top of my skull with it. Then he peered into the hole and pronounced me dead. My devotees accepted the verdict and buried me in a *samadhi* pit which was dug near the temple. I then died from being buried alive. I had been fully aware of the activities of the man who had drilled the hole and of the devotees who had finally buried me, but I was not able to respond in any way because I was so deeply immersed in *nirvikalpa samadhi*. It was uncannily like the experiences I had had as a boy in my current life, those experiences in which I had been immersed in peace and happiness, aware of what was going on around me, but unable to make any response.

Many years ago, when I was in the South, I went to have a look at this temple. I remembered enough of the route from my last life to direct the driver of the taxi from the local station, even though it was a long way from town with a lot of turnings at various junctions along the way. It was just as I had remembered it. The white Krishna statue I had installed was still there. I went off to look at my old *samadhi*, but it had gone. The local river had changed its course slightly and washed it away.

The Maharshi had taught me that I should not run after the forms of Gods such as Krishna because they are ephemeral. Though I have followed his advice since he showed me who I am, nonetheless, images of Gods still continue to appear to me. Even now, decades after my spiritual search ended, Krishna still regularly appears to me. I still feel a great love for Him whenever He appears, but He no longer has the power to make me look for anything outside my own Self.

Let me explain. When I was a young boy I thought that the body of Krishna was real because I could touch it. I now know that this is not the true criterion of reality. Reality is that which always exists and never changes, and only the formless Self meets that definition. With hindsight I can therefore say that, when I was a boy, the appearance of Krishna in my bedroom was a transient, unreal phenomenon which arose in consciousness, the one reality. All the other appearances of Krishna in my life can be classified in the same way. Now, abiding as the Self, I cannot be tricked or deluded by the majesty of the Gods, even the ones that manifest right in front of me, because I know that whatever power or beauty they may appear to have is illusory. All power and beauty are within me as my own Self, so I no longer need to look for them anywhere else.

After my final experience in the Maharshi's presence, my outer life went on much as before. I went back to Madras, carried on with my job, and supported my family to the best of my ability. At weekends, or when I had accumulated enough leave, I would go back to Tiruvannamalai, sit at the feet of my Master and bask in his radiant presence. The cynical, sceptical seeker who had aggressively confronted the Maharshi on his first visit had gone for good. All that remained was love for him.

In the first few months after my realisation, I didn't have a single thought. I could go to the office and perform all my duties without ever having a thought in my head. It was the same when I went to Tiruvannamalai. Whether I was sitting in the hall with the Maharshi, walking around the mountain or shopping in town, everything I did was performed without any mental activity at all. There was an ocean of inner silence that never gave rise to even a ripple of thought. It did not take me long to realise that a mind and thoughts are not necessary to function in the world.

When one abides as the Self, some divine power takes charge of one's life. All actions then take place spontaneously, and are performed very efficiently, without any mental effort or activity.

I often brought my family and business colleagues to the ashram at weekends. Out of all the people I brought, the Maharshi seemed to be particularly fond of my daughter. She had learned quite good Tamil during her time in Madras, so she could converse with him in his native language. They used to laugh and play together whenever we visited.

On one of my visits she sat in front of the Maharshi and went into what appeared to be a deep meditative trance. When the bell for lunch went, I was unable to rouse her. The Maharshi advised me to leave her in peace, so we went off to eat without her. When we came back she was still in the same place in the same state. She spent several more hours in this condition before returning to her normal waking state.

Major Chadwick had been watching all this with great interest. After her experience ended, he approached the Maharshi and said, 'I have been here for more than ten years, but I have never had an experience like this. This seven-year-old girl seems to have had this experience without making any effort at all. How can this be?'

The Maharshi merely smiled and said, 'How do you know that she is not older than you?'

After this intense experience my daughter fell in love with the Maharshi and became very attached to his form. Before we left she told him, 'You are my father. I am not going back to Madras. I will stay here with you.'

The Maharshi smiled and said, 'No, you cannot stay here. You must go back with your real father. Go to school, finish your education, and then you can come back if you want to.'

The experience had a profound impact on her life. Just a few weeks ago I overheard her telling someone in our kitchen that not a day has passed since then without some memory of that event. But if you ask her about it, she can't give any kind of answer. If anyone asks her, 'What happened that day when you were in a trance in front of the Maharshi?' her response is always the same. She just starts crying. She has never been able to describe or explain, even to me, what exactly happened.

On another visit I brought a Muslim *pir* I had met in Madras. As a professor in Baghdad he had had an inner awakening and taken to the religious life. He had come to India because he had suddenly felt an urge to visit some Hindu holy men to see what sort of state they were in. I encouraged him to join me on one of my visits to the Maharshi since I could not imagine a better example of a Hindu saint. At Tiruvannamalai we sat in the hall together for some time, looking at the Maharshi. Then the *pir* got up, saluted him and walked out. When I caught up with him and asked him why he had left so suddenly, he said, 'I have smelled this one flower in the garden of Hinduism. I don't need to smell any of the others. Now I am satisfied and can go back to Baghdad.'

This man was a *jnani* and in those few minutes with the Maharshi he was able to satisfy himself that the flowering of *jnana* in Hindus was no different from the highest experience attained by Islamic saints.

Such enlightened people are very rare. In the last forty years or so I have met thousands of *sadhus*, swamis, gurus, etc. I have been to *kumbha melas* which millions of pilgrims attended; I have been to many of the big ashrams in India; I have toured the Himalayas, meeting many reclusive hermits there; I have met yogis with great *siddhis*, men who could actually fly. But in all the years since my realisation I have only met two men, apart from the Maharshi himself, who convinced me that they had attained full and complete Self-realisation.[5] This Muslim *pir* was one. The other was a relatively unknown *sadhu* I met by the side of a road in Karnataka.

I was waiting for a bus in an isolated location near Krishnagiri, a town located midway between Tiruvannamalai and Bangalore. An extremely disreputable-looking man approached me. He wore tattered, filthy clothes and had open wounds on his legs which he had neglected so badly they were infested with maggots. We talked for a while and I offered to remove the maggots from his leg and give him some medicine which would help his wounds to heal. He wasn't interested in having any assistance from me. 'Leave the maggots where they are,' he said. 'They are enjoying their lunch.'

Feeling that I couldn't leave him in such a miserable condition, I tore a strip off the shawl I was wearing and tied it round his leg so that at least he could have a clean bandage. We said 'good-bye' and he walked off into the nearby forest.

I had recognised this man to be a *jnani* and was idly speculating on what strange karma had led him to neglect his body in such a way, when a woman approached me. She had been selling iddlies and dosas at a nearby roadside stall.

'You are a very lucky man,' she said. 'That was a great *mahatma*. He lives in this forest but he almost never shows himself. People come from Bangalore to have his *darshan*, but he never allows anyone to find him unless he himself wants to meet them. I myself sit here all day, but this is the first time I have seen him in more than a year. This is the first time I have seen him approach a complete stranger and start talking to him.'

I have digressed a little into the story of the bedraggled *jnani* because he and the Muslim *pir* illustrate a couple of points that I want to make. The first I have already alluded to. Though many people have had a temporary direct experience of the Self, full and permanent realisation is a very rare event. I say this from direct experience, having seen, quite literally, millions of people who are on some form of spiritual path. The second point is also interesting, for it reflects great credit on the Maharshi. Out of these people, the only three I have met since my realisation who have satisfied me that they are *jnanis*, it was the Maharshi alone who made himself available, twenty-four hours a day, to anyone who wanted to see him. The Krishnagiri *sadhu* hid in his forest; the Muslim *pir*, when he stayed at my house in Madras, kept himself locked up and refused to see visitors who wanted to see him. Of these three, the Maharshi alone was easy to find and easy to approach. My own early visits demonstrate the point. He could have kept quiet on my first two after-lunch visits and allowed his attendant to send me away. Instead, sensing that I had an urgent problem, he allowed me to come in and talk about the things that were bothering me. No one was ever denied access to him because they were immature or unsuitable. Visitors and devotees could sit in his presence for as long as they wanted, all of them absorbing as much grace as they could assimilate. Through his *jnana* alone, the Maharshi was a towering spiritual giant. By making himself continuously available, the lustre of his greatness shone even more.

On my visits to Sri Ramanasramam I would sit in the hall with the Maharshi, listening to him deal with all the questions and doubts that devotees brought to him. Occasionally, if some answer was not clear, or if it did not tally with my own experience, I would ask a question myself. My army training had taught me that I should keep on questioning until I fully understood what was being explained to me. I applied the same principles to the Maharshi's philosophical teachings.

On one occasion, for example, I heard him tell a visitor that the spiritual Heart-centre was located on the right side of the chest, and that the 'I'-thought arose from that place and subsided there. This did not tally with my own experience of the Heart. On my first visit to the Maharshi, when my Heart opened and flowered, I knew that it was neither inside nor outside the body. And when the experience of the Self became permanent during my second visit, I knew that it was not possible to say that the Heart could be limited to or located in the body.

So I joined in the conversation and asked, 'Why do you place the spiritual Heart on the right side of the chest and limit it to that location? There can be no right or left for the Heart because it does not abide inside or outside the body. Why not say it is everywhere? How can you limit the truth to a location inside the body? Would it not be more correct to say that the body is situated in the Heart, rather than the Heart in the body?' I was quite vigorous and fearless in my questioning because that was the method I had been taught in the army.

The Maharshi gave me an answer which fully satisfied me. Turning to me, he explained that he only spoke in this way to people who still identified themselves with their bodies. 'When I speak of the "I" rising from the right side of the body, from a location on the right side of the chest, the information is for those people who still think that they are the body. To these people I say that the Heart is located there. But it is really not quite correct to say that the "I" rises from and merges in the Heart on the right side of the chest. The Heart is another name for the Reality and it is neither inside nor outside the body; there can be no in or out for it, since it alone is. I do not mean by "Heart" any physiological organ or any plexus or anything like that, but so long as one identifies oneself with the body and thinks that one is the body, one is advised to see where in the body the "I"-thought rises and merges again. It must be the Heart at the right side of the chest since every man, of whatever race and religion, and in whatever language he may be saying "I", points to the right side of the chest to indicate himself. This is so all over the world, so that must be the place. And by keenly watching the daily emergence of the "I"-thought on waking, and its subsiding in sleep, one can see that it is in this Heart on the right side.'[6]

I liked to talk to the Maharshi when he was alone or when there were very few people around, but this was not often possible. For most of the day he was surrounded by people. Even when I did approach him with a question, I had to have an interpreter on hand because my Tamil wasn't good enough to sustain a philosophical conversation.

The summer months were the best time to catch him in a quiet environment. The climate was so unpleasant at that time, few visitors came. One time in May, at the height of the summer, there were only about five of us with the Maharshi. Chadwick, one of the five, made a joke about it: 'We are your poor devotees, Bhagavan. Everyone who can afford to go to the hills to cool off has left. Only we paupers have been left behind.'

The Maharshi laughed and replied, 'Yes, staying here in summer, without running away, is the real *tapas*'.[7]

I would sometimes accompany the Maharshi on his walks around the ashram. This enabled me to talk privately with him and to observe firsthand how he dealt with devotees and ashram workers. I watched him supervise the sharing out of the food, making sure everyone received equal portions; I watched him remonstrate with workers who wanted to prostrate to him rather than carry on with their work. Everything he did contained a lesson for us. Every step he took was a teaching in itself.

The Maharshi preferred to work in a low-key, unspectacular way with the people around him. There were no great demonstrations of his power, just a continuous subtle emanation of grace which inexorably seeped into the hearts of all those who came into contact with him.

One incident I witnessed illustrates very well the subtle and indirect way that he worked with us. A woman brought her dead son to the Maharshi, placing the dead body before the couch. The boy had apparently died from a snake bite. The woman begged the Maharshi to bring him back to life, but he deliberately ignored her and her repeated requests. After a few hours the ashram manager made her take the corpse away. As she was leaving the ashram she met some kind of snake charmer who claimed that he could cure her son. The man did something to the boy's hand, the place where he had been bitten, and the boy immediately revived, even though he had been dead for several hours. The devotees in the ashram attributed the miraculous cure to the Maharshi, saying, 'When a problem is brought to the attention of a *jnani*, some "automatic divine activity" brings about a solution'. According to this theory, the Maharshi had done nothing consciously to help the boy, but at a deeper, unconscious level, his awareness of the problem had caused the right man to appear at the right place. The Maharshi of course disclaimed all responsibility for the miraculous cure. 'Is that so?' was his only response when told about the boy's dramatic recovery. This was typical of the Maharshi. He never performed any miracles and never even accepted any responsibility for those that seemed to happen either in his presence or on account of a devotee's faith in him. The only 'miracles' he indulged in were those of inner transformation. By a word, a look, a gesture, or merely by remaining in silence, he quietened the minds of people around him, enabling them to become aware of who they really were. There is no greater miracle than this.

In 1947 the British Government, under pressure from the Muslims, decided that after independence India would be partitioned. The areas with a Muslim majority would form the new state of Pakistan; the leftover territory would be the new, independent India. In the Northwest, the border ran roughly north-south and was located to the east of Lahore. This meant that my family would find themselves in Pakistan after independence, which was scheduled to occur in August. In the months preceding independence many Muslims from India migrated to the embryonic state of Pakistan. At the same time, many Hindus who were living in areas that would be in Pakistan left to live in India. Feelings ran high in both communities. Hindus trying to leave Pakistan were attacked, robbed and even killed by Muslims, while Muslims trying to leave India were subjected to the same treatment by Hindus. The violence escalated to the point where whole trainloads of Hindus leaving Pakistan were hijacked and gunned down by Muslims, while, in the other direction, Hindus were attacking trains of fleeing Muslims, and murdering all the occupants. I knew nothing about all this because I never bothered to read newspapers or listen to the radio.

In July 1947, a month before independence, Devaraja Mudaliar approached me and asked me which part of the Punjab I came from. When I told him that I came from a town about 200 miles to the west of Lahore, he informed me about the forthcoming partition, stressing that my family and my father's house were going to end up in Pakistan.

'Where are all the members of your family at the moment?' he asked.

'So far as I know,' I answered, for I didn't have much contact with them, 'they are still all in my home town. None of them is living in a place which will be in India.'

'Then why don't you go and fetch them?' he asked. 'It is not safe for them to stay there.' He told me about the massacres that were going on and insisted that it was my duty to look after my family by taking them to a safe place. He even suggested that I bring them to Tiruvannamalai.

'I'm not going,' I told him. 'I cannot leave the company of the Maharshi.' This was not an excuse; I felt it was quite literally true. I had reached a stage in my relationship with the Maharshi where I loved him so much, I couldn't take my eyes off him or contemplate the thought of going to the other end of the country for an indefinite period.

That day, as we accompanied the Maharshi on his evening walk outside the ashram, Devaraja Mudaliar turned to him and said, 'Poonja's family seems to be stranded in Western Punjab. He doesn't want to go there. Nor does he seem interested in trying to get them out. Independence is less than a month away. If he does not go now, it may be too late.'

The Maharshi agreed with him that my place was with my family. He told me, 'There will be a lot of trouble in the area you come from. Why don't you go there at once? Why don't you go and bring your family out?'

Though this amounted to an order, I was still hesitant. Ever since the day the Maharshi had shown me who I am, I had felt great love for him and great attachment to him. I genuinely felt that I didn't have any relationship in the world other than the one I had with him. My attitude was,

'I feel so much gratitude towards this man who has removed my fears, shown me the light and removed the darkness from my mind, I can't have any relationship any more except with him'. I attempted to explain my position to the Maharshi.

'That old life was only a dream,' I said. 'I dreamed I had a wife and a family. When I met you, you ended my dream. I have no family any more, I only have you.'

The Maharshi countered by saying, 'But if you know that your family is a dream, what difference does it make if you remain in that dream and do your duty? Why are you afraid of going if it is only a dream?'

I then explained the main reason for my reluctance to go. 'I am far too attached to your physical form. I cannot leave you. I love you so much I cannot take my eyes off you. How can I leave?'

'I am with you wherever you are,' was his answer. From the way he spoke to me I could see that he was determined that I should go. His last statement was, in effect, a benediction for my forthcoming trip and for my future life in general.

I immediately understood the deep significance of his remark. The 'I' which was my Master's real nature was also my own inner reality. How could I ever be away from that 'I'? It was my own Self, and both my Master and I knew that nothing else existed.

I accepted his decision. I prostrated before him and for the first and only time in my life I touched his feet as an act of veneration, love and respect. He didn't normally let anyone touch his feet, but this was a special occasion and he made no objection. Before I rose I collected some of the dust from beneath his feet and put it in my pocket to keep as a sacred memento. I also asked for his blessings because I had an intuition that this was our final parting; I somehow knew I would never see him again.

I left the ashram and made my way to Lahore. The atmosphere there was every bit as bad as I had been led to expect. Angry Muslims were running around shouting, 'Kill the Hindus! Kill the Hindus!' Others were shouting, 'We got Pakistan so easily, let us now invade India and conquer it! Let us take it by the sword!'

I went to the station and bought a ticket for my home town. I found a seat in a nearly-empty carriage, put my bags there and went outside to have a drink at the platform tea stall. Surprised at finding the train so empty, I asked one of the passers-by, 'What's going on? Why is the train so empty?'

He gave me the reason. 'The Hindus are not travelling any more. They are afraid to go anywhere by train because they are in the minority here. So many train passengers are being murdered, no one wants to travel that way any more.'

In those violent days, Hindus and Muslims were travelling in separate carriages so they could protect each other in case there was any trouble. The nearly-empty carriages I was looking at were those occupied by the Hindus.

And then an inner voice, the voice of my Master, said to me, 'Go and sit with the Muslims in their compartment. Nothing will happen to you there.' Superficially it seemed like a good idea, but I had doubts about my ability to fool my Muslim fellow-passengers into believing that I was one of them. I dressed very differently and I had a highly-visible 'Om' tattooed on the back of one of my hands. I came from a community of brahmin Hindus which thought that all Muslims were polluted and impure because they ate beef. Anyone who wanted to come into our house had to show the back of his hand first. All the local Hindus had an 'Om' tattooed there; the Muslims did not.

The Hindus were allowed in, the Muslims were excluded.

I listened to the voice and took my seat with the Muslims. No one objected or questioned my right to be there. Somewhere in the countryside the train was stopped by Muslims and all the passengers in the Hindu carriages were gunned down. No one paid any attention to me, even though, to my own eyes at least, I was clearly a Hindu.

I disembarked from the train when it reached my destination and made my way to my family home. When I got there it was locked and barred. Nobody answered my knock. Eventually my father appeared on the roof, demanding to know who I was.

'It's your son,' I called back. 'Can't you see? Don't you recognise my voice?'

He recognised me and showed his astonishment at my return. He knew that my family obligations had never rated highly in my priorities before.

'What have you come back for?' he asked, somewhat incredulously. 'The Punjab is burning. Hindus are being murdered everywhere. Anyway, how did you get here? Are the trains still running?'

'Yes,' I called back, 'the trains are still running. That's how I got here.'

My father thought for a while before coming to a major decision. 'In that case,' he said, 'you must take the family out of the Punjab and get them settled somewhere in India. If the trains are still running, I can get railway passes for you all.'

The following day, equipped with the relevant passes, I took thirty-four members of my family, virtually all of them women, out of Western Punjab into India. The train we took from Lahore was the last one to leave that city for India. After partition, the trains never crossed the border again.

The Maharshi had sent me to the Punjab to do my duty. That was typical of him because he never permitted his devotees to abandon their family responsibilities. Telling me, 'I am with you wherever you are,' he sent me off to fulfil my obligations. When I first heard this remark, I only appreciated its philosophical significance. It did not occur to me that physically I would also be under his care and protection. Yet this was manifestly the case. He had told me where to sit on the train. For more than twenty hours after the massacre I had sat unrecognised in a Muslim carriage, despite having pierced ears and an '*Om*' on my hand, both of them classic Hindu identification marks. In an environment of utter anarchy I had secured seats for a vast contingent of my family and got them out of danger on the last train that ever left Lahore for India. After independence the cross-border railway lines were pulled up and the border itself was closed.

I took my family to Lucknow because I had a friend there from my time in the army whom I knew I could rely on for help. With his assistance I found suitable accommodation. There was no question of my returning to the Maharshi because I was the only potential earner in our group. Refugees fleeing Pakistan for India were stripped of all their possessions before they left. Even personal jewellery was taken. Arriving in India with little more than the clothes we were wearing, it became my responsibility to feed, clothe and support this vast group of destitute refugees. Having listened to the Maharshi for several years, I knew by heart the advice he always gave to householders: 'Abide as the Self and do your duties in the world without being attached to them in any way.' For the next few years I had ample opportunity to live this philosophy.

I had to work night and day to keep the family going. I have always been a big, strong man, and in my youth I was a successful wrestler. But even with all this strength at my disposal, I had a gruelling, arduous time trying to keep up with all the needs and expectations of thirty-four dependants, all of us stranded in a strange land. It did not help matters that my family did not feel any need to economise. On the rare occasions I came home I would find a houseful of women, drinking cups of tea and frying mountains of *pakoras*. I remember buying an eighteen kilo tin of cooking oil for them almost every week.

At 8.47, on the evening of April 14th, 1950, I was walking down a street in Lucknow. I suddenly felt an enormous spasm in my chest which nearly knocked me to the ground. I thought it must be some sort of heart attack. A few seconds later I saw a few people pointing up to a large meteor which was trailing across the sky. This was the meteor which thousands of people all over India saw in the first few seconds after the Maharshi's death. Many people have said that they knew instinctively that the appearance of the meteor signified that the Maharshi was dead. This never occurred to me at the time. I only found out about his death when I listened to the news on the radio the following day.

There is one final episode I must tell before I complete the story of my association with my Master. Many years later, sitting on the banks of the Ganges, I had an extraordinary vision of myself, the self that had been H.W.L. Poonja, in all its various incarnations through time. I watched the self move from body to body, from form to form. It went through plants, through animals, through birds, through human bodies, each in a different place in a different time. The sequence was extraordinarily long. Thousands and thousands of incarnations, spanning millions of years, appeared before me. My own body finally appeared as the last one of the sequence, followed shortly afterwards by the

radiant form of Sri Ramana Maharshi. The vision then
ended. The appearance of the Maharshi had ended that
seemingly endless sequence of births and rebirths. After
his intervention in my life, the self that finally took the
form of Poonja could incarnate no more. The Maharshi destroyed it by a single look.

As I watched the endless incarnations roll by, I also experienced time progressing at its normal speed. That is to
say, it really felt as if millions of years were elapsing. Yet
when my normal consciousness returned, I realised that
the whole vision had occupied but an instant of time.[8] One
may dream a whole lifetime but when one wakes up one
knows that the time which elapsed in the dream was not
real, that the person in the dream was not real, and that the
world which that person inhabited was not real. All this is
recognised instantly at the moment of waking. Similarly,
when one wakes up to the Self, one knows instantly that
time, the world, and the life one appeared to live in it are
all unreal. That vision by the Ganges brought home this
truth to me very vividly. I knew that all my lifetimes in
samsara were unreal, that the Maharshi had woken me up
from this wholly imaginary nightmare by showing me the
Self that I really am. Now, freed from that ridiculous
samsara, and speaking from the standpoint of the Self, the
only reality, I can say, 'Nothing has ever come into existence; nothing has ever happened; the unchanging, formless
Self alone exists'. That is my experience, and that is the experience of everyone who has realised the Self.

A few months ago, at one of the satsangs I conduct in
Lucknow, someone gave me a note which concluded: 'My
humble respects and gratitude to you, especially to one
who was a disciple of Ramana Maharshi.'

I couldn't let this pass. 'Why do you say "was"?' I exclaimed. 'Please correct your grammar! Please correct your

grammar! I *am* his disciple! He *is* my Master. How can I throw him away into the past? There is no past and no future for the Master. There isn't even a present because he has transcended time.'

When I left him physically in 1947 he told me, 'I am with you wherever you are'. That was his promise and that is my experience. There is no one called Poonja left anymore. There is only an emptiness where he used to be. And in that emptiness there shines the 'I', the 'I' that *is* my reality, the 'I' that *is* my Master, the 'I' that he promised would be with me wherever I am. Whenever I speak, it is not someone called Poonja who is speaking, it is the 'I' that is the Maharshi who speaks, the 'I' which is the Self in the Heart of all beings.

I tried to explain this to the person who sent me the note. 'Who am I? What am I? I never think it is I, Poonja, who am speaking. It is he, the Maharshi, the Master who is speaking. If I ever thought that this person called Poonja was speaking to you, I would have no right to sit here because whatever would come out of my mouth would be false. It is my own Master who speaks; it is your own Master who speaks. It is your own Heart speaking; it is your own Self which is speaking to you. There is no one here claiming to be an intermediary. There is no one here claiming that he once had a Master called "Sri Ramana Maharshi". There is only emptiness, and in that emptiness the "I" which *is*, not was, my Master speaks.

'I am sitting here introducing you to my teacher and his teachings. He is the teacher, not I. He is your own Self. He is the teacher of the world. He was the teacher before you even knew him. He was there, waiting for you, smiling within your Heart. Now you are attracted by him, not me. I, Poonja, am not in the picture at all.'

Poonja has gone for good, but the Master remains and

will always remain. He is seated in my Heart as my own imperishable Self. Shining as the 'I', he alone is.

Sources

1. Personal interviews, 1990-92.

2. *The Secret of Arunachala*, Swami Abhishiktananda, 1979 ed., pp. 80-95.

3. 'How I came to the Maharshi,' H.W.L. Poonja, *The Mountain Path*, 1965, pp. 155-6.

4. Sri Poonja satsang transcript, 10.3.92.

5. 'Plunge into Eternity,' Catherine Ingram, *Yoga Journal*, September/October 1992, pp. 56-63.

6. *Day by Day with Bhagavan*, Devaraja Mudaliar, 1977 ed., pp. 201-2.

Notes

1. Though they may sound absurd, these sequences are quite common in *Vedanta*. The second paragraph of *Who am I?* (an early work by Sri Ramana Maharshi) begins 'Who am I? The gross body which is composed of the seven *dhatus* (chyle, blood, flesh, marrow, bone and semen) is not "I".' It continues in a similar vein for another fifteen lines.

2. In one of my interviews with Sri Poonja he told me that this quote had been mistranslated in his article in *The Mountain Path*. There it appears as 'You, that is me, is Bhagavan'.

3. The account of this experience was given in response to the following question: 'Ramana Maharshi sometimes said that there is a very small hole in the spiritual Heart. He said that in the *sahaja* state it is open, but in other states it is closed. Did your Heart open in this way in Bhagavan's presence? Bhagavan also once said, in describing the realisation process, that, "the downward-facing Heart becomes upward-facing and remains as That". Did you have any experience akin to this?'

4. A very similar idea can be found in *Who am I?*, answer ten. 'By the enquiry "Who am I?" the thought "Who am I?" will destroy all other thoughts, and like the stick used for stirring the funeral pyre, it will in the end get destroyed. Then there will arise Self-realisation.'

5. In the course of a conversation I had with him Sri Poonja told me that he thought his mother's Guru was also a *jnani*. Since this section deals with people he has met since his own realisation, his mother's Guru is not mentioned.

6. Part of this answer was recorded in *Day by Day with Bhagavan*, 23.5.46. The compiler, Devaraja Mudaliar, came into the hall as the answer was being given. He therefore missed the original question, its context, and the first part of the answer.

7. To do *tapas* is to undergo some severe form of spiritual

discipline, often involving mortification of the body, in order to make spiritual progress. Since the word *tapas* is derived from a Sanskrit word meaning 'heat', Bhagavan was probably making an intentional pun.

8. Sri Poonja informed me that many years later, when he was visiting Paris, he read a Buddhist *sutra* in which the Buddha describes an almost identical experience.

Catherine Ingram and Papaji

Plunge Into Eternity

by Catherine Ingram
Lucknow, 1992

oonjaji, what is freedom?

Freedom is to know your own fundamental nature, your own Self. Nothing else. Freedom is the easiest thing of all to get. You don't even need to think.

And what is that Self?

This is indescribable. It is not intellectual, not even transcendental. Think of one without even the concept of two. Then drop the concept of one.

You often speak of surrender. Surrender to what?

To that Source through which you speak, through which you see, through which you breathe, through which you taste and touch, through which this Earth revolves and the sun shines, through which you have asked this question itself. Everything happens through that consciousness in which even emptiness is housed. That Supreme Power which is beyond the beyond—your own Self—to that you have to surrender.

Is the consciousness of which you speak eternal—unborn and undying?

Consciousness is beyond the concepts of birth and death, beyond even any concept of eternity or emptiness or space. That which accommodates the space, the emptiness or the eternity, is called consciousness, within which everything exists.

Yet there is the appearance of birth and death.

Creation and destruction happen ceaselessly. All these manifestations are like bubbles and waves in the ocean. Let them happen. The ocean doesn't find that they are separate. The bubbles, the eddies, the waves—they may appear to themselves as separate, but the ocean itself has no trouble with them. Let them move on it, let them have different shapes and different names, let them come and go. This body will be the food of worms and ants. From earth it came and to earth it will return. You are That which shines through it. The consciousness is untouched.

Do you propose that we identify with the ocean—that Source— instead of with the waves?

No, you need not identify with anything. You only need to get rid of your notions. Do not identify with any name or form which is not real. No name or form is real. Now, to reject name and form you need not make any effort or employ any kind of thinking or identification. You have been identifying with names and forms. These have caused you to feel separate from the fundamental nature which you always are, so you have to disidentify with something which is not true. No need to identify with the ocean or the Source. You *are* the Source. When your identification with the unreal has vanished, you will be what you have been, what you are, and what you will be.

What is mind?

Never mind! [Laughing] Show me the mind. You have used the word 'mind'. No one has seen what the mind is. The mind is thought, existing as subjects and objects. The first wave is 'I', then 'I am', then 'I am this, I am that', and finally, 'This belongs to me'. Here the mind begins. Now, keep quiet and do not allow any desire to arise from the Source. Just for one instant of time, don't give rise to any desire. You will find you have no mind and you will also see that you are somewhere indescribable, in tremendous happiness. And then you will see who you really are.

When you enquire 'Who am I?', this will take you home. First reject the 'who', then reject the 'am', then you are left with the 'I'. When this 'I'-thought plunges to its source, it ceases to exist and finds Being Itself. In that place you can very well live without the mind. If you do it, you will find that something else will take care of all your activity. That 'something else' will take care of you much better than the mind ever did.

We can see today what the result of using the mind is, how the world is behaving by using the mind. I believe that if you keep quiet and let the Supreme Power take charge of all activities, you will then see how to live with all beings. The one who knows himself will know what it is to be animals, plants, rocks—everything that exists. If you miss realisation of your own Self, you have not known anything.

People who are spiritually oriented struggle with what is called the 'ego'.

Let us see where the ego is rising from. The ego has to rise from somewhere to become the ego. The ego arises, then mind, then senses—seeing, smelling, tasting, hearing, touching. There must be 'I' before the ego arises. This notion of 'I' is the root cause of the ego, the mind, manifestation, happiness, and unhappiness—*samsara*. Return to 'I' and question what this 'I' is. Where does it rise from? Let us try.

I have done this many times, but....

You may have done it, but now don't do it. Just land into it. Do nothing. When you get enmeshed in the process of doing, you must return back to it again and again. Ego, mind, senses—these are called 'doing'. What I am talking about requires no doing at all, just intelligence. You have only to be watchful, vigilant, attentive, serious. No doing, no thinking, no effort, no notions, no intentions. Leave everything aside, simply keep quiet, and wait for the result.

This result happens here and now with you, but....

Then start from now with this happening. With this happening you have at least broken this process of ego, mind, senses, and manifestation. You can return from the happening. You can step out of this, but do it like a king when he rises from his throne and goes to his garden. He is not a gardener; he is still the king. You *are* this happening wherever you are.

The Buddha spoke about practising this awareness. He taught a meditation practice to enable people to taste this.

I have not found any results from these practices, but they are going on. I don't give you any practice. I just remove your old burdens. Don't expect me to give you something new. If you gain something new, its nature is not eternal, and you will lose it. Freedom cannot be the effect of any cause. You already have everything. You are an emperor. Throw away your begging bowl.

Practice is needed when you have some destination, something to attain. Abandon this concept of gaining something at a later date. What is eternal is here and now. If you find freedom after thirty years of practice, it will still be only here and now. Why wait thirty years?

Just sit with a cool mind and see where you have to go and where you are now. Question yourself: What do I practise for? For practice you need somebody to practise and some intention for practising. What is that thought through which you practise? Through what do you derive this energy to put anything into practice? Do you get my point? If you want to go somewhere, you have to stand up and walk to reach your destination, so there must be some energy to stand and walk. What makes you stand up?

Some desire.

Yes, but where is the desire rising from? Who makes the desire arise and from where does it come? People are doing practices for freedom. I want you to see, here and now, before going to your destination, what you really want. If you want freedom, then first find out what is bondage. Where are the chains? What are the fetters? Sit down calmly, patiently, and question, 'How I am bound?' What binds you except these notions, concepts, perceptions? Forget about all these things. Don't give rise to any notion, any intention, or any idea. Just for a second. Get rid of these notions, instantly. Then, who is seeking freedom? The seeker himself has not yet been tackled.

There's a saying, 'What you are looking for is what is seeking.'

Yes, find out who the seeker is. Find out 'Who am I?' You don't have to move anywhere because it is here and now. It has always been here and now. You are already here and you are already free. You think or have a notion that you have to search for something, to meditate to get something. You have been told this many times. Now, just for a short while, sit quietly and do not activate a single thought. You will discover that what you are searching for through methods or *sadhanas* is already here. It was what was prompting you to meditate. The desire for freedom arises from freedom itself.

Most meditation is only mind working on the mind. Your reality is somewhere where the mind cannot trespass. The real meditation is simply to know that you are already free.

Yet thoughts come uninvited, as unwelcome guests. And it seems that through meditation practice there is a lessening of thoughts. By systematically keeping quiet, in a calm place, thoughts slow down and even go away altogether.

Then you have a tug of war with the thoughts. So long as you are powerful and you are checking them, they are not there. But when you don't check, the thoughts come back again. Don't worry about the thoughts. Let them come and play with you as the waves play with the ocean. When the waves disturb the tranquillity of the ocean, it doesn't mind. Let the thoughts arise, but don't allow them landing space.

So much emphasis is placed on getting rid of thoughts, as though a mind without thoughts is tantamount to an awakened state.

No, no, no. Let the thoughts come. If you reject them, they will invade forcibly through your door. Remove the door.

Remove the wall itself. Who can then come in? Ideas about in and out are due to the wall, and this wall is the idea, 'I am separate from consciousness'. Let the thoughts come; they are not different from the waves of the ocean. It is better to be at peace with thoughts, the ego, the mind, the senses, and manifestation. Let us not fight with anything. Let us be one. Then you will see your own face in everything. You can speak to plants. You can speak to rocks, and you are the hardness of the rock itself. You are the twittering of the birds. You have to see, I am the twittering of the birds. I am the shining of the stars.

Isn't a still, silent mind more conducive to reaching this depth?

There is no depth. It is immaculate emptiness. No inside, no outside, no surface, no depth. No place to go. Everywhere you go is 'here'. Just look around and tell me the limits of this moment. Go as far as you can go. How is it measured? Its length? Breadth? Width? This moment has nothing to do with time or depth.

Is it really so simple?

Yes. When you know it, you will laugh! People go to mountain caves for thirty years just to find Being Itself. Being is just here and now. It is like searching for your glasses while wearing them. What you have been searching for is nearer than your own breath. You are always in the Source. Whatever you are doing, you are doing it in the Source.

Poonjaji, religions always promise some afterlife. Is this Source that you speak of a promise of everlasting Beingness?

I don't believe in these promises which will happen after death. This experience I am speaking of is here and now. What is not here and now is not worth attempting to get. To enjoy this here and now you have to get rid of the notion that you are not here and now.

Truth must be simple. Complication arises in falsehood. Where there are two, there is fear, and there is falsehood.

Ramana Maharshi, Nisargadatta Maharaj, and even the Buddha referred to this life as a dream. Why?

Because it is not permanent. Nothing has been permanent. Therefore they don't differentiate between this waking state and the dream state. In a dream you are seeing mountains, rivers, and trees which appear real. It is only when you wake up that you say, 'I had a dream'. Upon awakening, those things are seen as transitory, and you call them a dream. The state you have woken up into now seems real, permanent, and continuous when compared to that dream. Like this, when you wake up into consciousness itself, this so-called waking state will also appear to be a dream.

What is the function of the Guru or teacher?

The word 'guru' means 'that which removes ignorance, that which dispels darkness'—the darkness of 'I am the body,' 'I am the mind,' 'I am the senses,' and 'I am the objects and manifestation'. That person who has known Truth himself and is able to impart this knowledge, that person who gives this experience, he is called 'Guru'.

Many people think of you as their Guru.

They are speaking of the body, then. Guru sees only the Self. You are my very own Self. I am your very own Self. This relationship is no relationship. Your Self and my Self, what is the difference? I am speaking to that Self which you truly are. I am speaking to my Self.

Others may be preachers from some sect, they may give you some dogma, but a Guru gives you his own experience, and this experience is timeless consciousness, nothing else. Guru does not give you any teachings, any method, or anything that is destructible, impermanent. One who does this is not a Guru. You are not to follow anyone. You are a lion, and where a lion goes, it cuts its own path.

There are many Osho [Rajneesh] students here in Lucknow with you and more come every day. As you probably know, he was a very controversial teacher with a bad reputation. What are the differences between you and Osho?

I don't indulge in any kinds of differences. The divine is playing. Whatever It is doing, is being done by the commands of that supreme Source. All are my own Self, having different roles to play. It is being beautifully played.

You say that this divine is playing itself out, but let's look at the suffering on this planet. For instance, there is an ecological destruction that is creating a living hell for people and other beings who are not awake in this dream, as we can easily see here in India. We are creating a desert of this Earth and poisoning our land, waters, and air. Many more people will face starvation and live in degraded circumstances. World-wide tensions will increase, and so on. People who are primarily interested in spiritual matters, are, at this particular point in history, sometimes accused of being selfish. What do you feel about rendering service to the world, and from where does the passion arise for service if this manifestation is seen as a dream?

Having known the supreme state, our own Self, from inside there arises compassion. Automatically we are compelled. It's not service. Service has to do with somebody else. When the command is compassion, there's no one doing any service to anybody else. When you are hungry, you eat. You are not in service to the stomach, nor are the hands the servant when they are putting food into the mouth. We should live in the world like this. Service is the responsibility of the Self. Otherwise, who is doing this service? When the action is coming from the ego, there is hypocrisy, jealously, crises. When the doer is not there, compassion arises. If a person is realised, all his actions are beautiful.

What are the main obstructions to freedom?

The main obstruction is that the total, absolute desire for freedom is missing. This is because the relationship with the world has not been absolutely cut off. In a dream, sometimes, we have a wedding, and then we have children, and we of course love our children. When we wake up, we see how we instantly detach ourselves from our dream wedding, from our dream wife, and from our dream children. Like this, when we wake up from this dream, and the relationship terminates, there is freedom. *Viveka* [discrimination] is to discern the real from the unreal.

Do you think there is a danger in people seeing this manifestation as only a dream? If they have this attitude, they may not take responsibility for their actions.

That would be a misunderstanding. In 1947, when India was being partitioned, my home area was going to fall within Pakistan. At that time I was with Ramana Maharshi in Tiruvannamalai.

He said to me, 'There will be a lot of trouble in the area you come from. Why don't you go and look after your family?'

I replied, 'Since meeting you I have no family. It was a dream, and I have no more interest in that dream.'

He told me, 'If you know it is a dream, what difference does it make if you remain in that dream and do your duty?'

Then I said, 'I do not want to leave you'.

He replied, 'I am with you wherever you are'. This I understood then, and still it is true.

Now, when you have discerned the real from the unreal, then do not doubt. Doubt is a wall between you and freedom, and even this doubt is only a concept, a phantom. Plunge into eternity. This is the nectar. People are afraid of tasting the nectar. What to do?

Some teachers propose that there is merit in burning out desires, fulfilling desires until we are sick of them and don't want the objects anymore. You're saying that we need, rather, to see that this reality is just a dream, and then we will lose interest.

Yes, some teachers say that you must fulfil desires. I don't think that to extinguish a fire, you go on pouring gasoline on it. This only makes the fire bigger. Fulfilling desires will not cause them to end. The best way is to know what is real. Once you know what is real and what is not real, you will not desire that which is not real. Then you will stand with only one weapon in your hand: that is, discrimination between the real and the unreal and the desire to be free.

When you have this desire, it merges with freedom itself.

It seems that doubt and the inability to discern the real from the unreal are often perpetuated by psychological habits and a lifetime of conditioning, often leading to various forms of mental suffering. What do you suggest in those cases?

This suffering denotes that you are digging in the graveyard of the past. If you don't touch the past, you can't be unhappy. If you are living in the present, you are happy. In between the past and the future, who are you? You are bliss.

Is it love that is fuelling the cosmos—a gigantic pulsation wanting to unite with Itself?

I don't even call it love. When you utter the word 'love', if you carefully watch, you will see it is taking you to some previous experience which took place in the past. As far as my experience goes, it's not even love, not even love. It is something else—a fullness as when there are no waves in the middle of the ocean. The word 'love' is misused. There is love when there is no lover and no beloved. No subject, no object. This is true love.

To what does the concept of devotion apply?

It is not from any individuality toward something else. The silence is itself surrendering to its Source.

Poonjaji, are you still going beyond and beyond in your life?

Even now. Every moment. Every moment.

Who's Asking the Questions Here?

by Wes Nisker

ind is nothing but thought. You can't separate thought itself from the mind. So first you have to find out which is the first thought that arises from the mind. Which is the first thought?

'I'

Yes, 'I' is the first thought. This 'I' is ego. When we use the word 'I', there is ego. Then there is the mind, then there is a body, then there are senses, then there are sense objects, and then all manifestation arises.

And then there is suffering.

Of course. Where there is a separate being, there is suffering. Where there is oneness, then there is no suffering.

So, understand where this 'I' arises from. The question is this: 'Who am I?' Keep alert and then you will know. Pay full attention and then wait for the answer. Keep quiet and wait for the answer. It only takes one instant of time. Question where the 'I' is arising from now. Previous notions and concepts will not help you. This is a question you have not yet asked yourself. You ask questions to others about something else, but not this question to your own self.

I think that in fact I have asked this question.

'I think I have.' Who thinks that 'I have'? You will have to solve this question in order to solve everything.

I am using the term 'I' in a relative sense, just to....

'I am using. I am using.' Here is the 'I' again.

You are telling me to ask 'Who am I?' And that is exactly what I have been doing in my Buddhist meditation practice for the past twenty years. I have been investigating 'Who am I?'

Yes. 'I have been investigating. I have been investigating.' But you have not really investigated. Investigation means to go in.

Now? You want me to do it now?

Yes, now. Don't run away from 'now'. Just catch hold of this 'now'. You can try to step out of this 'now', but it will follow you—behind, in front, this side, that side, up and down. So what do you see in this 'now'?

I see me.

'I see me, I am me, I am now.' What does it mean? Who is the seer, and who is the seeing? Tell me what you see? 'I see me.' Is it an object, is it a subject? What is the form? What is the form of 'I'?

[Pause for some investigation] This 'I' I am referring to doesn't seem to have a solid form.

When a word has no solid form, then there is no more word. The previous 'I' you were using is no longer there. Now you have come to the real 'I'. Now you are working from 'now'. This previous 'I' was a fake 'I'. That 'I' represented the body and was the egotistic 'I'. But just now, when it went and jumped into the beyond, it was finished. And now this 'now' is finished. You have to start afresh all over again.

Every moment I have to start over.

To see the real 'I' means to see total consciousness, which in reality is representing emptiness. Before, the 'I' you were using was from the body, ego, mind and senses. But when it is arising from emptiness, it is emptiness itself. And this is the fathomless 'I'. When you see this 'I', then you will see everything as 'I'. Then there will be love, then there will be wisdom, then you will see your own reflection in animals, in birds, in plants, in rocks.

Now what about the twenty years of your practice of investigation? What have you been doing for these twenty years?

I've been looking in. I feel like I have experienced emptiness, and have dissolved into emptiness during meditation. I have seen the emptiness of all phenomena.

That emptiness you have been seeing was full of egotism. That was not emptiness. That was only a word, a concept. The emptiness which I am speaking about is not even emptiness. Emptiness has got nothing to do with where I am taking you, but I am using the word. I don't allow you to use the word emptiness even. Where did you learn this word emptiness? You must have learned it from some *sutras*.

Many Mahayana sutras talk about emptiness.

But that belongs to the past. It has nothing to do with this emptiness which I speak about. Now I tell you, don't use the word emptiness either. This emptiness is the finger pointing to something else. You have to reject the finger to see the moon. Now, reject this word emptiness if you want to go beyond.

So, do you think my twenty years of vipassana meditation practice was wasted effort?

No. Those twenty years have brought you to me. [Laughs] And not only twenty years have you been doing this, but for thirty-five million years. But there's no time wasted. In emptiness nothing at all exists. This is the ultimate experience. Emptiness is only a concept. To have this concept is just the pride of the mind. Once you touch the word 'I', simultaneously time will arise and you will have past, present and future. When the 'I' ceases, everything ceases. 'Nothing ever existed' is the ultimate truth. It is something unspeakable and it will remain unspeakable. Buddha spent forty-nine years speaking, speaking, speaking. And I don't think he touched the point. Why should he speak for fifty years after enlightenment?

He said he taught in order to end suffering. To free people.

He was trying to express that which he could not.

We all try to say it in order to pass it on. That is why the Buddha gave out various practices.

All practices involve the ego. In all practices you are working from the ego. You identify with the body and say, 'I am so and so', and you separate yourself from the ultimate truth. The absolute is something else altogether, and in any kind of practice you miss it.

Would you say that all sadhanas *or practices are a hindrance? And is this true for all people?*

Sadhana is not for freedom. It can remove some old habits, such as identification with the body. But *sadhana* is not for freedom, not for truth, not for the absolute. All the time you are doing *sadhana*, the truth is standing in front of you, smiling at you. The barrier in practice is your past concepts, such as the idea that you are bound. You say to yourself, 'I am bound, I am suffering'. And you are only doing *sadhana* to remove the suffering. Not for freedom. Freedom doesn't want any practices. It is there as it is. And you are already free.

Some Zen Buddhist Master once said, 'Now that I'm enlightened, I'm as miserable as ever'. In other words, you get the understanding, you get enlightenment, and still you have to live in the world.

Maybe the Zen Master said that because he suddenly realised that he had suffered needlessly for thirty-five million years, when all that time he had actually been free. [Laughs]

So then, how would you define enlightenment? I think a lot of people believe that they can achieve a steady state of realisation, always living in 'now', always in emptiness. Is that how you would define enlightenment, or does it come and go?

Whatever you do and whatever you don't do, it is all empty. Every day I see people who have had many different teachers and have done all kinds of practices, and they say, 'We are here seeing you because you don't give us any practices. Now we don't have anything to do. We just laugh.' [Laughs]

Maybe they laugh just from being around you. After all, some people say that realisation comes through the grace of a teacher. Would you say that it depends on the grace of the Guru?

It depends on the grace of grace itself. The teacher himself will draw you when you have a desire. First of all, you have to grace your own self.

Are we free to do that?

Your next-door neighbour did not come here and sit next to me to ask this question. So you do have grace.

I may have grace, but did I choose to have that grace? Was I free to have grace?

Grace and freedom are the same thing. Where does grace come from? The grace comes from within. But you do not understand the language of that grace. The grace makes you feel, 'I want to be free'. You said you have been doing meditation practice for twenty years. What was it that was driving you? Your neighbour did not feel this need. Why have you been picked out? Why have you been chosen? It is the grace from within. And this grace takes you to a person who will apprise you of the truth and speak to you in your own tongue. This person will only tell you that you are already free. Anybody who tells you to do this or that should not be regarded as a teacher. He should rather be called a butcher. The teacher relieves you from all activity, from all concepts, all precepts. You have done enough. For thirty-five million years you have been doing, doing, doing. When you come to a true teacher, he will not tell you to do anything more.

You tell us to enquire within. Isn't that doing something?

Going within means just listening to your own Guru. And this Guru is your own Self. You don't know him, you don't recognise him, you don't understand his language of silence. The real Guru will introduce you to the Guru within and ask 'you' to keep quiet. This is your own grace. It comes from within you. No one else can give you this grace.

Who gets this grace? Who is graced with this grace?

Everybody.

Everybody has it?

Yes, everybody has it.

Then why do so few people hear it? Why are so many people living in delusion?

Everybody is already free, but there is a wall hiding the truth from them, and that wall is desire.

That's exactly what the Buddha said. Desire is what clouds the eyes.

Yes. But you can very simply just throw away this desire.

You don't have to do anything. All desires belong to the past. When you don't have any desires from the past, your eyes are open. Try now. Do it yourself and tell me. Don't let any desire stand between you and freedom. Remove this wall of desire just for one second and tell me.

Now?

Yes, now.

[Long pause] There's nothing much here....

Then you have seen. The wall was desire.

When I came here, I had a desire for a good interview.

Any desire is a wall. Even the desire for freedom.

Poonjaji, many people seem to be in a devotional relationship with you, in the tradition of bhakti. *Do some people arrive at truth more easily through devotion than through enquiry?*

The most direct method—only meant for a very few, very sharp people—is enquiry. Nothing more is needed. You can be instantly enlightened through it. You can be free. All practices will bring you ultimately to this. Maybe in this life, or maybe after several other lives. You will eventually have to come to the place of absolute freedom. In devotion there is duality between the devotee and the Guru, or the devotee and the divine. Ultimately, the devotee has to surrender completely, but very few actually do this. Too often devotion is only ritual.

But if one surrenders totally to the Guru?

If the devotee truly surrenders, then he is finished. No more karma will be accumulated. From then on the divine will look after him. It is a love, a romance which always continues, a romance you can't forget. It is really a love affair with your own Self. Enquiry means you have to investigate, 'Who am I? Where is the ego arising from?' It's really the same thing, surrender or enquiry. There are hundreds of other paths, such as yoga and tantra, but I don't think they lead to the ultimate. Enquiry is the true practice. It is a short-cut method.

We all want a short cut.

The shortest. A real teacher can finish his student's work with one word.

You tell people to just be themselves. It sounds like the Zen masters who say, 'Just be ordinary'.

Be ordinary. Yes, just remove the doubt that says you are not awake or not enlightened. Because you are, and it's that simple.

Why then do so many people live in delusion? Is this just the leela, the play of the gods?

Yes.

Unfortunately there is a lot of suffering in this play of the gods.

Because people take it as reality. Therefore they suffer.

Poonjaji, finally, would you give me some advice on how to open my heart and love the world more?

To love the world you have to first learn how to love your own Self. If you love your Self then you love the whole world, because your Self includes everything. Also, if you know your own Self, you know everything there is to know. So, know your own Self. And this knowing is being. That's all you need to know. Knowing is being.

Shanti Devi

This article was written for *Odyssey*, a South African New Age magazine. After reading it out in satsang, Papaji commented that it was an excellent article because it was written from the heart and not the head.

Here and Now in Lucknow
by Shanti Devi

uck-now! Definitely an appropriate name for the city where H.W.L. Poonja resides. It wouldn't seem so at first sight as it is a rather polluted and large Indian city which can easily repel non-serious seekers. Who is coming here? Those who seek freedom! More than two hundred people every day, the amount varying with the seasons of the year. Many of them are Osho *sannyasins*, but there are also many others who come from all parts of the world, sometimes for only a couple of days. What brings them here? Grace. The Self. Themselves. The Universe. Whatever name you want to give to that force which propels us to our destiny. Whatever is to be fulfilled—That which is—that's what we discover in Lucknow: ourselves, who we are!

First of all, who is Poonjaji? He defines himself as 'That'. He is a saint, a Master, a teacher, a Guru (although he himself claims to be none of these). He brings us to the end, the end of *samsara*, the end of millions of years of searching and suffering. His message? Enlightenment is here and now! We are all enlightened, but we don't know it. Bondage is only a concept, he says. It is not real. We can wake up from that dream, from the illusion of life and the world, right now. There is no need to postpone it, all we need is a desire for freedom and one moment of inner silence. One moment between two thoughts, two breaths.

No need to meditate or practise. Nothing to learn, nothing to do. Nothing to attain, reach, grasp, or understand. One only needs to keep quiet. That means not doing anything, not stirring a single thought, having no desire, no wanting, no attachment, no expectations.

All this can be accomplished by self-enquiry. Asking oneself 'Who am I?' is the key to being in the Here and the Now. The question attacks the root of the mind. In fact it bypasses the mind completely and reveals to us what we really are.

If we are not this bag of bones, blood, and flesh that forms our bodies—if we are not our senses, nor the mind, which is only a bundle of thoughts, ideas, notions—who or what then are we? What we really are cannot be understood or even experienced. It can only be realised. Because it is beyond the mind, no words can describe it. That which we are is timeless, infinite. It can be called awareness, consciousness, space, love, silence, or rather, what is beyond silence. We are One, we are God, we are nothing. Total emptiness and nothingness. No word, no name. A total wonder and a total mystery.

Our troubles arise because we identify ourselves with our body, our senses, and our mind. This creates the separation and the duality that is the cause of suffering. 'When there are many, there is falsehood,' says Poonjaji.

In self-enquiry one looks at the root of this 'I'. After that we do not need to touch it again. That is freedom, freedom from the mind. Freedom to be who we are, totally unrestrictedly, enjoying forever serene fulfilment, peace, love, joy, happiness, and bliss. In this state one accepts oneself as one is—without notions, concepts, and judgements. There is no past and no idea of how things should be in the future. There is just a surrendering to what is, to the reality of the Here and the Now. This is knowledge, this is Truth, and this is also very simple. Only our minds want to make us believe it is difficult.

Who convinces us that it is easy? It is the Master, a being who is already enlightened. Only a few very rare beings, such as Ramana Maharshi, have spontaneously realised the Self without a living human Master. And even those who *have* realised with a Master are rare. That is why it is the most wonderful luck to have a living Master like Papaji, a being whose grace can give us the necessary push to jump into the Here and the Now. That grace is what he is offering us from the bottomless depths of his Heart.

Defining Papaji is like talking about the Self: words are lacking, inadequate, inappropriate. How to describe that unconditional love, that infinite wisdom, that kindness, that patience, and sweetness? How to talk about his silence, a silence which communicates so richly? How to speak about the unnameable beauty of the Self that shines through him?

He is now eighty-three years old and probably the happiest man on earth. His happiness is contagious, overwhelming. His sense of humour is spot on, sharp, hilarious. His satsangs are always an occasion to roar with laughter. He never condemns, criticises, or judges. He is egoless, mindless. What comes through him is the clarity of his Heart, which is the Truth. He has that wise ability to see the essence, the Heart, and not the name and form of those who come to him. As a real sage his words and deeds sometimes surprise and puzzle, but the passage of time will inevitably vindicate him and demonstrate the grandeur of his wisdom. He is delightful, mischievous, playful and has incredible fun by just being who he is. His satsangs are touched with beauty, with songs and music that people offer gratefully to him. There are moments of love, moments of truth. In satsang with Papaji we return home, to the *now* that has always been our true home.

∽

Papaji and Madhukar

For many years, up till 1992, Papaji held satsangs with small groups of people in his own house. When increasing numbers of visitors made this impractical, he began to hold satsangs in a large rented house about a kilometre from where he lives. Up to 300 people attend during the winter months. As the numbers grew, various projects were started for the benefit of the visitors. A restaurant, a bookstore and a bakery were opened, video and audio tapes of Papaji were marketed, and several book and film projects were started.

Throughout his years of teaching Papaji refused to let anyone set up an ashram around him because he felt that such organisations inevitably become corrupt. This attitude, which he often affirms in public, led many people to wonder what he thought of all the ashram-like activities which were springing up around him. To clarify the situation, Madhukar, one of the devotees who was most actively involved in the setting up of these projects, submitted a written questionnaire to Papaji and asked him to answer all the questions during one of the public satsangs.

No Building in the Transit Lounge

by Madhukar

eloved Papaji, as we enter 1993, please allow me to submit to your feet the following questions. Would you please answer them in satsang for the benefit of all of us.

For the last two years you have been making yourself available to many people who relate to you as their teacher, Master, Guru. Did we make you our Guru?

This is for them to decide. I do not know.

Do you have any part in this?

Yes, to lend you my hand. No one is a 'part' of anything. My role is to apprise you of the fact that you are not a part, that you are the whole. The parts will eventually disappear, but right now they are dangerous.

Who is asking this question, 'Do you have any part in this?' Who has created this idea? Who is the one asking the question? If you find the answer to the question 'Who am I?' you will also find the answer to the question you have just put to me. Your question, your idea that there are 'parts'—all this is your own creation. If you don't enquire who you are, you become not merely a 'part', you become creation itself. Enquire and find that place where no parts

---

have ever been created. By enquiry, move towards that place of wholeness.

What are the 'parts' I am talking about? They are all the people who think, 'I am so and so. I am separate from the whole.' When you don't enquire you become 'parts' and you become manifestation. You become something that will eventually be destroyed. So, proceed towards your own source by asking, 'Who is the questioner?'

The first and most obvious answer is, 'I am the questioner'. But when you say, 'I am the questioner,' you are surely still speaking of the body and the senses, your desires, your belongings, your hopes. This collection of identities seeking its source can be compared to the waves on the surface of the ocean wondering what they really are and where they come from. When the waves first make this enquiry they initially think that they are parts of the whole. 'We are all parts of the ocean,' they will say. 'Some are big, some are small; one is in front, one is behind; all of us are in constant motion.' These waves will never find out what they really are if they restrict their enquiry to studying their relative sizes, their relative positions and their relative speeds. Looking at names and forms can never take you back to the essence.

So, they try something new. The waves get together and decide to have a satsang in which they will all seriously enquire, 'Who are we really? What is our source? What is our real nature?' Then, each part, each wave, will suddenly discover 'I am water'. When this discovery is made, the names, forms and dimensions of the waves suddenly cease to exist. The waves have discovered their common essence, nature and reality, a reality which they ignored when they previously assumed that they only existed as names and forms. The names and forms were not created by the water, they merely arose out of ignorance. They arose because the waves never understood what they really are.

Water is the source and substance of the waves. If a wave rises with the knowledge 'I am only water', it has no problem when it takes the form of a wave because it never forgets that its real nature is only water. If it forgets, and suffers as a result, it can be helped if it is told, by another wave which understands the real situation, 'You are water and water alone. Stop pretending that you are merely a wave.'

Waves forget who they really are. Thinking themselves to be a name and a form, they search endlessly for truth, for knowledge, for their own identity. But this search never impinges on reality itself. Ocean always remains as ocean. The searching, suffering waves are always water, always ocean, even if they are not aware of it.

People who suffer on account of the wrong ideas they have about themselves have to be apprised of the truth by one who knows the truth. A wave will arise in the ocean and, speaking from its own direct knowledge and experience, will say, 'I am ocean, I am free. You are also that same ocean. You are also free.' Out of compassion that wave will spread the message of freedom: 'As I am, so you are. You are already free.'

You became attached to name and form and imagined that you were a wave. Never mind. Every day, when you sleep, you forget about name and form for about six or seven hours. Why don't you extend that forgetfulness into your waking state? Now itself, forget that you are a name, a form. You are not the body, not the mind, not the senses, not the ego. Try to forget all these wrong ideas you have about yourself. If you can do it while you sleep, why can't you do it while you are awake? Make your decision now, in this moment. Whatever you can forget, whatever can be changed, leave it aside, because what is real cannot change. Find out what that reality is by looking within yourself. There must be something real within you, otherwise you couldn't speak, see or even move. What is it that makes you move? What is it that makes you speak? Go towards it and see for yourself. If you do you will find a place somewhere within you. In that inner cave you will find an 'indweller' hiding. He is not really hiding. He is merely hidden from you because you don't want to look at him. And why don't you want to look at him? Because you are always engaged elsewhere. When you finally get exhausted with that 'someone' who is always looking elsewhere, He will reveal Himself. Hope and desire are concealing your kingdom.

Who is who in this creation? The real 'Who', the real 'You' is whole. The real 'Who' is everything. This 'Who' is itself empty, but millions of creations can take place within it. Once you know this directly, you will know that there are no parts and no whole. This 'Who' is beyond everything, beyond imagination, beyond any calculations, and beyond any description. You are that which cannot be described, which cannot be imagined, which cannot be touched, which cannot even be thought about. You are so pure, so secret, so sacred, nothing has ever touched you. When you touch something else, you get polluted. And what is that something else? It is 'I'. When you touch 'I', you become proud. This is the correct word, I don't want to use any other word.

When you touch your pride, your arrogance, you become arrogant: 'I am doing this, I have done that. I want this, I want that.' This and that, desire and hope—all these are arrogance. Once you decide that you are not all these things, you are peaceful, you are free.

You had a Guru yourself: Ramana Maharshi. What was his function and what is your function as a Guru?

Out of his compassion he made himself available to everyone. Anyone who had doubts about his own freedom or his own true nature could go to him. He solved all such problems merely by sitting quietly. All doubts were cleared in his silent presence.

He is my Master and I had the good fortune to be with him during his lifetime. Now, I am his humble servant. I am in his service giving help to whomsoever comes to me. The work he started is being carried on. Somewhere, somehow, someone will always be continuing with this work. The candle he lit will be passed on. It will always be bright. It will never go to waste.

Who is this 'someone' through whom the Master's teachings will always flow? That 'someone' is not known to anyone. It is not the mind, not the body, not the ego. It is something else, something that is never known. What is it? You are That Itself. Don't take yourself to be anything else. You are that light, you are that wisdom. Don't pretend to be anything else. Don't deny your own reality. There is no difference between him and you.

He used to speak and teach in silence. In that silence he convinced people, and gave them the experience, that what they are is Truth Itself. This Truth is called existence, knowledge and bliss, and you are That.

A new satsang hall has been created in Lucknow as well as a canteen and a bookshop. A daily programme is to follow. More and more of us are staying for a long time in Indira Nagar. An ashram-type organisation seems to be appearing.

'A new satsang hall has been created in Lucknow.' If it is a real satsang hall, then I am very happy to hear the news. Generally, these things don't work. I have seen many spiritual organisations begin which later ran into many difficulties. Whenever something like this is going on, problems and quarrels eventually arise. People start to have disagreements. Troubles and misconceptions arise. Many ashrams start with a good Guru, but afterwards there is always some kind of trouble. I have seen many such ashrams in Rishikesh, in Haridwar and also in the South. Somehow these places lost their way and acquired a bad reputation. If people who have their own interests get control of organisations like this, it is better to close them down. I am not interested in having an organisation like that. If individual interests take over here, it will be better to close down the satsang.

I have only been here for the last two or three years. Before I got health problems, I used to travel to the West, return, and then spend some time in the Himalayas. I have also travelled in the South, because I know many places there. I have never stayed in Lucknow until recently. Now, because of my health problems, because of some trouble in my legs, I am staying here continuously. I can't walk well any more, so I have stopped travelling. Now I stay here permanently in order to serve you. But if the people here, for any reason, suddenly get interested in fame or in gaining anything other than freedom, then I will not be interested in helping them. I am only here to serve those people who come here with a genuine desire for freedom. I am here to clear their minds of any doubts they may have.

It is very difficult to find people who have no self-interest. This Satsang Bhavan came up by itself. There are some people here now who have no self-interest. But later on that may not be the case. I was recently asked if I wanted my own building here. I refused because I know that such a building, such an institution, will not work.

This place is an airport. Everyone here is in a transit lounge, waiting for his flight out. No one stays permanently here. I don't want to start bricklaying in the airport. Why should I make any permanent building here? I also have to leave. I am also waiting for my flight to leave.

This house is rented. I am very happy that some good people are paying the rent and offering me a place. So long as they offer their service I can continue to come here. Otherwise the house I am staying in is enough for me. I used to give satsang there to thirty or forty people. There was no problem when I met them there.

Recently, because many foreign people are coming here, we have started a restaurant. It was opened because I could see that many visitors were not accustomed to the spicy food that is served in town. Some of the oils which were used there made the visitors sick. So, for the benefit and convenience of these visitors, I was asked if a restaurant could be opened for them. I agreed simply because I don't like to see people get sick because they can't find suitable food. This restaurant was started for the benefit of those visitors who wanted to keep up their good health while they were here. It serves good food, prepared by the devotees themselves. It is free of injurious oils and spices. Also, very little salt is used. The food is well-prepared and well-cooked. All visitors can avail themselves of this facility.

What is our part in this?

Selfless service must be your motto. Only then does it become worship. Whatever you do, even cutting vegetables in the restaurant, is worship. Sweeping this hall is worship.

I believe that there is no difference between meditation, sweeping the floor and dusting the shoes outside in the shoe rack. You can have a taste of true meditation when you are selfless. By doing lowly service with the right attitude, you can attain freedom itself.

I will tell you a story. There was once a saint who had an ashram. Early in the morning, at five a.m., people used to come to him. This teacher, this Master, was an educated man, a good poet. His poetry used to flow from his inner silence. Whenever he spoke his verses, the people nearby would note them down on pieces of paper. His devotees were planning to bring out a book containing all the Master's poems, but before it could be completed a wind blew through the room of the saint and scattered all the pages. The devotees had wanted to print the poems in chronological order, but they had not put the date on any of the pages. After the incident no one could remember what the proper order was. The two hundred people who used to visit the saint were all consulted, but not a single one of them knew how to reassemble the pages in the correct order. Finally, the saint said, 'Call that man who cleans the ashram'.

It was this man's job to sweep the floor of the ashram and remove cowdung from the cowshed. The devotees, knowing that he was totally illiterate and that he never attended satsang, wondered why he was being consulted. They told the saint that this man could not possibly help to solve the problem.

The saint said, 'He is the only member of the ashram who has so far not been asked. Perhaps he can help us.' So, somebody went and brought him into the saint's presence.

The saint told him, 'Last night a wind blew through my room and scattered all the papers on which my poems were written. They are all out of order. Do you know the correct sequence?'

'Yes, Guruji,' he replied, much to everyone's astonishment. 'I know. I can begin from the beginning, from the day you started speaking. I know all the poems and I know the order they should go in.'

Then, after asking the other devotees to listen to his words and put the papers in the right order, he recited the entire collection from beginning to end in the sequence in which it had been composed. Everyone was astounded because he had not attended any of the satsangs in which the poems had been composed and dictated.

One devotee asked the saint how it was possible for this man to know all the poems. The saint replied, 'Ask him yourself. I myself do not know the answer. I was as surprised as you were when he recited the poems.'

They asked him and he replied: 'I am a manual labourer. I know that I am illiterate. I cannot sit with all you educated people because I am always dirty as a result of my work in the cowshed. But at the same time I felt that each word was so beautiful, I didn't want to miss a single one. So, what to do? How to remember words which I have not even heard? I solved the problem by putting my ear in the Heart of my Guru, in the place where the word has yet to emerge.

'My ear is now in the Heart of the Guru. When Guruji speaks these words, I am at the source of these words, in his Heart. I know everything that has gone on here this morning because I am now in the Heart of all. The Lord of the Universe is the indweller in the Heart of all beings. You can know this Lord by abiding in the Heart yourself. When you are known to the Lord in this way, you yourself are the Lord in all beings.'

Everyone who has to work here should work like this man. Only then will the work be of benefit to the whole world. If the work is not selfless, there will only be confusion and quarrels. Sister will quarrel with sister, mother with son. We have gathered here today from all over the world. We all know how worldly affairs are being conducted, how quarrels can arise even between blood relatives. To avoid this happening, we have to meet in satsang with love in our hearts—love for the Truth and love for each other. There is no use in having a satsang if the spirit of love is not present.

If you want to have this satsang, I will come here as a humble servant to do service for as long as I am in this body. I will not refuse. I will come. But you will have to take care if you want this satsang to continue. You will all have to be absolutely selfless servants. Only then will it work. If you start thinking, 'I am in charge of the Satsang Bhavan,' or 'I am running the restaurant,' the satsang itself will not work, and I won't want any part of it. You have to have the right attitude towards the work. Then, everyone will be benefited and I will be happy to come here. I have no other business to do, and I am always happy to hear that people are benefiting from these satsangs.

I am happy to see so many people discovering who they are. I don't think that anything like this has ever happened before, at any time in the past. What is happening here is absolutely new. Perhaps it is the blessing of your own Self. Your own Self is very happy with you and that is why we are all meeting here. This is a very blessed occasion, and that is why we call it satsang—association with Truth. Because that Truth is one, we have to be one here. We cannot be strangers with each other. It is as one that we must be here, it is as one that we must listen, with nobody lower, and nobody higher. We must not think, 'He is from this country, she is from another'. I don't have any concepts about frontiers, no divisions of any kind. I don't accept differences based on caste, religion or any political differences.

We have to be very free when we are here. With everybody who comes here we have to speak about Truth. If we gossip and waste our time, it will be of no use to anyone.

About two hundred and fifty people are here with you every day in satsang. I have heard you say, 'Wherever there is a crowd, there must be falsehood'. How can the crowd in satsang and your statement be reconciled?

I have often said, 'Wherever there is a crowd, there is some falsehood'. I don't deny it. You don't even need a crowd for falsehood to rise. Even when there are only two people together, there can be confusion and quarrelling. If you want to disprove my statement, 'Wherever there is a crowd, there is some falsehood,' you will have to prove that when you are in a crowd, you are always happy. This you cannot do. I am always prepared to listen to anyone who says that he is always happy in a crowd. But I don't think that I will believe him.

What does this crowd really mean? 'Crowd' is mind itself. You are always crowded with thoughts. Every single second is full of thoughts. Is anyone ever free of thoughts? In this crowd there is always falsehood. Who can be happy in a crowd of thoughts, sense-impressions, objects, relationships between subject and objects? In both the waking and the dream states the dense crowd of thoughts prevents everyone from being happy. Not a single person is ever happy in this crowd of six billion human beings.

We all have five senses. There are millions of things to see through the eyes, millions of words to be heard by the ears, millions of things to be smelled by the nose, millions of things to be touched by the hands. All these constitute the crowd of thoughts and words. Do you know how many pieces of information the eye registers in each second, just to make one fleeting image in the brain? It is millions. So, how many images will you absorb in one minute or in the rest of your life? The amount is incalculable. Each image enters your memory and, collectively, they constitute the vast crowd you call memory. Each impression in the memory is one incarnation. Not only that, each of these impressions has the power to create a new incarnation for you. At the moment of death, your last thought will take a form, and that form will be your next birth. Crowd upon crowd, incarnation upon incarnation. You are never free of them. Not when you sleep, not when you dream, and not even when you die.

Imagine that you are alone in your apartment, asleep and dreaming. In your dream you see many people having a fight. In this case, even though your door is locked, and even though you are alone in your bed, you are not alone. You cannot escape the crowd anywhere. Not even in a five-star hotel room. The people who work in these places are trained to keep unwanted people away from you, but they cannot protect you from this crowd of thoughts.

All the billions and trillions of objects you register through the eyes, ears, nose, hands and mouth come through five channels. The five senses alone are responsible for this crowd. Let these five senses go towards that which sees through the eye, which hears through the ear, which smells through the nose and which tastes through the tongue. If I ask you what that is, you will say that it is the mind. When your mind is not there, you don't enjoy food, you don't see, you don't smell, you don't taste. The mind alone is responsible for the crowd: five senses and millions of objects.

What is this mind? All the millions of thoughts are

only equal to one 'I'. All is condensed in 'I'. Mind, body, senses, sense objects, the crowd of thoughts, the subject who sees these objects—all of these are 'I'. The past, the present, the future—these are also 'I'. You are never free from the crowd. You are never free from the 'I'.

If you want to be free, if you want to be happy, if you want to be alone, you have to find out who this 'I' is who is generating this vast crowd.

Now I want to take you to a very solitary place. Ask yourself, 'Where does this "I" rise from?' The source of that 'I' is a solitary place, a place of rest, peace, love and freedom. You can go to that place here and now. It will reveal itself to you when you really want it. If you want to find that place urgently enough, you can locate it in less than a second, but if you want anything else out of life you won't locate it. If you keep putting off the search for it to some future date, you will never locate it. It doesn't exist tomorrow, it only exists now.

In ordinary life there is no peace. In childhood there is ignorance, in youth lustful passions. Then family life with its own problems. Whatever stage of life you are in, you are always dependent on someone else for your well-being. When you are dependent in this way, there is never any peace.

After birth, people are prone to all kinds of diseases. People who are healthy in both body and mind are very lucky, but not so lucky as those who have a desire for freedom. The very best human birth is one in which you have good health, a strong discriminative mind, and a great longing for freedom. If you have these qualities, you can get out of the crowd. If not, you will always be in it. Finish your quest for freedom and be happy. You don't need anyone else's company on your journey to freedom. Having the company of others is always troublesome.

We are a family here, but this family does not belong to *samsara*. Some outsiders may come here and say, 'There is a big crowd here,' but that is not what I see. There may be a thousand people here, but if our thoughts are one, then we ourselves are one. You are what you think. If the common thought here is of truth or freedom, then that is what we all are. We are here to find freedom. By having that desire, we belong to the family of freedom. In that state there are no differences between us. When we all have that same thought, we cease, at that moment, to belong to a crowd. So, I hope I have clarified what I mean by the word 'crowd', and I hope you now understand what I mean when I say, 'Wherever there is a crowd, there is falsehood'. If you don't believe me right now, you may have to wait years and years before you understand. I don't wish this delay on you, I sincerely hope that you are getting that right understanding in this present moment. If you want to stay in the crowd, though, you will have to experience its consequences.

I am not giving you any predictions for the future, I am only giving you facts. I will repeat the main fact again: 'Wherever there is a crowd, there is falsehood.' I will continue to uphold this statement until somebody can prove to me that it is not true.

Those of us who have any role in the functioning of this satsang must be the humble servants of those who come to satsang. Then it may work. It has never worked before in any other spiritual organisation. If it works here, it will be the first time ever. We all know the results of other people who have tried to set up an organisation like this. They have all failed. Knowing this, it may seem foolish to make another similar experiment. Still, we have to try.

As your devotee I can't help but be of service to you, out of gratitude. Would you please say what your role is in this?

A true devotee has no right to ask me. To be a devotee means to be in a state of devotion. Having merged in this devotion, he has become That Itself. One becomes a true devotee only after fully surrendering. One then gives up one's identity in the same way that a river gives up its separate nature when it flows into the ocean. After merging, the river has no right say, 'I am a river,' because that identity disappears when it becomes the ocean.

A devotee becomes whatever he is devoted to. If he is devoted to the Divine, he becomes the Divine. That divineness then stays in the Heart of the devotee, for the devotee is the Heart of the Divine. What can be my role in all this? When the devotee and the Divine merge, my role also merges and disappears. There, in that place, I do not know what part is left for me to play.

Aum, shanti, shanti, shanti.

Papaji and Henner Ritter

No Questions, No Answers
by Henner Ritter
Lucknow, 1993

et me ask you something about what is beyond Self-realisation and awakening.

In Self-realisation there is no you and there is no me. No one is a questioner and no one is questioned. No questions are there to ask. What are you going to ask when you are beyond, beyond this manifestation? When you have realised the truth, when you are 'beyond', what can you ask and to whom?

No questions.

OK. At this moment, let the questions arise from the state of 'no questions'. You cannot; the questions are still there. This is an interview, 'no questions' will not do.

Mankind is desperately looking for answers to overcome the global crisis.

Very good question. 'Man-kind' has to become 'kind-man'. If this is achieved there will be no trouble. All other approaches have failed because they are not kind. Kindness is lacking. How to be kind?

The East, especially India, has always emphasised unmanifested being and infinite consciousness. It wants to transcend what appears to be a corrupt and material world.

113

But consciousness is the source and nature of this world. Everything you see in this so-called material world has arisen from and appeared in consciousness itself. So, we must start with this fundamental consciousness and the understanding that whatever arises in this immaculate, pure consciousness cannot be anything except consciousness itself. It is like the ocean. Whatever forms appear in the ocean, whether they be waves, bubbles, eddies or foam, the fundamental substance in each manifestation is the same. They are all forms of water. Similarly, everything that arises from consciousness must be consciousness itself.

We always have to keep in mind that we are that consciousness and we have to go on playing, with the conviction and the knowledge that all these different names are forms of consciousness. If we know that the substance is the same, there will be no conflict. If we are without this knowledge, if we only take note of external names and forms, we will go on quarrelling with each other.

Time and space arise from consciousness. How? When you sleep you are not aware of anything, not even the passage of time. There is no consciousness of time and space during sleep. But when you wake up, you instantly give birth to time and space. This division has caused the difference between east and west, north and south. Don't forget: wherever you go there is consciousness, and in consciousness there are no spatial divisions at all. It is immaculate, pure. It cannot be divided into any regions. Establish yourself in this knowledge and go on with your life.

Different forms made of gold, such as rings or bracelets, never lose their fundamental nature, which is gold. Only the names are different. Similarly, whatever forms appear to exist are really consciousness only. When you look at a ring, you don't see the gold. You see the form instead and call it a ring, a bracelet, a chain or a gold watch.

This gold is ignored when you give a name and a form to anything that is made of it. But whatever the form may be, the fundamental common property is still pure gold.

Misunderstandings and clashes arise in the world because we only take note of the 'ornaments', the external names and forms, and ignore the gold, the common underlying consciousness which comprises them all. Gold can be melted down and recast into many forms without having its fundamental nature, its 'goldness', changed. Likewise, though consciousness appears continuously to change its forms, its real nature never changes. Gold still exists as gold, even when it has not been shaped into ornaments. In the same way, consciousness remains as consciousness when there are no forms appearing in it. It does not matter to consciousness if forms are present or absent. It is always the same.

The West has emphasised becoming, leaving eternity to the Pope and hypocrites, meanwhile exploiting the world into self-extinction. How can we serve the wholesome integration of East and West? Is there a promise? What is your vision?

In my vision I don't think that we are disintegrated at all. Rather, we are fully integrated. How do you demonstrate that we are disintegrated? Only by taking note of the names and forms which are not your real nature. Consciousness cannot be divided or 'disintegrated'. If you see or feel disintegration, look within yourself. Turn within and find that indwelling reality which has never disintegrated and which remains timelessly the same both before and after the creation and the destruction of all physical forms. Creation and destruction are merely phenomena which rise and fall in the ocean of consciousness. In the same way that the ocean is unaffected by the waves that appear and disappear on its surface, similarly, name-and-form creations will appear in consciousness and will eventually be destroyed there without the underlying consciousness changing or being affected in any way.

Concepts such as 'there is disintegration' or 'I am separate from consciousness' are erroneous. They arise in ignorance. When you see through these concepts, when you realise their falseness, they dissolve and disappear. Ignorance has no beginning but it can and does have an end. If you mistake a rope for a snake you can say that the snake had no beginning because it was never born. It may appear to exist but it has no real existence. Though it had no beginning, it can and does have an end. It disappears as soon as the knowledge dawns in you that it is a rope. Similarly, when you realise directly 'I am consciousness,' the concept of disintegration will vanish. So will the false ideas that there are eastern and western nations and that there are differences between them.

After one remembers and realises the ineffable truth and oneness, one also realises that it is not an end but the beginning.

Imagine a circle, and imagine that you are travelling around its circumference. At whatever place you start your journey, that place is your beginning. But once you start moving, there is no end; you just go round and round in circles. If you want to get out of this endless circling, you have to be aware that the circle has a centre, and you have to be in that centre, instead of on the circumference.

What is this centre? It is the indwelling reality in the Heart of all beings. It is consciousness; it is truth and love. All people have to know this centre if they want to terminate the endless circling, the continuous moving from point to point. There are no points in that centre, and so, no movement. When you arrive at that centre, everything is finished for you. There are no beginnings and no ends in that centre because there all directions, all distinctions, and all movements have ceased. Very few people know where this centre is or how to stay in it.

Once, Kabir, a realised man who lived in the sixteenth century, saw his wife grinding wheat grains in a stone hand-mill. He watched all the grains being poured into a hole in the centre and he noted how they all became ground and crushed into flour. As he looked on, he began to cry. He was such a kind man, he had so much compassion, he could not even bear to watch grains of wheat being crushed. I mentioned at the beginning of this interview that 'man-kind' had to become 'kind-man', a man like Kabir who, because he was one with consciousness and knew that consciousness is the common substratum of everything, could feel empathy with all living things, even grains of wheat.

His wife asked him, 'Why are you crying?' and he answered, 'I cannot bear to see all these grains being put into the mill and crushed'.

His wife, who was also enlightened, removed the upper part of the grinding stone and said, 'Look! There are a few here which have not been crushed. I cannot crush them because they are near the pivot, close to the centre.'

In this world the ones who will be saved from being crushed are those who are near the centre, near the Heart of their own beingness. If you go away from this centre you get crushed. Most people distance themselves from this centre, and on account of this alone, they suffer. It is best to stay near the pivot and to rest there in motionlessness. If you stay in this place, the world will circle around you, but you will not be ground and crushed by it. If you rest in that centre, the world cannot affect you or touch you in any way.

117

How to make use of Self-realisation in the world and in the body?

After realising the Self you will understand that it is the Self alone, and not the ego, which performs all activities. This same Self is animating the activities of all people. When you realise the Self you will have full trust in it and full trust in the activities it makes you undergo.

Realising the Self is the most worthwhile accomplishment. If you want to help the world, this is the best way to do it. In that state the Self will reveal its plans to you. After realisation, you yourself do not decide, 'I am going to help the world' or 'Now, through my activities, I can benefit humanity'. If, after realisation, the Self needs to make use of you, it will do so.

To let the Self use you in this way, you have to surrender to it, you have to be devoted to it, you have to have great obedience to it. If you succeed in this you will know that you and the Self are one. Knowing this, you are then aware that whatever actions your body performs, it is the Self alone which is doing them. In that state you, the person, are not responsible. Everything which gets done in this state is perfect, excellent, because the Self can never make a mistake. It does not even have the capacity to judge whether activities are good or bad.

Surrender to the Self with great devotion and keep quiet. That's all you need to do. If you succeed you will find, instantly, within yourself, a flame of energy that will give you strength. It will permeate your nervous system, giving you a thousand times more strength than you could get merely from your own resources. In this surrendered state, if you allow this energy to work through you, you will know that there is no 'you' who is working. The body will work, but you will know that you are not the body. Some other energy, some eternal force, will work through your limbs.

Even now, before that surrender has taken place, it is the same force which is working through your body, but your ego is appropriating it by saying, 'I am working'. Dissolve this feeling and the idea that you yourself are doing something no longer arises.

Imagine you are holding a piece of paper. When the idea 'I am holding this paper' is dissolved, holding, in the way you have always understood this idea, is no longer possible. Where then does the strength come from to hold the paper? Go back to this energy which is keeping the paper between your fingers. Where does the finger get the energy to hold that paper? And from where did the intelligence come to hold it in that particular way? How are all these things going on? There is a lesson to be learned in everything we do and everything we think, a lesson that can be learned if we can be one with this underlying energy without claiming it as our own. At every moment this energy is giving us a lesson. Realisation can happen at any moment. It will happen in the instant that you master the lesson that the manifestations of this energy are trying to teach you.

That energy rises within us. Intelligence rises from the same source. Don't obscure your awareness of it by thoughts such as 'I should do this' or 'I should not do this'.

Every one of us has to live in peace and love with all beings of the universe, not only with humans but also with the animals and plants and rocks. What is the difference between humans and animals?

When you look into the centre of both you realise it is the same.

The Buddhists promote the way of the Bodhisattva *to develop*

119

virtues: generosity, patience, discipline, wisdom, etc.

When you realise the truth these virtues will automatically follow. The *Bodhisattvas* practise to develop them, but I don't think they can be developed. They will arise as a consequence of realising the truth. Then, these virtues will be helping you. Whatever you do then will be wise and virtuous.

Everyone who is realised automatically has the compassion of a *Bodhisattva*. *Bodhisattva* means a compassionate person who defers his own liberation until all other beings are enlightened. This degree of compassion is what each of us must have in order to give happiness and peace to others. How can you help others when you are not wise yourself? I believe they go together. There is therefore no difference between a Buddha and a *Bodhisattva*. Whoever is a Buddha has also to be a *Bodhisattva*. Even at the end of his eightieth year the Buddha was still helping people. In his dying moments some poor man appeared before him and Ananda, his disciple, said, 'The Master is dying, you can't see him'. But the Master, who had already seen him, invited him to come near. In the last minutes of his life he spoke to him, gave him great love, and then died. This man got enlightened in the final moments of the Buddha's life. Ananda was the first to get enlightenment from the Buddha. This man was the last.

Others claim that you can and should do kriya yoga *exercises in order to build an immortal body like Babaji's or Ramalingar's so that one can live eternally to help the rest of mankind.*

I don't think that these exercises have worked, even on themselves. No exercise can work until you realise the truth yourself. Then, everything is fine. If you teach others without having known the truth yourself, what will be the result of these yogas?

Should one aspire to the supramental transformation of the human race to take it into the next superhuman stage of evolution, as Aurobindo has maintained?

This also has not happened so far. There have been no results. You can go to Pondicherry and see for yourself.

I have been there.

What was your impression? What revolution did you see there?

They are still aspiring.

Still aspiring, yes. This aspiration is a trick of the mind. There is no difference between aspiration and mind. In this place I don't ask anyone to aspire to anything, or desire anything. I want people to stop the mind in this instant, and not after lengthy practices. I say, 'Keep quiet, don't think. Direct your mind towards its origin, consciousness, and immediately you will be enlightened.' When the mind faces its source, there is instant enlightenment. So, this advice, merely to turn the mind towards its source, is it not reasonable?

You do not have to practise any *sadhana* and waste your whole life on it. You can be free instantly because freedom is already there. If it is not, it means that we are wanting something which is not here now. If you have this wrong attitude, it will result in your wanting to gain something. If it is not here and now, and if you want to gain it, then, when you get it, it becomes your acquisition. Whatever you get anew cannot be consciousness because consciousness is already there. This consciousness cannot ever become an acquisition because it is not a thing to be acquired. Whatever is not always there should be left alone because it is not eternal. What is eternal must always be there. You should not aspire for anything that is not eternal.

What prevents us from realising the consciousness that is here and now? It is only a preoccupation with gaining and aspiring for transient, external things. Once we get rid of this preoccupation, reality, consciousness, will reveal Itself to Itself.

Some vehemently propagate renunciation, particularly from sexual matters, in order to gain salvation and to save the world.

I think that any person who propounds sexual renunciation must himself be the product of a sexual union. Now, for some reasons best known to himself, possibly personal ones, he is advocating celibacy.

Enlightenment is immortal, it cannot be tainted by anything. It is not embarrassed by anything; there are no warnings and prohibitions in it; there are no differences in it. Freedom cannot be attained merely by abstaining from sex. If this were so, eunuchs would have been the first people to become Buddhas. So, I don't believe in renunciation of sex. It is a natural way of life, and what is natural need not be abandoned. But, having said that, there should be some regulation in all human activities. Diet, sleep, sex, and so on, should be regulated in such a way that they conform to healthy and acceptable standards of human behaviour.

What is the difference between animals and human beings? They sleep, we sleep; they eat, we eat; they have fears, we also have fears; they have sex, we also have sex.

So, these four things—sleep, eating, fear and sex—are common to both. The one thing we have which distinguishes us from animals is the faculty of discrimination. It is this faculty which allows us to call ourselves human beings. We should make the best use of this faculty.

That faculty has brought you here today because you want to find out how to live in peace with all people. That discrimination has also given rise to the desire, 'I want to be free right now'. It is solely because of this discriminative faculty that everyone has the chance and the possibility to be free. But out of the six billion people on this planet, very few take up that option. Those who can exercise their discrimination and become truly free will never suffer again. They will be that consciousness which is light, love and beauty.

People search for that consciousness but they can't find it even though it is under their own feet, within their own Self, in the breath itself, behind the retina itself. It reveals itself only when we keep quiet. Quietness doesn't merely mean an absence of talking. Real quietness is when everything is quiet.

Kabir says, 'Be quiet in your mind, quiet in your senses, and also quiet in your body. Then, when all these are quiet, don't do anything. In that state truth will reveal itself to you. It will appear in front of you and ask, "What do you want?"'

You have to keep quiet. In that quietness something will arise, reveal itself to you and give you satisfaction. But if you run after it and try to catch it, you won't be able to hold onto it. If you turn your back to the sun and try to catch up with your shadow by running after it, you will fail. The faster you run, the faster your shadow will run.

We are trying to get satisfaction by running after the shadows of name and form. What you have to do instead is turn your face towards the sun. Your shadow, which you can take to be the shadowy names and forms of this world, will also turn and face the sun because wherever you go, your shadow follows. When you face the source and vanish in the Self, your shadow, the names and forms of the world, also vanishes. This is the ultimate offering of yourself.

You don't have to run after it, you only have to face your own sun, your own Self. Then, everything will be done for you, everything will be given to you, everything will be added to you, even if you don't want it. Just keep quiet, don't ask for anything, and everything will be added to you.

If you go on asking like a beggar, 'I want a kingdom,' nobody will give you a kingdom. Nobody will even give you a dollar, let alone a kingdom. It is better to sit on the throne. There, everything belongs to you. This throne is freedom.

Others are convinced that suppression of sex instincts is the main cause of suffering.

I have already told you about this. There are people who run away to monasteries. They reject all kinds of sexual contact. You must have seen this in your country also. I have visited Maria Laach, a very big monastery. I looked at all the faces of the monks and the nuns, and I also saw the abbot. Some woman came to see him while I was there and shook hands with him. For one hour after that he forgot everything except the fact that he had just been touched by a woman. What could I do? I had come to see him to talk to him, but all the time I was with him I could feel that his mind was not on me. It was dwelling on the happiness he felt at being touched by a woman. I could feel his thoughts: 'I have entered forbidden territory; I have intruded; I have put my hand in hers.'

So, people like this have an external facade of rejecting women, but they are still keeping them inside. When thoughts of women arise, they can't leave them alone.

I don't accept the living of an unnatural life like this. If the whole world becomes a monastery, what will be the outcome? Just imagine. God will then have to create some other method for instantly producing us.

Right now, in these bodies, which are the outcome of a sexual union, we have a life-span of a hundred years. That is more than enough time to win freedom. We should make the best use of this life-span and not waste our time with thoughts such as, 'This should not be there, that should not be there'. In consciousness there can never be any rejection nor any acceptance. Let there be a free flow and you will find that it will start from consciousness itself. You will always be very well guided by that flow. But when you use your ego, every step that you take will be disorderly. That is why man is killing his fellow-man. Even a pig does not kill a pig. No horse ever kills a horse, but many men now pride themselves on how many other men they can kill, and how quickly they can do it.

Nowadays governments are talking about banning some kinds of weapons that can kill millions of people. The talks may not produce any results, but at least they are a step in the right direction. We should become human beings first, before we think about becoming free men or wise men. It is not human to kill our own race.

In the light of the Self, suffering is just an illusion.

Even when you are sleeping, the suffering ends. The suffering is only in the waking state and in the dream state. But when you sleep the physical suffering ends. If we are free, all sufferings will end.

But a child who is really beaten, abused and abandoned actually suffers and is conditioned to further suffering. Therefore in the West psychotherapy was developed to decondition and heal the wounds of the soul. Can you imagine a partial cooperation between self-enquiry and psychotherapy?

You say, 'a child who is really abused and abandoned...'. First of all, whose mistake is this? Is it the mistake of the parents who do the abusing, or is it the mistake of the child? It is the parents who have to be looked after and treated. They are the ones responsible. But the parents themselves are not responsible people, otherwise they would not maltreat their children. As a psychiatrist, whom should you help, the child or the father?

Let me tell you a story as an example. I apologise in advance for telling you such a gruesome story, but it really happened, in Germany. I read about it in the papers. There was a family comprising a mother, a father and a daughter. The daughter, who was thirteen years old, took her father's revolver and shot him and her mother. Then she surrendered herself to the police and was arrested. At her trial the judge asked her why she had shot her parents, and the girl replied, 'My father raped me. So I took his revolver, shot him, and he died.'

'So, why did you shoot your mother as well?' asked the judge.

The girl answered, 'I was shouting to my mother to intervene and save me. She was watching what happened, but she didn't come to help me. So I shot her as well.'

The judge dismissed the case and set her free. Now, is your therapy going to help the child or the parents? What would you do in such a case?

Treat both.

Parents have to be responsible for their children. They should not misbehave with them. From the beginning of their lives, children are spoilt by their parents. I was once travelling on the subway in New York when I saw a couple with their child, who was probably about six months old. The father was smoking and kissing the child at the same time. Seeing this hurt me very much. I am only telling you this story because it still troubles me that he was exhaling smoke and kissing the child at the same time. At that early age, the child was inhaling smoke and the taste of nicotine. Who is responsible if the child gets cancer early in its life? Who has to be taught about this? Not the child because it was only six months old. It is the father who should know that he should not kiss the child in these circumstances.

I was going to stop him but I kept quiet. What to do in such cases? If I had spoken, he would probably have said, 'Who are you to tell me how to treat my son?' So, I kept quiet.

In many cases it is the parents or other older people who damage the children. Something has to be done with these older people. I am very sorry to have to say it, but I have seen many such cases. One mistreated girl is here today in satsang. She is only twenty-one years old. She told me that she couldn't stay in her country. When I asked her why, she told me, 'When my father misbehaved with me, why should I stay in that country?' So, she is here.

I am happy that therapists are working, but at the same time I also believe that therapy only takes a person into their past. In therapy you are taken slowly backwards in order to locate and dig out the cause of your troubles. What we do here in satsang is bring a person from the past into the present. In that absolute present everything will be dissolved.

Your work is beautiful. I would like to talk to you

about it, but unfortunately you don't have much time. I have heard that you are doing very good work, and that you are doing it selflessly. Because of this I am interested in telling you how to work with compassion. There is a kind of compassion through which, without even speaking a word, you can help anyone who comes to you. Once you have learned it, you will help everyone in the world, without even uttering a word.

Let me tell you a story. A realised man, a *sadhu*, was walking in the forest. Because it was sunny he wanted to find somewhere to have a rest. He sat down under a tree, leaned back against the trunk, and had a short nap. When he woke up, he was ready to continue his travels. As he was picking up his stick and his begging bowl he saw many people sitting near him. Much to his surprise they all stood up and thanked him for his satsang.

He told them, 'But I was sleeping. I didn't speak a word to you.'

They answered, 'This is a type of satsang we have never had anywhere else. Everywhere else people are barking and bleating: "You must do this, you must not do that! You must sit like this and look like this." Your satsang is different. We have not found anything like it anywhere else. We are all gods from different heavens, from different heavenly worlds. We found out that there was a *mahatma*, a realised person, sitting under this tree. We all thought, "Why not go and have satsang with him?" So, we all came down to this world to be with you.

'We are gods, but we still find ourselves engaged in many activities. We never have time to sit or meditate and we still have many unfulfilled desires. Our lives are long and we will not get old, even after a thousand years. So, we have plenty of time to enjoy ourselves.'

People who are due to be rewarded for their meritorious actions can, after their deaths, be reborn in one of these heavenly worlds so that they can enjoy themselves endlessly. But they will still have to be reborn again because these pleasures will not give ultimate satisfaction.

These gods, tired of their endless enjoyments, came down to the *sadhu* to have his satsang. The gods showered the *sadhu*, who had been silently sleeping during his satsang, with flowers. The nearby trees, which had no leaves, flowered out of season, and also shed their flowers onto this silent man. This is the force of satsang.

Gods came near to that silent person, and even the plants and the trees responded to him. Why will you not help people in this way? You have to learn the trick.

When you go back to your own country, I wish you bon voyage. If you wish to keep contact with me I will welcome it, and I will keep in touch with you.

I wish every being in the world could feel the blessing of your presence and the liberating power of your irresistible laughter.

I am thankful to you for coming to Lucknow. I invite all of you who are here listening to come again.

If you have anything more to say, you can say it now.

No questions, no answers.

This is where your therapy has to begin, from here, from the place of no questions and no answers. Go there and see what happens.

I will report it.

Papaji and Jeff Greenwald

Who are You?

by Jeff Greenwald
Lucknow, 1993

 *he first question is: Who are you?*

I am That from where you, me, she, he, and all the rest emerge. I am That.

What do you see when you look at me?

The seer.

Papaji, how does an awakened being like yourself see the world?

As my own Self. When you see your hands, feet, body, mind, senses, intellect, you know they are part of you. You say, 'My "I" includes all these'. In the same way you must see the world as yourself, as not different from who you are. Right now you regard your hands, your feet, your nails and your hair as being not different from you. See the world in the same way.

Are you saying that there is no place where 'I' ends and 'you' begin?

There is. I am taking you to that place.

Papa, you speak about freedom. What is freedom?

Freedom is a trap! A man who is imprisoned in a jail needs to be free, doesn't he? He is trapped in the jail and he knows that the people outside are free. You are all in prison and you have heard about outside from your parents, priests, teachers and preachers. 'Come to us,' they say, 'and we will give you freedom. Come to me and I will give you rest.' That is the promise, but this is only another trap. Once you believe it, you are caught in the trap of wanting freedom. You should be out of both these traps—neither in bondage nor in freedom—because these are only concepts. Bondage was a concept which gave rise to the concept of freedom. Get rid of both these concepts. Then, where are you?

Here.

Here, yes. 'Here' is neither a trap of bondage nor of freedom. It is not 'there'. In fact, It is not even 'here'.

Words seem to me to be a very great trap. Throughout the time I have been here, words have been inadequate to express the nature of the awakenings that take place here. They cannot even express why words are inadequate. I would have to compare them to what was adequate and I can't do that in words. But one word that is thrown around a lot in the West and in the East is the word 'enlightenment'. Is what you speak of enlightenment?

Enlightenment is Knowledge Itself, not knowledge of a person, a thing or an idea. Just Knowledge Itself. Enlightenment is there when there is no imagination of the past, no imagination of the future, not even an idea of the present.

I can't imagine a state with no imagination.

That is what is called bondage. It is called suffering. It is called *samsara*. I tell you, 'Don't imagine. In this present moment, don't have any imagination.' When you imagine, you are constructing images, and all images belong to the past. Don't recall the past and don't aspire to anything in the future. Then imagination goes. It is no longer in the mind. Everything in the mind comes from the past.

When you tell me not to think of anything, it is like telling me not to think of a hippopotamus. The first thought that comes to mind is, of course, a hippopotamus.

I am not asking you to think of anything. What I am saying is, 'Don't imagine anything that belongs to the past, the present and the future. If you are free from all imagination, you are also free of time, because any image will remind you of time and keep you within its framework. In the waking state you see images: of persons, of things, of ideas. When you go to sleep, all these vanish. Now, when you are sleeping, where are all these images? Where are the people? Where are the things?

In sleep these things are still there. They don't go away when I sleep.

You are describing the dream state. I am talking about the sleep state. I will show you. What time do you go to sleep?

About 11.30 at night.

Think of this last second, the one after 11.29 and fifty-nine seconds. What happens in that final second? Does the sixtieth second belong to sleep or to the waking state?

133

It is a zone in between, neither here nor there.

Now, let us talk about one second later. The sixtieth second has already gone. Just now you spoke of 'here' and 'there'. Where is 'here' and 'there' in that first instant of sleep? In that instant, you reject everything: all images, all things, all persons, all relationships. All ideas are gone in that instant when you jump into sleep. After that sixtieth second there is no time, no space, no country. We are speaking now about sleep. Now, after you have woken up, describe to me what happened while you were asleep.

There was dreaming.

Not dreaming, I am talking about sleep. Dreaming is the same state as you see here in front of you. In dreaming, if you see that a robber has robbed you or a tiger has pounced on you, you experience the same fear as when you are awake. What do you see when you sleep?

Nothing.

That is the right answer. Now, why do you reject all the things of the world, things you like so much, merely to offer yourself up to a state of nothingness.

I do it because I become tired.

To regain energy you go to the reservoir of energy, to that state of nothingness. If you don't touch that reservoir, what will happen to you, where will you go?

Crazy!

Crazy, yes. Now I will tell you how to stay continuously in that state of sleep, of nothingness, even while you are awake. I will also tell you how to be awake while your body is asleep. That will be good, won't it?

Let us talk about the end of that last second before you woke up from sleep. Waking has not yet come, and the sleep state is about to end. Now, what is your experience in the very first moment of the next waking state?

My senses call me back to the world.

OK. Now tell me what happened to the experience of happiness you had while you were sleeping? What have you brought from the hours of nothingness?

It is gone. I am relaxed, refreshed.

So, do you prefer the tension of the waking state to the relaxation of sleep?

I have a question about that later.

If you understand what I am trying to convey to you, you probably would not ask me this next question. Imagine that you have just come out of a cinema after seeing a show from ten till five. You go home and your friends ask, 'How was it?' What will you tell them?

'It was a beautiful show.'

You can bring the memory of those images to them, but you brought nothing from your sleep. Who woke up? Who woke up from that state of happiness? You were happy while you were sleeping. If it were not a happy state, no one would be willing to say 'Good night' to their loved ones every evening before going to sleep. No matter how close you are to them, you still say, 'Good night, let me sleep'.

There is something superior, something higher, something more beautiful about being alone. Ask yourself the question: when I wake up, who wakes up?

When you woke up, you did not bring the impression of the happiness that you enjoyed for six or seven hours of dreamless sleep. You can only bring with you impressions of the dances you saw in your dreams.

You have to create a new habit, a habit you can create only in satsang. You were taken to the theatre by your parents when you were a small boy. Through such trips you learned how to describe the impressions your senses received, and you also learned how to enjoy them. But your parents could not tell you or teach you about what goes on when you are free of the senses. This can only be known in satsang, and that is why you are here. So, I will ask you again: when you wake up, who wakes up?

It is the 'I' that wakes up.

OK. The 'I' has woken up. When the 'I' wakes up, the past, the present and the future also wake up. This means that time and space also wake up. Along with time and space the sun wakes up, the moon wakes up, the stars wake up, mountains wake up, rivers wake up, forests wake up, men, birds and animals all wake up. When the 'I' wakes up, everything else wakes up. While this 'I' was sleeping during the sleep state, everything was quiet. If you don't touch the 'I' which woke up, you will experience the happiness of sleep while you are awake. Do it for one single second, half of a single second, a quarter of a single second. Don't touch the 'I'. The 'I' is something that we can well afford to be without. Don't touch the 'I' and tell me if you are not sleeping.

That is right. In that instant, everything is like a dream.

This is called waking while sleeping and sleeping while awake. You are always in happiness, always awake. This awakening is called Knowledge, Freedom, Truth. Don't touch the names, though. Get rid of all the words that you have so far heard from any quarter. And you will see who you really are.

[Silence]

Now, don't sleep!

Papaji, I live next door to a car repair shop by your house. Sometimes I feel that my only impediment to spiritual progress is the racket of the mechanics banging on the cars. How can we remain quiet when the senses are continually drinking in the environment? After all, that's their job.

When a child is learning how to walk, his parents give him walking aids. When he grows up and learns how to walk independently, he throws them away. So, in the beginning, if you find that you are disturbed when you are meditating, it will be better to change the environment. I will give you the following advice. When you choose a house or an environment to live in, you must first look at the neighbourhood. Is it full of garbage and pigs? Noisy people? A fish market? A supermarket? You must avoid all these things in the beginning. You can go to the forest to meditate. Then, when you have learned the art of meditation, you can sit in the middle of a fish market or on Shalimar Crossing or Hazrat Ganj. Once you have mastered the art of meditation, you will not hear noise. You will not hear anything. When you are truly meditating, you will be in the same state that you were while you were sleeping. But you will be awake at the same time. This is called sleeping while being awake. Until you have learned this, it is better to avoid uncongenial environments. See what your neighbourhood is like before you move in. The neighbourhood has to be good. The neighbourhood is even more important than your own apartment. Find people to live among who are following your own way of life. Teachers like to be with teachers, philosophers with philosophers, workers with fellow workers. They all very much like to be with each other. But once you have learned the art of true meditation, you can do whatever you like, wherever you like.

What is meditation to you? Many different kinds of meditation are practised. Many of them rely on looking at phenomena such as watching the breath, or seeing thoughts rise and fall.

You are not speaking of meditation, you are speaking of concentration. Meditation only takes place when you are not concentrating on any object. If you can manage not to bring any object of the past into the mind, that is called meditation. Do not use your mind—that is called meditation. If you use your mind to meditate, it is not meditation, it is concentration. The mind can only cling to some object that belongs to the past. Have you been told to meditate without the aid of the mind?

That is hard to answer. Most of the meditation that I have done involves techniques for dealing with thoughts that arise. But the aim of the meditation seems to be a thoughtless state, where no thoughts arise.

Yes, that is called meditation. When no thoughts arise, that is called meditation.

But thoughts arise, inevitably. How does one deal with thoughts that arise?

I will tell you how to deal with them. I think you can devote an amount of time equal to a finger snap. That is all the time I need to stop your thoughts. What is a thought? What is mind? There is no difference between thought and mind. Thought arises from mind and mind is merely a bundle of thoughts. Without thoughts there is no mind. What is mind? 'I' is mind. Mind is past, it is clinging to past, present and future. It is clinging to time, clinging to objects. This is called mind. Now, where does the mind arise from? When the 'I' rises, mind rises, senses rise, the world rises. Now, find out where the 'I' rises from and then tell me if you are not quiet. Go on, comment on what is happening while you do it.

I am listening to you speak.

After that. We have arrived at the fact that the mind is 'I', and that mind arises from 'I'. When the 'I' rises, the mind rises. This is what happens in the transition from sleeping to waking. Now, find out that reservoir, the place where the 'I' rises. Where does the 'I' rise from?

It is the name.

Wait, wait. You don't follow. I will repeat it again. If there is a canal which comes out of a reservoir, you can follow this canal back to the place where it emerges from the reservoir. I am telling you, follow the 'I'-thought in the same way. Where does it rise from? I will tell you how to do it, how to find the answer. You don't have to box like Mohammed Ali for this. It is very simple. To know yourself is as simple as rubbing a rose petal. This knowledge or realisation is as simple as a rose petal in your fingers. It is not difficult at all. Difficulties only arise when you make an effort. So, you don't have to make any effort to go to the reservoir which is the source of 'I'. Don't make any effort and don't think either. Reject effort and reject thought. When I say reject thought, I mean, 'Reject the 'I'-thought and any kind of effort'.

It feels like a comet that is skirting the atmosphere. It flashes briefly and then disappears back into space. It is like a momentary spark of flame which is followed by the darkness of 'I' again.

Not again. For 'again' you have to go to the past. 'Again' is past. I am telling you to get rid of this 'I'. Don't make an effort and don't think either for one single second. Even half of a second or a quarter of a second is quite enough. My dear young Jeff, you have not spent this much time on yourself in thirty-five million years! Here and now is the time to do it.

I find it impossible not to make an effort. There is always a trying. There is an expectation, a sense of trying, always.

All this 'doing' has been taught to you by your parents, by your priests, by your teachers, by your preachers. Now, instead, keep quiet for a quarter of a second and see what happens. You have inherited doing from your parents: 'Do this and do that.' You went to the priest and he told you, 'Do this and don't do that'. Then you heard the same thing from society and from everywhere else. I am telling you to get rid of both doing and of not doing. When you indulge in doing, you are back in your parents' world. You first learned doing from your mother. If you did not handle your spoon and fork correctly, she slapped you at the dinner table and said, 'Don't do this!' Do's and don'ts first came from your mother. And then from the priest: 'You have to go to a particular church. Don't go to somebody else's church. If you do, you will go to heaven. If you don't, you will go to hell. You are a sinner.'

I say, 'Get rid of both doing and not doing'. Have at least a taste of it. You have already had a taste of doing. There are six billion people and they are all tasting doing. Tell me, what is the result of all this doing? Recently we have seen the result of doing in the Gulf. We have also seen three wars. The result of this doing is hatred between man and man, and lots of killing. Let us instead see what can be done by not doing. In not doing, there will be love, not hatred. Let this love spring up once again as it did in the time of Buddha and Ashoka.

Papaji, now that I am calling you 'Papaji', I am putting you in a parental role. It feels a little awkward.

This parent tells you: 'Don't make any effort.' Listen to this Papaji, to only one of his words. If you don't listen to this Papaji, you will have many other Papaji's for another thirty-five million years!

I am a writer and I find it very natural to write. People are always coming to me, asking for advice on writing and I tell them:

'Just do it naturally. Just write as you would speak. There is nothing that is easier.' But they can't do it. They need to make some effort to do it.

Papaji, you awakened spontaneously and completely naturally at the age of eight. Why are you so confident that it will be so easy and so natural for others? We have spent thirty-five million years trying with little success.

I must also have spent that long. I know it because I have seen many of my past lives. Buddha also said that he spent many, many incarnations trying to wake up. He also knew them very well. He remembered very clearly a slight mistake he had made 253 incarnations ago. He also had been doing and doing.

You asked me a direct question. I do not know what caused my awakening. It was very spontaneous. I did not have any background, I did not do any meditation, I had not read any book about enlightenment. I was in Pakistan, so these books were not available. They are mostly written in Sanskrit, but I had not studied Sanskrit. I had only studied Persian. It came to me, but how I do not know. Perhaps it chose me. The Truth reveals Itself to a holy person. I did not have any qualification. I was not educated at that time. I was only eight years old, studying in the second standard. What I saw then I am still seeing. What is it? What is it? What is it? I am more and more in love with It with each passing moment.

All my life I have wondered what it would have been like to have lived in the time of the Buddha, and to have sat at his feet. Here with you, I feel I know the answer to that question.

You have been with him, you must have been with him. Otherwise you would not have asked these questions, you would never have come here. What about the other people, the other six billion people? Why don't they come to satsang? What about your neighbours, what about your parents, what about your society? Why only you? You have been chosen, you have been chosen for this purpose.

When you know It, you will know It in an instant. In that instant, you will know that nothing ever happened before, and that nothing will ever happen in the future. In one moment you thought you were bound. In that same moment you will find that you are free. In that instant of awakening, you will know that there is no freedom, no bondage. You will know, 'I am what I am'.

Papa, can the mind assist in the process of realising freedom?

Yes, it can. Mind is your foe and mind is your friend also. When attached to sense objects it is your enemy. But when it aspires to come to satsang, the same mind is a friendly mind. It will give you freedom.

That's a big relief for some reason. When we speak of realising freedom, who is realising freedom?

This 'who' itself is realising freedom. The 'who' who is asking the question is the same 'who' who feels that this 'who' is now bound. After having known this, 'who' will show its oneness. 'Look here, Jeff,' it will say, 'I am the same "who" who brought you here!'

It was Saint Francis who said, 'What you are looking for is who is looking'.

Yes, yes. When you only say 'Who?', w-h-o, where do you find it, tell me? Where? You have to add something. Only then will the reply come. Who are you? If you simply say 'Who?', who then will appear to you? Simply say 'Who? Who? Who?'

I'm going to start sounding like an owl in a minute. You say that the force that has brought us here, that brought us to satsang, will take care of us. What force is that?

The force which has brought you here, the force which is speaking your words, the force which is asking the questions: that force is the same. The force has now become the questioner. The same force is now asking. And this force is also telling you, 'Keep quiet!'

[Shaking his head] After you, Papaji, I could interview anybody.

In the scientific view everything that we perceive, from an apple to pure grace, is the result of neural signals and chemical processes. From the biological perspective the miracle of consciousness has a direct physical cause. How can we be certain that consciousness, awareness, awakeness is not just a chemical reaction, and that the realisation of emptiness is no more than a mere quieting of our brain cells?

Science has done very well in its researches. I don't have any quarrels with science. We are living in the twentieth century and we are very lucky to enjoy the benefits of the results of scientific research. I can't reject scientific discoveries. Without them you could not have come here from California in just twenty hours. So, we should accept them. But where does the intellect which discovers come from? Discoveries have been made about the nature of the cells in the brain. But where these cells get their energy from has not yet been discovered. I hope that this will one day be discovered.

It is emptiness itself which animates these cells. These cells then send signals throughout the body to the billions and trillions of cells in the body which activate thoughts, movement of the limbs, the senses, the mind, etc. This is creation. In the beginning there is emptiness. Emptiness animates the cells, and the cells then make the intellect and the mind work. Then, once there is mind, the body, the senses and the objects they see, arise. All these perceptions are registered via the cells.

Each cell is giving you a new incarnation. Each cell. Because what you desire will enter directly into the cells and lie hidden there. These desires will emerge from the cells at the appropriate moment and reincarnate in other cells. It is the cells which have reincarnated and become mind.

Your question was that maybe emptiness is just something chemical happening in the brain. But who is aware of this chemical happening? Some higher force, some force which is subtler than the cells is conscious of what is happening to the cells. It is aware. What is that force?

Grace, atman. The larger context in which we are all existing in all forms. In asking this question I want you and everyone in this room to understand that I feel grace in your presence, Papaji. I am not denying that, I am just trying to understand and to remove the doubt. So my answer would be 'grace'. It sounds to me like a force that must encompass everything, even more than everything. It is something that is larger than everything. But it also sounds to me like something I am being asked to believe in, something I must have faith in. Is faith in the supreme force a prerequisite for freedom? Must we have faith in this force to awaken to freedom? Does what you are giving us require faith?

The word 'faith' is used by the founders of religions. When you say the word 'faith' you must go back to the founder of some particular set of beliefs. Faith means following someone from the past. When you speak the word 'faith', you must see that your mind goes to the past. Tell me any instance where there is a question of faith that doesn't belong to the past.

For me, the word 'faith' is associated with religions, dead religions.

This word takes you to images from the past. 'Have faith in this god or that god, in this statue or that statue.' I don't tell the children who are here to have faith in anything from the past. I don't teach faith at all. I teach Knowledge. Knowledge has nothing to do with faith. Faith brings you to the past, Knowledge to the present moment. Between *atman* and grace there is no difference. When you use the word *atman*, the mind does not hold onto any person, any thing, any concept. When you utter the word 'grace', you should not think that it is coming from such and such a person, or an image or a thing. Grace is more than space, higher, subtler, more supreme than even space. Where does the space arise from? That is *atman*. Through whose grace does the sun shine? The shining of the sun is a manifestation of that grace. The moon in the night, the hardness of a rock, the softness of a flower, the flow of a river, the movement of air and the waves of the ocean. What is this thing which moves the air? Not the movement itself, not the movement of the waves on the surface of the ocean. I am talking about that ultimate power which is the source of the movement: That.

It is the ultimate mystery.

Call it mystery if you like. That mysteriousness is called grace. There is no difference. It is a mystery and it will always remain a mystery. This mystery, this secret is so very sacred, you will not be able to tell me about it. When I took you to that place, you could not tell me about it. If it were not a secret, surely you would tell me about it, because you know me. I will not deceive you. You did not tell me what was happening in this instant because you couldn't. It is so secret, two cannot walk abreast there. Not even one. Not the body, not the mind, not the senses, not even the discriminative intellect. That is That.

I have been trying for the last sixty years, but I cannot solve this mystery. I have never been able to solve this secret. I am an old man. You are very young, so please speak to me. I want to see that secret, that mystery face to face. I want to kiss Him, I want to kiss Her, because I have not seen a beauty like this beauty anywhere on the face of this planet. I am in love with someone, but the Beloved I have not seen.

How did I end up sitting at your feet like this? What kind of miracle is this that put me here?

You have called. It is your invitation.

Papaji, you recommend that we don't read books about awakening because it just creates the preconception and expectation of what awakening will feel like, taste like, of what it will be like. What then do you hope to convey about it in an interview?

I don't recommend that you read any sacred books or books about saints. When you read a spiritual book, you will probably like some part of it. If you read it and like it, you store it in the memory. Later, you sit in meditation, trying to get freedom. You want to be free, and you have a conception of freedom which you have acquired from your books. When you meditate, this preconceived idea will manifest and you will experience it. You forget that what you are experiencing is something that is stored in your memory. What you get is a past experience, not enlightenment. The real experience is not an experience of a past memory. The mind deceives you when you meditate. The mind is always going to deceive you and cheat you, so don't depend on the mind. If the mind wants or likes something, don't listen to it. Whatever the mind likes, dislike it. Memory means past. When you meditate, you are trying to execute a plan which is in your mind: 'I have to arrive at the place I have read about.' Your later experience is therefore preplanned and that is what you get, because whatever the mind thinks, it manifests.

When you have a thought of *samsara*, manifestation arises. This is your thought, your wish. That is why the world manifests. It looks so real to you because you have faith in its reality. Once you experience that Reality is somewhere else, you will reject *samsara* instantly. You will have a very new, very fresh experience. Each moment will be new. You will not experience it with the mind. Then there will be no mind, you will be all alone. This and this alone is called 'experience'. I won't use the word experience again because all experiences are planned from the past. It is not really going to be an experience, it is going to be a very direct meeting. For the first time you will meet That. You will go to meet It after denuding your mind, after denuding all the concepts of the mind. You have to go there undressed. Undress everything. Be nude. Even denude yourself of the nudity. Do you understand? The chamber of this Beloved is so sacred, this is the only way you can enter. If you want to meet your Beloved, go there. Who stops you? Do it now itself. It is so simple. To dress up takes time. To undress is much easier.

Yesterday you told a story about a Guru who was so deeply engrossed in meditation, he didn't care for his sick son. Someone asked you about responsibility. I also want to ask you the same question: 'Is freedom also freedom from responsibility?'

The man who asked me about this came to me again. I told him that this was a story of a saint, his wife and his son. I told him, 'You do not relate to any one of these three, neither the son, nor the wife, nor the husband. This is a story of a saint and his wife. You have to become either a saint, or his wife to know. Or at least his son.' Then he kept quiet and said he was satisfied.

Responsibilities have been there for a long time. You have a mind and an ego which says, 'This belongs to me and that belongs to him'. From this, responsibility arises.

Who is the father of all this creation? Before your birth, this *samsara*, this creation, was already there. It has been here for millions of years. Who looked after it during all this time? You have been looking after your own responsibilities, your own liabilities, for about thirty years. After seventy years you will not be looking after them any longer. Your responsibilities and liabilities, the span of your duty, cannot be more than a hundred years. What about the millions of years before you? Who is responsible for the billions of activities that went on before you were born?

If you accept responsibility for your family, your son, your wife, your society, your country and all others in the world, you have to move your mind, your body and your intellect. Don't you? To fulfil these responsibilities you need three things: good health, which means a good body, a good mind, which means good intentions, and compassion. Where do you draw these things from? Where do you get the energy to move the body so that you can help others physically? Where do you get the energy to move the mind to send compassion to others? Where do you draw this energy to act?

It is drawn from grace.

If you know that you are drawing the energy from grace, how and why do things become your own responsibility? This bulb is shining, light is there. Can the lamp say, 'It is my light! If I want to shine I will shine, and if I don't there will be darkness'? The light does not come from here. The reservoir, the source of it, is somewhere else. If this lamp says, 'I am bright. Because of me you can see,' it is mistaken. It doesn't know. Where does the current come from? Where does the electricity come from? There was a chief electrical engineer who worked in this place, so I asked him: 'What is electricity? If you break the wire through which the current is passing to give us light, I don't see anything.'

He answered, 'We do not know yet. Somehow it works. Electricity is generated, but where it ultimately comes from, that we still do not know. We do not know what is the original source of that power which flows through the wires.'

When you are five years old, your parents look after you. When you grow older and you feel that you can look after yourself, you leave your parents and work for yourself. Your parents are happy when you start to be independent. If you have trouble, you can always go back to them for help and advice, and you will always be welcome. Why am I telling you this? There is an energy, a grace, which nurtures you and looks after you. You can go back to it at any time for sustenance. That reservoir is the source of all energy. It is the source of electricity and the source of your own energy as well. Don't forget that all your energy, the energy through which you do work, comes from *atman*, from grace. When you tap into that source, you will have two hundred percent more energy to work with than you have now. Go back to your country and see for yourself.

When you let this grace run your life, you will know, 'This is coming from grace. It is my good luck that I have seen this grace working. Through it I have been given the opportunity to look after my children, my wife, my relations, my society, my country.' When you function from that place, you will have a new life. Many people who leave here write to me: 'Where does this energy come from? We were busy before but now we have taken on more jobs and we still don't fatigue ourselves. We feel very young now. It is as if we were thirty years younger than when we came to Lucknow.'

Then I would be eight years old. A good time for an awakening!

Yes, yes. Otherwise you will be too old. It has to be got in childhood or youth. In old age there are responsibilities. Children will trouble you, society will trouble you, diseases will trouble you. The body is a disease itself. It is full of complications. When you are old, your mind will be dwelling on your diseases. It will not be able to concentrate. There will be mental ailments, physical troubles, relationships—so many things. So you have to do it in your prime, in your youth. Childhood is the best time, but youth is also good. Some old people have also come here. They will be all right next time.

Yesterday a woman came and saw you. She was a bit older than I am and she seemed to have a wonderful visit with you. When I saw her, I was very confident because I thought, 'I still have time'.

Why time? What for? You get rid of time here. Why depend on time? Time is the past. When you go from here, you throw away time. You don't need time.

This has actually happened here. A man about fifty years of age came from L.A. because he was not happy that his son was always here. He was a rich man and wanted to take his son away and make him work in some business. He had brought hundreds of questions and wanted to fight with me. He wanted to know why I had taken his son from him. They had three rooms in the Clarks Hotel and spent the night there before coming to see me. The next morning his son introduced him to me. He sat down in front of me in my house.

The father said: 'You came to me last night. You sat by my bed in the Clarks Hotel and you answered all my questions. Now I have nothing to ask.'

He had a watch on his wrist which he placed next to me, saying, 'I don't need time now'.

He stayed here for twenty days. Have you ever seen an American with no watch? Even while going to sleep they have a watch under the pillow. Even when they go to the bathroom the watch is there. They are so careful, so punctual, even in the bathroom.

When he was leaving, I said to him, 'What about the time? If you don't have a watch, you will have to ask other people the time.'

He replied, 'No, it is all the same. Getting up and sleeping—now it is all the same. I have forgotten time. I don't need it anymore.'

I told him, 'No, take my time now,' and I fastened the watch on his wrist.

When you have time, the mind and all these other things, you have to be responsible for them yourself. But when you know the beauty of no-mind and no-time, who will look after you? If you rely on the supreme power, it will take care of you very well.

Papaji, nearly all of us are very well-to-do people from free countries. Visiting you in Lucknow is a privilege that all of us can afford. For many people, though, freedom still means relief from political oppression, from imprisonment, from torture. Is external bondage an impediment to internal freedom, and if it is, do you see a place for political activism in the world?

External circumstances are no impediment. The impediment is the ego. Impediments are created by the ego. 'I have to do this.' 'I must not do that.' This idea that you are doing something is the impediment. If you act without feeling that you are the doer, there will be no impediments. The supreme power is working through you. It will guide you as the circumstances arise.

I spend some time working for human rights. People in other countries like Burma and Tibet are being terribly oppressed. They are being killed or hurt by people who have taken control of them. You say that the body itself is a disease and that sometimes, in old age, the body exerts a tyranny that makes it very difficult to wake up. There are some places where one could be killed just for attending satsang. There are places where meetings like these are prohibited. In these places the government agents would gun us down if we tried to assemble for a satsang. These external circumstances must be an impediment. And since they are, there must be a need for people to take action against their oppressors. You yourself did that in your twenties, if your biography is accurate. How do you deal with that kind of action?

The world is moving towards disaster. We are moving towards the destruction of the human race itself. Atom bombs and chemical weapons are taking us there. This is not the way to go. Let us try instead broadcasting compassion and love towards all human beings and to all other beings. Let us try this. Here in satsang we are making a trial. We are spreading the message of peace and love. I hope that the message will spread. All those who are here are ambassadors of their respective countries. They will give this message to their parents and to the people in their country. This fire will spread. One day you will see its results. You yourself are going home. You will speak to your people, to your friends, and they will find out what is happening. You will see a tremendous change. I am very sure about it. These times are now coming.

We have to learn the lessons that previous destructions have taught us. We have still not forgotten Hiroshima in Japan. People are still suffering there. We can't forget.

We must learn the lesson and spread the message of love as it was done during the time of Ashoka, when there was peace everywhere. There were no wars then. He sent his own daughter and son to Sri Lanka, to China and the eastern countries. This is how the message was spread. This message of peace was started by one man sitting under the bodhi tree. The flame of love is very powerful. Once it is ignited, it will start a conflagration that cannot be stopped, even by chemical weapons.

Simply meditate alone. You can do it anywhere, even in your own apartment. You will see the results. Keep quiet, send the message of peace, 'Let there be peace,' all over the world. 'Let all beings live happily in peace.' This wavelength has to work.

Let's hope that it does.

Not hope, no. I don't believe in hope. Hope is about the

future. Let us trust in the supreme power. It will look after this world very well. It can bring about instant change. Pray to the supreme power: 'Please help us to be in peace with all living beings. Please teach us.' It is very easy to teach others, to give others advice. Help yourself first. Find out for yourself what peace is. Don't bother trying to help others until you yourself have learned what it is.

What have you learned from your years as a teacher?

I am not a teacher. Who told you I am a teacher? A teacher's teaching is always of the past. A teacher is someone who tells you to do this and to do that, and that if you don't you will go to hell. This is a teacher. I am neither a teacher nor a preacher.

I'll rephrase the question: What have you learned from sitting in this spot in satsang over the years?

Love, love, only love. I love them [gestures toward the satsang].

Why 'them', Papa, don't you love me, too?

I don't include you in this, because you are the Beloved. I love them, and you are my Beloved. What does it mean? Because you are my Beloved, you are seated next to me.

[In a later interview Papaji explains what happens when people approach him in satsang: 'I absorb them all and give them a seat in my Heart, in my Heart. As the lover gives a seat to the beloved in his Heart, you are always seated in my Heart.']

155

Thank you, Papa.

Thank you for coming here. On behalf of myself I thank you, and on behalf of my children I thank you again and again. I am very happy with your questions. We have all benefited from these questions. The vibration from this satsang is not confined to this building. It has already been transmitted all over the world. You will see.

Papa, you have a very broad wavelength. Any kind of dish can receive this signal.

No dish and no signal! You don't need any signals. For signalling you need two—one to send and one to receive.

Of course. When will I ever learn?

[Silence]

[Laughing] You are answering my question now. You asked me so many questions. I asked you only one question, and this is the answer to it. Here is the signal without signalling. Beautiful. What is this? At least you can tell me now. The interview is over. What is this?

[Silence]

What is this? What is happening inside? What is this enjoyment? You can feel it. All the cells are enjoying it. Do you see now? They are enjoying nectar. [Picking up the question paper] I will take these questions with me.

To my amazement, Papaji, you answered them all. I thought there were some pretty tricky questions, but they all have exactly the same answer.

(l-r) Ron Stark, Papaji, and Henry Baer

Leap into the Unknown

by Ron Stark and Henry Baer
New Delhi, 1990

 ou say that to get enlightenment one does not need the understanding mind, the analytical mind or the feeling mind.

No mind is needed to get enlightenment.

What, then, is needed?

Nothing is needed. You are already That. I don't want you to start from here and arrive somewhere else. You must know who you are right now. What is the problem with you right now? The idea that there are different types of mind, the idea that you must use them to reach somewhere, even the desire to reach enlightenment, all these are preconceptions. All these preconceptions belong to the mind, and whatever is in the mind is in the past, not in the present. The preconceived ideas keep you digging in the past.

To make an effort, even to meditate, you must have a preconceived idea or object in your mind. I tell you, 'Take away the object and see what remains'. To do this you have to stay as you are. You are already That, you don't need to do anything to reach It or attain It. Anything that you want to achieve must be something you haven't got now, otherwise you would not be wanting to get it. And if you can 'get' it, you can also lose it because it is not your own nature, your own reality. Your own inner reality, that which you really are, is the only thing that you can never gain and never lose.

Look at all the things you have stored in your mind, everything you have learned, remembered, thought, believed. These things are not 'you'. If you do away with them all, what is left? You just talked about 'analytical mind' and 'intuitive mind'. Do away with them as well. Do it this instant and tell me what is left.

I will tell you what is left. No words, nothing.

There is peace, here.

Peace, light, wisdom, intuition.

How do you do that?

By not doing anything.

Very difficult, not to do anything.

Not true. It is the easiest thing to do. It is not difficult because it is here, right now.

But the mind is very active.

I am not speaking of the mind at all. Don't use your mind. Don't do anything with the mind and let us see where we end up.

The words coming out of your mouth must have been preceded by a certain amount of thought.

I don't agree.

You must think in order to formulate your thoughts.

The words you are speaking now, where are they coming from? I will tell you: from unknown emptiness. It is the birthright of everyone to speak like this.

If I ask you a question, your brain has to process my words. It has to sort through all your knowledge and all your experience in order to come up with an answer.

My experience is that whenever I speak I don't utilise anything that is stored in my memory.

But the memories are still there, at a non-conscious level.

Yes, at a non-conscious level. Go to that non-conscious level and jump into it.

Past and future are fundamentally the same. They are both mind. If you stay only in the present moment, you don't have to deal with the past at all. Memory is of something that is in the past. Mind is also past, it is a collection of images of things that have already gone. When you speak you are always summoning up images from the past. I never dig into the past in order to find an answer to a question. The questions you ask will come from your mind, but my answer will not come from the memory. Everyone can do it. Everyone can talk like this.

It is just being more spontaneous?

It is being absolutely in the present. Walk through life without thoughts, without preconceived thoughts. It works immediately. When you have no conceptions, that is called enlightenment. Now, carry on with your questions.

When I try to think up a question to ask you, I have to go into my mind, into my past. In order to formulate a question I need to ask myself, 'What don't I understand? What do I need to know? What questions are needed?' To find answers to these questions, I have to search my memory, my mind, my past experiences. I can't even formulate a question without doing all this.

That is all right.

If we are totally present, if we are experiencing the totality of this moment, there will be no need to talk.

If you are in emptiness, you can still talk. You can be two hundred per cent efficient there. All work can be done more effectively from emptiness. You don't know this because you have never been there. First jump into emptiness and then see how you respond.

I quite agree with you when you tell me that you are thinking, and that you are asking questions from your memory. That is because you have not yet leapt forward to that emptiness. Go to that emptiness and talk. In that place both your questions and my answers will be in the present.

My mind is still active because whenever you speak I am making judgements: 'This makes sense, this does not make sense.'

Don't try to make sense of anything.

Something in my mind says, 'Wait a minute. Something is wrong here. I don't understand.'

You are talking from a level of the mind. Your understanding comes from a particular level. I say, 'Jump into that place where there are no levels at all'.

This is difficult.

This is a word you have heard or read in the past. Now, in this present moment, don't use that word 'difficult'. Don't go into the past, your past experiences. Leap into the unknown. From there, speak to me, ask me a question.

I agree. It feels the right thing to do. Then the thought arises, 'I want to do that. I want to let go of my preconceptions, I want to let go of my conditioned thoughts. I want to live and function some other way.' But how do I do it? I am being controlled by all these thoughts, by the mind saying, 'Is this right? Is this useful?' How do I let go and just be here now?

You are saying, 'I want to do it'. That is the wrong attitude because to get it you have to do nothing at all. Letting go does not involve achieving anything new. You don't have to try to reach some new state. Because even now you are what you seek. You cannot work at or make an effort to be yourself because when are you not yourself? All this trying, this seeking, this wanting to achieve and attain, is unnatural. What you gain by these unnatural activities will sooner or later be lost, but you can never lose your own Self. Find out who you are right now and put an end to all this useless seeking.

I am pure awareness.

Absolutely right. When you are pure awareness, where will the questions come from? In pure awareness there are no problems. Everything is included in pure awareness. Your gestures, your words, everything you do comes from that pure awareness. This is beyond all levels of thought. It is a non-level. Be in that place, speak from there, carry out all your normal, everyday activities from there. Be that consciousness, be that emptiness.

Kindness, wisdom, compassion. Are they in that place? Will they flow naturally from it?

In that place wisdom, compassion and kindness will be your own inherent nature. When you eat, your hand picks up the food and puts it into your mouth. The mouth is not grateful to the hand. It does not say, 'Thank you, Mr. Hand. You have fed me. Without you I would have starved.' When you live in that place, you will cooperate with humanity in the same way that the hand cooperates with the mouth. You will have compassion for all beings, you will be helpful and kind to them all, but at the same time you will never feel, 'I am being compassionate. I am being kind.' Your actions will be rooted in kindness, love and compassion, but you will never be aware that you are doing them to help other people.

You mean there will be no conscious intentions?

This is the natural state. In this state you help everyone, all beings, and you do it automatically.

Does everyone have this same nature?

Yes, the same nature.

What about those people who have an ugly nature, people who are not kind?

That is not the nature I am speaking about. I am speaking of one's own fundamental nature which is awareness, light, wisdom, humanity. To be compassionate, you first have to experience That.

That is the nature of all of us? Do you feel that That is your inner nature?

Inner nature. Cosmic nature. Eternal nature. *The* nature.

And do we get in the way of it? Does the analytical mind and everything else get in the way of it?

These other things are just confusion. Don't call them 'nature' at all. They are not natural.

People rape, kill, steal. Where do these impulses come from?

They come from unnatural dirty actions. They are acquired from society. Society tells us to take revenge and to do all the other violent things. They are not manifestations of Self-nature. Even people who kill get remorseful. They know, somehow, they have violated a natural law.

Prisons are filled with convicted criminals. I don't think that most of them feel shame or remorse for having killed, or for having stolen, or raped. They feel that that is their nature. They are not in harmony with other people. They are selfish, they want things only for themselves. People have different natures. There is not one common nature.

I am not speaking of different natures. These arise due to outer circumstances. The nature I am speaking of is awareness, your own inherent inner nature. If someone commits a violent crime, it is not an expression of that inner nature.

Even your external nature gives you a knowledge of right and wrong behaviour. You know that it is not natural to kill a man or rape a baby. You know that you are going against nature when you do it. When you transgress nature's laws with acts of violence you have to pay for them. If not now, then at some future date.

You say, 'Let go, just be'. It sounds right, and I agree with what you say. Nevertheless, after hearing you and agreeing with you, I go back to my mental programmes, my conditioning, my reactive mind. I wonder why. I know I should do nothing, and it sounds very simple. How can I learn to do that more and more, to be that way all the time?

You haven't understood what I am trying to tell you. You are still talking about getting something at some future date. You talk about being spontaneously in the present. Why do you have to wait and plan to get into the 'now', the present moment? Trying takes you out of it, into the future.

Right now my mind is in twenty different places.

The mind cannot go to different places at the same time. It can only go in one particular direction. Tell me where your mind is now. What are you thinking at this moment? Where is your mind going now? Show it to me.

I am listening to what you are saying.

OK. You are listening to what I am saying. I will work on this. What you have listened to, where has it sunk?

It sank into the part of me that is judging what you are saying. I am judging what you are saying.

'I am judging.' 'I' is the subject and 'am judging' is the predicate. Now, from where within you did this 'I am judging' rise? 'I am judging' is three words. Rephrase it: 'Judging am I.' Where did this 'I' come from? Trace it back to its source. Every time you ask me a good question, this will be the answer. This is the answer to every problem.

...You have suddenly gone quiet.

I am trying to come up with an answer.

You are Ron and Henry. Mr. Henry, for a little time you were quiet. In that quietness, was the 'I am judging' present or not?

It was not.

OK. This statement was not present. And you were quiet because you couldn't find an answer for this question I asked you. At that moment, who were you?

...Now you have gone quiet again. Again you are quiet.

I feel....

'I feel'—two words. 'Feel' means what? 'I feel'—two words. What is prior to 'feeling'? Who is prior to feeling?

Words fail me.

OK. 'Words fail me.' What is that 'me' whom words have failed?

Behind the thoughts, somewhere there is....

No! No! Stick to your quietness. This is a repetition of the question. Who is this 'I' which has 'feeling'? To whom does this feeling occur? Who is this 'I'? Where is it? Chase back this 'I' to the place it came from and all problems will be solved. Who is this 'I'?

The answer to this question is the answer to everyone's quest.

Is the 'I' these glasses? Is the 'I' this body? Does it have skin, limbs?

No.

What is this 'I'? You have said 'I feel' many times. Let us first solve the problem of what this 'I' is. To whom does this feeling arise when you say 'I feel'? It is 'I'. What is this 'I'? Let us pursue this matter. Let us get acquainted with and be friendly with our own Self. Try to do it now! It is not far away. My dear friend, it is not in San Francisco. Where is the 'I'? How far away from you is the 'I' situated? How far?

It is here somewhere, but I....

Trace it in here [pointing to the chest]. Remove what is on the outside, and go into that place. Do it now! It is very practical. Do it! Who is this 'I'?

There is no 'I'.

No 'I'? In that case the problem is solved. If there is no 'I', you will spontaneously question, spontaneously think, and spontaneously function. You will be spontaneously compassionate.

Because none of it refers back to anything. There is nothing behind it.

Nothing behind it. That is right.

It is so easy to let go [laughing].

Correct. It is so easy to let go.

There is no 'I', or belief or feeling.... There is no 'I'. I think. Can I use the word 'I' in a specific way? If you are alive, you have an 'I'. It is the life force.

I am not talking about a physical 'I', something that has or is life. I am talking about the psychological 'I'. You are speaking now, where are these words coming from? You feel, 'I am speaking, I am working, I am thinking'. What is this entity, this 'I' to which you are attributing all these activities? Who is saying all these words? Where are they coming from?

The 'I'. It seems to be something we make up.

Something that you make up. Now then, what is the source of the 'making up'?

I don't know. Tell me.

No. I want you to go there yourself. I'm not going to tell you. I can't tell you.

I....

One word. [Laughs] Mr. Henry, that is a full sentence.

We have come from four sentences to one word. Not so far to go now!

How difficult is it to stay in that one word, Mr. Henry?

I can perceive this 'I'?

No, because it is the fountain, it is source of 'I am thinking'. You say, 'I will think, I will do this and that'. I say, 'Just return back to this "I"'. If you return back to this 'I' what will be there?

There are no questions there. Questions don't matter there.

There may be a thousand and one questions, one after the other. But this 'I'-consciousness is never affected by them or anything else.

So questions can still be there?

Questions will be there. Activity will be there. Everything will be there. But you yourself, you are *not* there. When you put an 'I' there which does not belong, confusion, unrest, disturbances and even wars arise. When the 'I' is not there, something still remains.

The word 'survival' has just come to me. I think the 'I' arises and persists because of our instinct for survival, for self-preservation. When the 'I' goes, what survives, what remains?

This is a different question. Let us go into it. If we go back to our source, we arrive at consciousness itself. Let us do it now. Let us go back into that source. Right now. It is not very difficult. Don't do anything else, don't go anywhere else. In this instant of time, be that consciousness. You are that Being right now. You don't have to study it or look for it.

My total being relates to what you are saying. I fully understand and agree that this is what I have to do. I hear what you say, I understand the necessity of doing what you say, I even want it to happen, but I still can't let go of the concept of 'I'.

I'm not telling you to let go. I'm not asking you to let go of anything. I am only asking you to be aware of your own beingness. Put your face into your own being. Look at your face in the mirror of consciousness. Instead of running out-wards, retreat inwards. Go back to that consciousness and see what is there. There you will see your own face. You will recognise it and you will love it. Establish yourself there and everything will be so simple and so natural for you.

Now, Mr. Henry, I want something more from you. When you speak your next sentence, please see where it rises from. Where does it rise from? When I take you there, we will be very near to our solution. Now, as you speak to me, see the whole process. Where does it rise from?

Looking where it rises from gives me understanding.

No! No! Reject the understanding. My dear Henry, go back to the source of understanding.

What you are saying is very difficult for me and also very confusing.

No, no. Do it first and then express your difficulties afterwards. You have not yet done it. Go back to the source of your being, from where everything comes. It all comes from within yourself, not anywhere else. Everything rises from there—past, present, future. Everything is located there. You should go there.

I am trying. I can't find it.

Don't try. You will find it neither in the past nor the future. Don't try. Give up all your efforts. Have you done it? You say, 'I am trying right now,' and I say, 'Give up all trying'. Have you done it?

For a second maybe, for a second, yes.

OK. That is enough. That one second is quite enough. For a second you have given up all trying. In that second, who are you?

I don't know.

Excellent! Excellent! Can you stay in that second and tell me, 'I am coming out of that second'? Explain to me how you leave this precious second. How do you get out of it?

That's easy. I go back to the concept of 'I'. It is so easy to become 'I' again.

Yes, this 'I' is just a concept. But I am speaking of this second where there is no 'I', where there is nothing. I am speaking of this present moment. If you are in that second, what do you perceive?

Openness.

Excellent. Do you want openness or closedness? Which do you prefer?

Open.

This is where we started. Please excuse me for dealing with you like this. What is arising in you now? What is the concept in your mind? What trouble? What problem?

To fully accept it.

Let us be gentlemen. When we arrive at a solution we should stick to it. You said first that you experienced openness. Then you said, 'It is hard for me'. Where did you go after this first statement, 'I am open'? What did you do with it? How did you throw it away?

I closed it. [Laughter]

Closing is what happens on Wall Street. When you say 'I am open,' you are happy at that time. When you say 'I am closed,' are you happy at that moment? Choose either! Choose! Come on! In the openness there is no choice at all. It is choiceless.

No choice.

So don't close. Keep open. Is that not reasonable?

Very.

Thank you. Let us have a cup of tea and continue talking.

When we notice 'closed', 'not open'....

When you notice where this concept of 'closedness' is coming from, you will be back in your awareness.

It is that simple?

Does it seem that simple to Mr. Henry as well? It is so simple, so natural. And that is what you are. What do you have to do to be like this? What effort do you have to make to be like this?

No effort.

If you don't make an effort, who are you?

[Laughter] The next question comes up: what else do I need to know? I want to know.

Be assured: there, in that place, all questions will be answered.

The concept of 'I' wants to know, wants to understand, wants to make an effort. When I feel bad I know I'm off-centred.

If your questions arise from the ego, they will only create confusion. We have arrived at that other place, from where 'I' doesn't arise. Right now you are speaking from that place.

From that place questions still arise, but no problems.

Questions will be there, the same difficulties will be there, but no problems.

I will have a different relationship to them?

You will be related to all the problems. From this vantage point you will solve them in a much wiser way.

What is the ego?

Ego is not Self. When your actions are not grounded in the Self, all kinds of misbehaviour arise: pride, hypocrisy, politics. When you are functioning through the ego you acquire knowledge and identities from your neighbours, friends, priests and teachers. These are not your real nature. You have just been conditioned to believe that this is what you are. Your teachers, your priests, your parents, society—they have all done this to you.

That is what makes it so difficult. My normal thought processes, my normal awareness is mediated through that conditioning.

You have to come out of that conditioning.

When I wake up in the morning, I look at my watch. I think, 'It is now eight o'clock. I have to do this, I want to do that.' All activities are filtered through that conditioning.

If you say that these thoughts condition you, then you are conditioned. If, instead, you acknowledge that they arise from the unconditioned source, they do not condition you. The same activity can either be conditioned or unconditioned. Now we are having tea. Activity is going on, but it is not giving us any hindrance.

So we can have the same routine, but a different relationship to it. Then there will be no problem.

In that different relationship there will be 'no problem'. Face it. Work it out a different way. Don't do it with a revolver in your hand.

The value of vipassana, I find, is that we learn to see thoughts as impersonal. We learn how we identify with thoughts and we learn how the thought 'I' is also a concept. In vipassana, which is the path of insight, we practise letting go of thought. If you learn to let it go, you don't get caught as easily in the concept of self, of 'I'. I find vipassana to be a useful tool.

By doing this a trinity is created: the meditator, meditation and the object of meditation. This trinity is maintained. I want you to be in unity. Let us be one, the whole picture, not divided into the meditator, meditation and the object meditated upon.

They are not. That is not part of the teaching, not part of the path. I know it from my own experience. But even if I concede that what you say is true, I could say that the method continuously reminds us, 'I am identifying with thoughts. I am creating a self, creating an "I" with its problems.' Thoughts will then vanish. Vipassana is a process which reminds us that thoughts are not real. It helps us to get back to no-self, to emptiness. But I still like your way.

Don't get enmeshed in vipassana, in this process of watching and doing. When you are aware that you are practising vipassana, ask yourself, 'Who is doing vipassana?' While you are doing it, you have to enquire 'Who am I?' in order to find out who is the one who is doing the practice.

You are observing objects, but I am asking you to remove the objects. If you remove the objects, everything goes. Then there will be consciousness alone.

What do I do to remember all this?

Nothing. Remembering belongs to the past. In order to remember, you have to dig into the past to get something.

That I understand. Everything must be spontaneous. If you go out onto the street, what do you do? How can you be spontaneous there?

You can go out there, and you can respond to everything there, but without forgetting the emptiness. You cannot go anywhere where this emptiness is not. You see things only because of the emptiness that lies behind them. There is nothing without emptiness. If you cannot go anywhere where there is no emptiness, why not accept that emptiness now by seeing that that is what you are.

The emptiness is the blank space behind everything.

That is what I am saying. You can't enclose it or exclude it. Look at this building we are in. Can you say, 'Outside there is emptiness, but inside there is no emptiness because this is my home'? Can the inside ever be without emptiness?

So, emptiness is the natural state?

Emptiness, awareness, wisdom, enlightenment.

If emptiness did not exist, there would be no house. Inside and outside are both emptiness. We put up four walls and call it a house. Then we say that we are living in it. But we are not living within the walls, we are living in emptiness.

All knowledge comes from That which is unknown. And it always stays in the unknown. Knowing this is enlightenment. To try for this is vipassana.

In vipassana we practise intensively for months at a time. It is very difficult to get this understanding.

No, no, it is not a problem. I did not go off to caves and meditate for months at a time. I just went to my Master and he said, 'What appears and disappears is not true'. Then I got it.

How did you arrive at this understanding?

I got it by the grace of the Master. I did not make any effort to understand. Instantly I got it.

Did you meditate before you met him?

I did a lot of things. Devotion, meditation, all sorts of things. There was nothing that I left out. I went on with my search very, very seriously. But when I met my Master, something happened that made me get it. Instantly.

Imagine that you are going to get married tomorrow. You go to the market, you shop and you make all your plans for the next day. Then you go home. On your way home you have to cross a forest. Suddenly a tiger appears right in front of you. What then happens to all your care-fully-made plans?

They change, quickly.

That is how it happens, Mr. Henry. What would happen if you were to remove all the ideas of what you are going to do tomorrow, of what you might reach or attain in the future? You need the sight of a tiger.

Any questions that come up seem to be irrelevant. They all come back to the same point. All these questions are tigers.

No, no, *they* are not the tigers.

Your questions command my attention. You are my tiger when you ask me, 'Who am I?' I was moving in one direction, plan-ning an answer to give to you. Suddenly, my answer is no longer useful.

That is the tiger.

[Laughter]

It just happens—by not making any effort, by not attend-ing to any external things. It does not come from reading books.

[Silence]

Now, what are you thinking, my dear Henry? Now, just now?

I am trying to....

No, no. Don't talk about trying. Tell me, what, in this instant, is appearing in your mind?

There was a space. There was an emptiness.

That is what I wanted.

That means that there is nothing there. So the 'something' is just a mistake.

It is an empty space. You can call it 'space', you can call it 'the source', you can call it 'enlightenment', you can call it whatever you want.

In that space there are no attachments. You don't have any ideas, you don't have any questions.

Now he is leading! [Laughs] OK! He got it!

I have had discussions like this for many years, and I have done a lot of vipassana. I have tried to explain it before, but I didn't get the sense of emptiness behind the question.

[Laughing] I caught him at the right moment. He found the space inside him, not somewhere else. Why should I ask him a question now?

You should not forget the space because you cannot ever get rid of it. You cannot throw away the space: it is always there. Life after life it is there. All these lives take place in that space.

Look at the waves in the ocean. Some are high, some are low, some are long. If you only look at the forms, you see separate waves, but if you look at the substance, you know that they are all ocean, all water. There may be distinctions in your mind, but you are not these distinctions, these waves. You are the ocean of the Self. You can't take the waves away from the ocean. You can't separate them.

What to do when I am not with you? When I am out in the world and I forget? How to remember this?

Don't remember! If you don't remember, then neither you nor I will be present. Right now, we are together, speaking. Don't have any concepts. If you don't record and accept concepts, everything will be fine. You will not be there, I will not be there. There will be no distance and no separation.

Is that how the Guru stays with someone?

Yes, yes.

So the idea of distance between us is just a concept. If I were to stay with you three days, one week, two weeks, what more would I get—other than what I just got?

Nothing new.

Just more?

No, no. No more and no less.

This.

I won't even call it 'this'. If I do, there will be confusion with 'That'.

The answer and the understanding that you have communicated

181

in the last few minutes.... My analytical mind....

You can still use the analytical mind. It is still possible. But now the answers will come from the space, 'I know'.

I can see how my mind operates through words, thoughts, ideas. And I can see how I give them reality. I can see now how I never gave credibility or understanding to the emptiness, the space behind that reality. I identified with a thing called 'me', and the thoughts, the concepts, the memories, the projections of 'me'. Now I understand and know that it is the emptiness behind them all that is really useful.

Then now you can think and do whatever you like.

It is not me, and it is not you.

Space, source, emptiness. You can't reject what is. The waves on the ocean look as if they are fighting and striking each other, but they are still only ocean.

I can identify—the ego says, 'It is my idea, it is my question, it is my answer'. That is the ego. But the ego cannot identify, cannot take credit for, cannot be proud of space.

When you call it space, there is no ego. When you jump into the space, everything is fine. I don't use any word to describe that space. It just is.

So, the ego creates problems. There is no way that the ego or the sense of 'I' can understand space or emptiness because it is prior to the arising of 'I'.

[Laughing] He explains it very well. It just knows Itself.

When I called you today, I wanted to find out what your future plans would be. I wanted to know where you would be so that I could come and see you. Now I wonder whether it is necessary. I'd like to spend more time. Yet I wonder: shall we spend more time together?

No, I don't think that you need to spend more time with me. If there is a problem, solve it right now. I will help you here. Make sure you have no problems before you go. If you have no problems, why do we need to meet again? If you are truly without problems, then we are always meeting. Don't waste your time coming to see me again!

Chokyi Nyima Rimpoche and Papaji

Nothing Has Ever Existed

by Chokyi Nyima Rimpoche
Kathmandu, 1993

 came to see you because the time was ripe for me to come.

We are all aiming in the same direction, moving towards the same attainment. We are all aimed at the same achievement.

I don't think so [laughter].

Why not? Why not?

Because there is no direction. No direction. Any direction, any direction, leads you to the past.

But non-direction is the right direction.

Non-direction is....

Right direction [much laughter].

I remove all the directions. 'Direction' means to have some starting point. Then a destination. Then a path. Then a direction: north, south, east, west. These are concepts. I remove concepts. 'Concept' means past. Past means mind. Mind means space. Mind means direction. Therefore don't give any direction to the mind. When you give it a direction it will take you into a thirty-five million year cycle.

Thirty-six million [laughter].

Any claim you make comes from the mind. It rises from the mind. Even the claim, 'I am free from the mind,' is mind.

Yes. Any claim one makes comes from the mind. To claim anything is mind. Not to claim anything is also mind.

Yes. 'I am bound,' is the mind. 'I am free' is also from the mind.

Certainly.

There is no difference between 'I am bound' and 'I am free,' because bondage and freedom are related to each other. The root is the same. And this root rises from somewhere, but the source is not known. So let us see the root. Let us see the source. The source from which rises the concept of mind, the concept of freedom and the concept of bondage. Let us see the root. If we see where it arises, if we go to the root, there will be no bondage and no freedom. Therefore I say, 'You are already free'. Already free.

In the Tibetan language we call this, 'the rootless and groundless'.

Any language is a 'ground'. This is beyond language. What I speak of is beyond language.

Without using words it's hard to show the meaning. But I agree: words are only labels, words are only superficial.

Therefore, if you use words, everyone will hold on to them.

Right.

Because everyone holds on to words, it is better *not* to use words.

That is why many Masters in the past would use no words but only a gesture, like pointing a finger to the sky. No words, in order to point out the ultimate Truth.

Yes, a word is like a finger pointing to the moon. People hold on to the finger and don't see the moon.

Yes, that's true. The finger is only there to help people to look towards the moon. But also, the moon is not the moon.

Reject both because both are words. Moon is a word. Finger also is a word. Now, where do these words come from? Any word? Where do all words come from?

Word is made by thought.

Achcha. Thought and mind, no difference.

Thought is a functioning of the mind.

OK. Then thought will function only when there is the 'I'. There is no difference between 'I', thought, mind, space, past. When 'I' rises, everything rises. The world rises, *samsara* rises, bondage rises, freedom rises. The main cause of all this is 'I'. 'I am bound,' 'I want to be free,' 'I seek a teacher for freedom,' and finally, 'I am free'. In each case 'I' is still there. 'I' is mind itself. Now, how to remove the 'I'?

The knowledge that sees no 'I', that realises egolessness is called prajna. *This knowledge, this* prajna, *that sees no 'I', is the remedy for 'I', for holding the notion 'I'.*

'I' or ego is the root of samsara. *When one holds on to the idea 'I', me and that arise, duality arises. Because of this 'I' there are disturbances, pleasures, karma, and suffering. So the knowledge, the* prajna, *that realises no 'I' is the remedy for everything. In short, liberation and enlightenment are arrived at through the knowledge that sees no-self. And what you just said before is exactly right. This knowledge is beyond thought, beyond mind.*

It is the nature which is free from the subject and object of meditation. And in this knowledge that sees no 'I', you cannot use the word 'meditating' because there's no act of meditating upon something. Why? Because it is the innate Truth, also called suchness, tathata. *It is present in everyone. And if we bring into our experience this nature which is already present, then that itself is the method of awakening to enlightenment. It is, itself, the nature of all things.*

It makes no difference whether an enlightened being comes into the world or does not, whether he teaches or doesn't teach. The nature of all beings is exactly the same. As you said, 'This nature is beyond thought'. So what does it look like? If it is beyond thought, we cannot find any words to really describe it.

I will tell you [laughter]. His Holiness speaks about knowledge. First of all, knowledge means knower, knowledge and known. Knower, known, knowledge. Now, who is the knower? The knower has to be there to attain knowledge, and whatever knowledge is there must be from the past.

There are two types of knowledge. Normal knowledge is with knower, the known, the act of knowing.

Yes.

But there's also transcendent knowledge which is called the 'prajna paramita'. This goes beyond the duality.

You say, 'There are two types of knowledge'.

Translator: Right.

So, [separating two glasses of juice in front of him] this knowledge is one type [pointing at one glass], and this knowledge [pointing at the other glass] is another type. Now, this is one and this is two. Wherever there is 'two' there is falsehood. The concept of 'one' and the concept of 'two' both belong to the past. Now, you say that there are two kind of knowledge. Remove one [removes one of the glasses]. Remove the other [removes the other]. Nothing is left now.

One can only be 'one' in relationship to 'two'. So one is also a concept. If both are removed, there is nothing. The concepts of both one and two are gone.

That's true. Everything is like that. One concept is always dependent on another.

Let me proceed further. What I speak of is emptiness. When 'this' and 'that' are both gone, there is emptiness. In this place the 'I' is finished. For any knowledge to come, the 'I' has to rise, but there is no 'I' in that emptiness. Don't give any names to the different kinds of knowledge because these knowledges are ignorance.

What you say is true. But we only use the word prajna— *supreme knowledge—when there is no knower and no known.*

Correct. This is called *prajna*. *Prajna* means beyond, beyond the mind.

Translator: The word that Rimpoche is using is the....

It is *'prajna'*. Beyond knowledge. But this 'beyond knowledge' is not a word. Don't even hold on to this word *prajna*. *Prajna* is not a word, not a concept.

Time is also just a concept.

What?

Time is also just a concept.

I agree. Time is a concept and time is mind.

So there is no going....

And no coming. So this *samsara*....

When there's no going, there certainly cannot be any coming. Definitely no going and no coming.

There has never been any coming. Not ever.

But you came [laughter]. You came here.

I will tell you why. You have brought me here [laughter]. I will explain. 'You are coming, I am coming.' This is *samsara*.

    After enlightenment, the Buddha was quiet. He sat under the bodhi tree and kept quiet. After the attainment of Wisdom, enlightenment, he didn't speak.

Translator: For seven weeks.

Then Ananda asked him, 'Sir, what's your experience?'
Buddha didn't answer. He just carried on being quiet.
What does this mean?

He was enlightened in his twenty-ninth year. Up till
his eightieth year he was speaking about enlightenment.
His speaking came from no-mind, no-thought. It came
from *prajna*. Was that speech coming from thought? No, it
was coming from no-mind.

Not everyone can speak from no-mind. Ordinary
people will use the mind to speak. In order to speak from
no-mind, one must know that one is already enlightened. If
there is the feeling that enlightenment is something that
has been gained, then it will be lost later, because whatever
is gained will be lost. If it was not there before, or if it is
newly-acquired, then one day it will be lost.

If you know that you have not gained anything, and
that you are not going to gain anything, you are aware that
nothing ever existed. This is the ultimate Truth: nothing
has ever existed.

Ultimate Truth, is it worth anything?

What?

*What is ultimate Truth good for? What is the use of ultimate
Truth? Are there any good qualities there?*

It is total Truth, total Truth. And now, Truth is asking
Truth, 'What is the use of this?' There is nothing else except
Truth. And It reveals Itself to a holy person. Truth Itself
reveals Itself to a holy person.

———

191

That is correct. But will you accept that ultimate Truth possesses wisdom, compassion, and an ability to help others?

Yes, yes. Yes.

Then are not these the qualities of ultimate Truth?

Ultimate Truth includes compassion, but this is not a compassion for someone else. True compassion does not recognise anyone else.

There are waves in the ocean. Each wave has a certain form—a length, a breadth and a height—and is moving in a particular direction. But are they separate from the ocean? The wave might feel that it is separate from the ocean, and it may go searching for the ocean, but is it ever separate?

I don't understand. How can there be compassion, but not for others?

I will tell you about compassion. Compassion and Truth are one and the same thing. If my hand is picking up food from the plate and putting it in my mouth, I will not say, 'My dear hand, thank you very much. You have put food into my mouth. [laughter]' Who is being compassionate to whom? The whole of *samsara* is one. The whole of *samsara* is one.

Buddha was compassion Itself. Buddha was compassion Itself. It forgot everything. It knew nothing other than Itself. It forgot about everything.

You must know the story of the diamond merchant whose son became a follower of the Buddha. His only son became a monk and followed the Buddha. When the Buddha walked through this man's town, the diamond merchant stood in front of him and started to abuse him. He carried on abusing him for six hours. The Buddha, who was compassion Itself, smiled at him for the whole period. He just smiled [laughter]. When his stock of abuses was finished, the Buddha said, 'Now it is my turn'. And he carried on smiling at him.

The diamond merchant went back to his shop, threw all his diamonds in the street, closed his shop, set fire to it and became a follower of the Buddha.

This is called compassion. True compassion burns the roots of the ego. When confronted with true compassion, suffering ceases forever.

This word 'compassion' has recently been adopted by Christian missionaries, but what they are practising is not true compassion. They are trying to help 'others'.

Yes. Compassion which includes the concept of 'others' is deluded, mistaken. But there is also a compassion which has no duality, which does not arise from mistaken concepts.

That is what I am speaking about. Compassion which has no relationship with the mind, with the ego.

To have 'compassion with concepts' is better than having feelings of anger or hatred. But I agree that compared to the compassion which is non-dual, the normal compassion with concepts is not clean, not sure. Non-conceptual compassion is only present when realising emptiness.

Very good! We agree on everything! [Laughter]

I have no place for disagreement. I have no place for disagreement.

Translator: Rimpoche says he's happy to meet you and also happy to talk with you.

Thank you very much. I am very grateful. I'm happy to see the work you are doing. I am happy to see that you are spreading a message of peace. I have seen many Buddhist groups in the States. The Buddha's teachings are needed now. The world is being destroyed by chaos. There is fighting everywhere. We should do what Ashoka did in his day—spread the message of peace. We need many people like Mahendra, Mitra and Bodhidharma, people who will spread the Buddha's message of peace to all corners of the world. This is my aim also. We can all work on this.

The children who come to see me [the audience laughs as he gestures towards them] are ambassadors. When they go back to their countries, they spread the message of peace. The *dharma* is being spread by these people.

The Buddha was my first Guru.

[At this point Papaji told many stories from his childhood. These have already been recorded in the first chapter of this book. He particularly emphasised the strong attraction he felt towards the Buddha in his early teens.]

If you did that when you were very young [referring to the time when Papaji dressed as a Buddhist monk and went out to beg] it shows good karma from a past life. You have a strong imprint from a past life. This is a proof that you have been practising Buddhist meditation in past lives [laughter].

[Papaji then told several more stories which are also in chapter one, including the one in which he saw all his past lives while sitting on the banks of the Ganges. He then talked about reading, in a Mahayana *sutra*, an account in which the Buddha went through a similar experience.]

I saw all my lives, right from a worm up to my previous life. I saw many human lives, and many other lives. And I saw them all in a split second. This whole cycle of birth and death which appears to take millions of years is, in reality, only a split second. In the moment of enlightenment one will know this to be true. All troubles, all sufferings, all cycles, all concepts of cycles, arise and disappear in this split second. If you do not touch the mind for a split second, you will know this directly.

Simply meditate. Be without thought for a split second and you will know who you really are. Thank you. *Buddham saranam gacchami.* [I take refuge in the Buddha.] Thank you.

Translator: It is Rimpoche's good wish to meet you again in future. [Rimpoche then put a prayer shawl around Papaji's neck.]

Very good, very good [laughter].

Rama Crowell and Papaji

No Teaching, No Teacher, No Student

by Rama Crowell
Lucknow, 1993

 apa...
*Shankara claimed that his teachings could be
summed up in half a verse. If you had to sum up
your teaching in one or two sentences, what
would they be?*

No teaching, no teacher, no student.

Then what are we doing here today?

To find out who you are. If you go for any kind of teaching,
you have to leave your own place and go to a forest. You
have to find some centre in the Himalayas, or some teacher
who lives there in a cave. Then, when you have found him,
you have to reject your old life and your family and stay
with that teacher. And what is he going to teach you? Only
some teaching that he has learned from his own guru or
read in some books. So, whatever he tries to teach you has
come from the past. Any teaching that he gives you will
come from his mind, and if you are a student who is re-
ceiving the teachings, you will have to understand them
with your mind.

You cannot avoid the mind if you have a set-up which
includes a teacher, a teaching and a student. Everything

197

pertaining to the mind is past. If the teacher takes his teaching from some books, the teaching will come from the past.

What I do, I don't call it a teaching. I tell people: 'Stay quiet. Don't run after any teacher, any teaching, any intention, any notion, any idea.'

Whatever walk of life you are in—it may be family life, army life or you may be a businessman—I tell you the same thing: 'Keep quiet and shun all notions and all ideations.'

What teaching do you need? If you want to go in search of a teacher, you have to leave one place and go to some other place. What are you going to get by moving geographically from Vancouver to Lucknow?

Master, what is wrong with the past? It has been said that those who do not learn from the past are doomed to repeat it. Can we not learn from the past?

The only thing you can learn from the past is how to remain in the past. How to get rid of the past? How to be in the present? What will you learn from the past?

The past is a graveyard. If you enter a graveyard and dig out the graves, what will you learn from those people who are under the ground?

You say, 'Be quiet'. This strikes me as tantamount to asking a man to stop breathing.

Man is a product of his past. The Dhammapada *says, 'Man is what his actions and thoughts have made him'. It is not so easy for most of us, for conditioned people, conditioned by the past, to escape from it, to deny it. Is there not something you can say to people who find themselves in such a situation?*

Everything in the whole universe is the past. Creation is

past, the planets and stars are all past, the Creator Himself is past. God Himself is past.

Some Hindu philosophies say that Brahma, the Creator, brings about the creation of the universe. Once it has been created, He needs to look after all the beings He has created, so He becomes Vishnu, the Preserver. Then, when it is time for the destruction of the universe, Siva, the Destroyer, comes along. Where do all these concepts of creation, preservation and destruction come from? Who created the Creator?

When you speak about anything in this world, you can trace it back to the Creator. But who created the Creator?

Master, for what reason do the scriptures exist? Why have the great ones of the past asked us to study the scriptures, and why do they make a distinction between worldly knowledge and spiritual knowledge?

They tell you to read all these things—the *Upanishads*, the *Vedas*, the *Sutras*, the *Shastras*—so that one day you will get fed up with them. Then, afterwards, you can be quiet. You will not get anything from reading books like the *Vedas*. Just keep quiet and see what happens.

Does the yearning for freedom arise spontaneously? Does one not first need to hear about the possibility of freedom from an authoritative source?

That yearning is already there. It is already there, but you cover it up with all your notions: 'This *Veda* says this,' 'There is a Creator called Brahma'.

Do not these ideas have some utility? If not, why do teachers teach them?

The teacher will teach you these things, but when you have learned them, he will say, 'This is not the ultimate teaching'. The *Vedas* are full of writings on all types of spiritual topics, but these same *Vedas* admit that ultimate Truth cannot be spoken about. '*Neti-neti*,' they say. 'It is not this, it is not this.' What does this mean?

Veda means knowledge. The *Vedas* are the books of knowledge. They are the most ancient books in the world, but they very honestly admit that Truth cannot be described. '*Neti-neti*,' they say. 'Neither this nor that.'

So, if you believe this very honest statement in the *Vedas*, you will not believe anything written in the *Vedas* is true. This tallies with what I am saying.

[Points to two metal tumblers on a table in front of him] Neither this, nor that. [Indicates the space between the tumblers.] In between this and in between that. This and that. [Removes the two tumblers from the table.] Now, 'this' is gone and 'that' is gone. What is there now?

Nothing.

Nothing. And this nothingness, was it there or not before these cups were there?

Yes, it was there.

It was there. It has got nothing to do with these cups. It is not affected by their presence or their absence. The cups appeared, but nothingness was not disturbed. And what is the cup? Name and form.

I see. So no amount of action from the past can deliver us from the past because action cannot counter ignorance, only knowledge can counter ignorance. Is this what you mean?

What is the origin of this avidya *[ignorance]? And where specifically does* avidya *inhere in the* jiva *[individual self]? Is it in the* ahankara *[ego] itself, or in the* manas *[the thinking faculty], or in the* chitta *['mind.' See the Glossary for more information]? You are saying that bondage is ignorance. Where does this ignorance appear in the* jiva*? If my true nature is ever-free, if I am pure consciousness itself, how does it happen that the* jiva *becomes bound? Where does this ignorance arise from?*

You are speaking of *avidya*. 'Navidyate iti vidya.' 'That which is not ignorance is knowledge.' When you don't see, there is ignorance.

Where is that ignorance in us, Master?

It rises from the same source.

The same source as knowledge?

From where the *vidya* [knowledge] rises, from there also *avidya* arises. There's no other place. Where else can it arise from?

Yes, that's my question. Is it coming from ahankara *or* manas*? From* chitta *or* buddhi *[the intellect]?*

Whatever exists must arise from one source because there is nothing else apart from It. If there is a reality, it has to be one. There cannot be two realities, one being the source of one thing, and the other being the source of another. Everything has to arise from the One, whatever It is.

I agree. There cannot be two infinite Absolutes.

No, there cannot be. The infinite must be one. I don't give any name to that place from which everything rises. Some people call it knowledge, others emptiness, 'I', light, consciousness. Which do you prefer that I use? You can call it *atman* [Self] or *Brahman*, if you want to convey some idea of it, but I prefer not to use any word at all.

Master, how does the atman *become clouded with* avidya?

Atman is ever pure. I will tell you how it happens. First consciousness is there alone—consciousness, awareness. From the awareness something rises which is like a wave arising in the ocean. Now, what is the relationship between the wave and the ocean?

They are the same and yet they are different.

Achcha. The same and yet different. The person standing on the beach may watch the waves and, seeing only forms and movements, forget that the waves are an inseparable part of the ocean. But they are still one and the same substance. The wave and the ocean are the same substance. Likewise, the wave that arises in consciousness is also consciousness. There cannot be any difference. Now this rising wave, which is consciousness Itself, wants to know what It is. It wants to know Its own identity.

This implies a lack of knowledge in consciousness. How then can consciousness be full and complete?

Consciousness Itself is questioning Itself. 'What is this? What is this?'

But It should know already. Is there anything lacking in consciousness? If you say that in consciousness a desire arises to know Itself, that implies that there is a lack of completeness in consciousness, since a desire implies a lack.

I'm going to tackle this point also. But for the moment, we are addressing the question of how this universe arises from consciousness and the related question of how bondage arises. Your question is about bondage.

This wave of consciousness is arising from consciousness and consciousness wants to know what It is. Consciousness is addressing consciousness and asking, 'What is it?' Consciousness is addressing Itself in the same way that you address your own reflection in a mirror.

You look at yourself in the mirror, you admire yourself, enjoy the reflection and ask, 'Am I Rama? Is this me?' And when you look and say, 'It is Rama, it is I,' separation has taken place in the mirror. Once the mirror is there and the reflection is there, separation has arisen within consciousness. It is all consciousness, but now separation is there. The wave has risen in consciousness, but the real nature of consciousness is concealed within it.

Is that reflection real or not? One school of advaita *considers it to be real, but another school thinks that it is unreal.*

It is unreal insofar as you don't recognise that the substance is the same. Then it's not real. Then it's different. The idea of separation conceals the original consciousness. You don't see that they are the same. [Takes a ring off Rama's finger.] This is a ring. It is round and about half an inch in diameter. It has a circumference and a particular function. It's name is 'ring'. It's form is something round which we put on the finger. Now, what else do you see?

What it's made of. It's made of gold.

When you say, 'It's gold,' you don't see the ring, you see what it is made of. It is the same with the universe.

Names and forms hide the reality.

Name and form is hiding the goldness.

And this comes from an act of consciousness Itself?

It came from gold, it was gold, it is gold. It was just an ore. I am a mining man, I know that once it was just an ore. And out of one ton of ore you may get one ounce of gold. It was just a stone, and when that stone was there, you didn't even see this gold. When you see the ring, you don't see the gold. The gold is concealed because of name and form.

Goldness is now concealed. Consciousness is now concealed because some wave has arisen in It and declared Itself to be 'I'. 'I' has now become separate, the wave has separated from the ocean. The waves give themselves identities and attributes: 'I am Rama, she is Bhakti. I have a body and a mind. I have intellect, I have limbs, I can do this, I can go wherever I like.'

You asked about ignorance and where it came from. Where does this 'I' arise from? It arises from the one source because there is no difference between the 'I' and consciousness.

Where does this 'I' arise from, Master? Where does the 'I'-thought originate? Ramana Maharshi says that it originates in the spiritual Heart, in the right-hand side of the chest. There, he says, is the cave of the Heart within which the aham sphurana [radiance of 'I'] throbs or shines. But you say that this Heart is neither inside nor outside the chest. Where then is it?

Neither inside nor outside.

This doesn't say much to me. If it is neither inside nor outside, it's nowhere.

It's everywhere, which is neither inside nor outside. It's everywhere.

But it must localise within the jivatman *[individual self] somewhere.*

[Picks up a cup] You say it has to be localised. This is a cup. There is emptiness inside the cup....

I am asking this question because you are advising us to find the source of the 'I'. Like your teacher, your own Master, you have asked us to ask 'Who am I?' and to trace the source of that thought. Now if that thought is neither inside nor outside....

I am asking you to find out because you have come to me, saying, 'I am afflicted with the suffering of the world. Master, please save me.' So I tell you that your burning affliction will end if you ask yourself 'Who am I?'

Yes, I agree I am burning.

Then I say to you, 'Find out who is suffering. Who is suffering?' You will answer, 'I am suffering'. So, ask yourself, 'Who is suffering?' Question yourself, 'Who is suffering?' Find out where the 'I' who suffers arises from. Your question is very genuine.

I say it from the heart.

It's a very correct question. If you solve it you will solve the problem of the whole phenomenal world. And you can understand it in a fingersnap. How? Let me show you. When you wake up from sleep, who wakes up first?

The 'I'.

The 'I'. And during the period you were asleep, before you woke up, where was the 'I'? Were you aware of it? When you go to sleep at 11.00 p.m. you send away everyone. You leave your library, your flat, your near and dear ones, and you go alone to sleep. You are so alone, you don't even take your body with you. You leave your name and form and everything else and go to sleep. You go to that place absolutely alone. There is no 'I', no mind, no ignorance, no wisdom, no God, no demons, no *samsara* there. You go alone.

What then is the dream state?

There is no difference between the dream state and this waking state. There is no difference because in both states you are seeing objects. When you see a tiger in a dream, you are genuinely afraid of it. If he pounces on you in the forest, you don't say, 'You are a dream tiger. I am a dream Rama. Come and eat me up.' You don't talk like that, you try to climb the nearest tree.

Master, where does the light in one's dreams come from?

That's the next question that I'm going to ask you. You went alone to your sleep. You did not know anything there. Then you woke up again. The 'I' arose. She was waiting outside for you. You kept her outside and bound yourself to her. If you cut this rope that binds you to the 'I', you will never wake up. Never again wake up to the waking state. Then you will wake up to the real state wherein there is no waking state, no dream state and no sleep state. It's some other state. You have an experience of it in the sleep state. When someone asks you, 'Rama, how did you sleep?', you reply, 'Oh, very well, excellent. I did not have any dreams. I forgot everything.' To speak like this, you must have been aware of the sleep. Who was aware while you were asleep? Who was enjoying while you were asleep? There was no *samsara* [manifestation] there. Nothing was there. Who is the one who enjoys when you sleep? Who is the enjoyer?

Self. Atman.

Self is there now. When you wake up, who is waking up? Is it the Self?

The Self is always awake!

It is the 'I' that wakes. But what about this Self that was there while you slept? The Self is seeing your sleep state also, and when you are dreaming, the Self is aware that you are dreaming. Now you say that you are in the waking state, but can you have any state without the Self?

The wave that is 'I' has separated itself from the Self and identified itself as a separate wave.

Therefore suffering....

Yes, therefore suffering.

And That which was the enjoyer is now concealed. When you say, 'I woke up,' this means the body, the mind, the intellect, activity. These woke up.

Master, you once said in an interview, 'Know your own Self, and this knowing is being. That's all you need to know. Knowing is being.' Now my question is: 'What makes knowing being?' The two are not co-extensive. Mathematicians, for example, can talk about a solid figure with fifty-four identical sides. For them it is a valid piece of knowledge, but in the real world it cannot exist, it cannot have being. Knowledge seems to be a mental act whereas being is something that may be mental, but is obviously something more as well. In what sense then do you mean that knowledge, knowing, is being?

Knowledge and knowing have to come from the past. Any knowledge you have comes from the past. Either from the books you have read, or from some sages, saints or teachers. You call this 'knowledge' and go on accumulating it. Life after life you go on accumulating it. This knowledge is now collected and stored in your memory. Now, tell me, where does this knowledge go when you go to sleep?

When you speak of knowledge, you have some definite subject or object in mind. Something you have learned in a university or heard from someone else. But this is not direct experience. Knowledge is gained through the mind, but it is not a direct seeing, a direct knowing. When I say that 'seeing is being' I am not talking about this kind of learning that is accumulated and processed in the mind. This knowledge is not true knowledge. True knowledge is the source which is beyond mental knowledge and learning.

Which is beyond mind.

Yes. Everything that arises comes from that place. Even inventions, things and ideas that are completely new. Every kind of knowledge comes from emptiness, from consciousness. Whatever it is, it arises there.

If it is not the mind that knows these things, to whom does this knowledge occur?

To no-mind.

I see. Do you mean the sakshi, *the witness? Is this no-mind the witness?*

Achcha. Mind has gone. When the mind goes....

By 'mind goes' you mean no manas, *no* chitta, *no* ahankara, *no* buddhi?

No, not even *buddhi.*

No memory....

Means no past....

In which case we would normally say that there is no knowledge also.

There is nothing there. Mind means knowledge....

It is necessary to have a mind to know. If you have eliminated mind, how can you know anything?

Everything that we know is from no-mind.

Who is sleeping? In the deep-sleep state, who sleeps? What is it that sleeps? What is it that witnesses that sleep? Is there not a witness here behind the mind?

It is behind the mind, beyond the mind.

What is this witness? You talk about the witness, the sakshi.

It is the *sakshi*. If I describe it, then it becomes described.

That's all right.

If it becomes described, how can it still be the witness? When it is taking part in the description, how can it still be the witness?

Two people were once fighting outside Kabir's house as he came out to have a bath in the Ganga. One of the fighters chopped off the hand of the man he was fighting. They were both arrested and brought before a magistrate. The man who had chopped off the other's hand said that he had acted in self-defence. He said that the chopper belonged to the other man, and that the other man had attacked him with it. Kabir was then asked to appear as a witness because he was on the spot when the quarrel took place.

When he was asked what happened, he said, 'The one who has seen cannot speak. Eyes have seen, but they cannot speak. The tongue can speak, but it has not seen.'

I like this story, but Papa, when you talk like this....

This is the answer to your question. Witness is someone else. It is within that person who carried out the attack, it is within the person who is not brought to trial. That is the best witness, but no one knows It. Neither the judge nor any of the other people there knew It. It is the best witness, but It is concealed because you don't listen. We don't listen to That. It is concealed because of the 'I'.

So how do we then remove the 'I'-ness that conceals the witness?

Now we are back to where we started. Before, when you raised this question, I was going to answer it. Now, where does this 'I' rise from? Find out the source of this 'I'.

To finish you have to come to 'I'. You have to go to the source of it. Now, what is next? After the 'I' has gone, what remains?

Why should I think that anything is next? Maybe all I know is 'I'. If I'm in thought, to go beyond thought is an impossibility.

No, no. You are not to think. Whether you say, 'I am thinking' or 'I am not thinking,' you are searching for the same 'I'. Find the source of this 'I'.

Right. But I say that this is like asking a man... when you tell a man to stop thinking....

I will tell you again. The 'I' is there. Now what I am saying is, 'Don't use the word "I".' Then let me see what happens to you.

Without that word....

Without that word. Don't use the 'I'. It's just a word. Don't use any word. And don't think for one second and tell me what happens.

Mind runs on.

This is mind. 'I' is mind.

How to stop the mind?

It is stopped.

But words don't make it stop.

I don't say 'Stop'. I say, 'Give me the result'.

The result is thought. Thought, more thought.

I say, 'Find out the source of thought'. 'I' itself is a thought.

All right. Supposing someone tries to do this....

Why someone? Why not you? We are both here now. If it holds good for you and me, it will hold good for everyone. [At this point the film in the camera was changed. When the dialogue was resumed, the subject matter changed]

Master, there are some people who say that the behaviour of a Guru is to be taken as an indication of that teacher's degree of realisation—that there is a one-to-one correspondence between the behaviour of a realised soul and his state of realisation. Do you believe that a Guru is responsible for his actions? Is this a valid way of determining the quality of a teacher?

First of all, the Guru is not commanded by any person. He is a free man. No one can command him. Not even God can command him. God listens to his commands.

Yes, sir!

This is an idea you have got from some religion. They all say, 'You have to behave according to our commandments, otherwise you will go to hell'. And each religion has a different set of commandments. A sinful act in one religion may be a meritorious act in another. So whom to believe?

But you are talking about the actions of a realised person. A realised person is one who has transcended all codes of conduct, all rules of behaviour. For him, nothing ever existed.

Behaviour is a part of ignorance. Whatever the enlightened man does, whatever he eats, wherever he looks, it is absolutely the finest behaviour, the way one should behave. He will look on every person, every animal and every rock with a beauty that no one else can match.

Are a teacher's actions to be taken in relation to his disciples? Are they a teaching or not? That is to say, when a Guru acts in a particular way towards a disciple, should the disciple regard all these actions to be specific teachings for him?

It is not a marketplace in which there is a seller and some customers. A Guru has no disciples. He is alone. Who is there other than himself? For him, nothing ever existed. There is no student and no teacher. This alone is wisdom. All the rest is preaching. Your questions pertain to preachers, not teachers. The true teacher has no teaching and no rules of conduct. He has transcended everything.

Sometimes you appear to be angry. Are you?

It is the anger that gets angry. Mr. Anger plays his part very well. He works very well on some people. He is my

Cat Commando. [The Black Cat Commandos are an elite force in the Indian Army. They often act as bodyguards for the Prime Minister.] He takes care of me. Mr. Anger is there, and so is Mr. Hunger. At the proper time he sends me to the table to eat. Mr. Hunger is a good friend. Miss Sleep is also a very good friend of mine. She likes to sleep with me. And I sleep with her.

All right. Now, let me ask you this. What are the three most important qualifications for a true disciple? What is important for a seeker who sincerely wants to be free?

Most important for the seeker is that he should seek freedom alone. Only freedom. When a girl needs a young boy, there is nothing else in her mind. Her parents have brought her up but when she gets to around twenty years of age, she falls in love with a boy and rejects everything she has known before—her neighbourhood, her friends, her teachers, everything.

So what Shankara calls mumukshutva *[the desire for enlightenment], the intense, burning desire for freedom, is necessary?*

Yes, intense burning. Not like the love a wife has for her husband. It is more like the love an unchaste wife has for her lover.

You mean like the gopis *for Krishna?*

The unchaste wife may be cheating her husband, but she still takes care of him very well. She gives him special massages, she knows all the good points. She takes good care of her children and sends them to school, but at the right time, when everyone in her house is asleep, she jumps over the wall to sleep with her lover.

So, don't show anyone else that you are a seeker after freedom. Don't show it. Don't give any smell of it. Hide it from everyone, from your family, from society. Tell no one. The unchaste wife doesn't even tell her friends that she is in love with this neighbour.

If you had to give one other qualification, apart from a burning desire for freedom, what would it be?

Number one is this strong, burning desire for freedom. If your clothing catches fire and there is a river nearby, you run straight towards the river. If you meet someone on the way who says, 'Come and have a cup of coffee,' you ignore him. Nothing will distract you because your desire to extinguish your burning takes precedence over everything else.

The one who is aware that the river has saved his life should not forget the river. He should be very grateful to that river because it saved his life. From then on, he shouldn't leave the bank of that river which saved his life.

Moving on to the Guru, what would you say is the most important qualification for a teacher, for a true Guru? How can we distinguish a true teacher? How can a person know that a teacher is the right teacher, a good teacher?

Suppose you are walking in a forest. A deer comes along and rubs your legs. You pet it, and then some more come. Then a rabbit appears and licks your foot. These animals are very friendly, and you are very friendly with them.

Then, suddenly, a tiger appears in front of you. Will you pet him the way you did the other animals? Why not? What will you think at that moment?

I'll run away.

Run away? Will he allow you to run away?

If I'm not fast enough.

He will run after you. Who is faster, you or the tiger? When you meet a tiger, he will take very good care of you.

That is the sign of a teacher. When the tiger suddenly appears in front of you, will you think, 'My wife is waiting for me with my dinner'? Will you think like this?

No.

No. Why not? Because that is the consequence of suddenly meeting a tiger. In front of him, you don't think. He will take very good care of you.

He who stops your thinking is the true teacher. That is the number one indication.

Ah, I see.

This is the symptom you should look for. He who stops your thinking is a true teacher. You go, you are struck dumb and you simply surrender to him.

Master, you sometimes say that the bird of freedom has two wings, jnana [knowledge] and bhakti [devotion]. We have spoken about jnana. What is the place of bhakti in your teachings?

It is not for the West. Therefore I don't speak about it.

I see. But if someone has an inclination towards bhakti, do you encourage or discourage him or her?

Very much encourage.

All right. So to the person who is on the path of love, who is treading bhaktimarga *[the path of* bhakti*], is it not better to begin with* saguna bhakti, *devotion towards a form, rather than* nirguna bhakti *[devotion to the formless]? This is what the* Gita *says. The* Gita *says that it is easier for a person to love form than no form. Is that not so?*

Yes, yes, there are steps.

Could you say something about nirguna bhakti? *About love of the formless. That is something that is very difficult for many people to understand.*

Let me start with *saguna bhakti.* In the beginning the mind needs some image or some statue to concentrate on. Later on the concentration turns into devotion. The devotee projects his devotion onto the statue. It doesn't matter what the image is, it is the intensity of the devotion that is the important factor. If the devotion is strong enough, the divine will begin to manifest through the image in a way that conforms to the devotee's conception of the divine. This is 'devotion with form'.

When you are a child you want to play with toys. Your parents will bring you toys. They don't want to play with them themselves, they just give them to the children and let the children play with them. When the children grow up, they don't want to play with their toys anymore.

So they move on to nirguna bhakti.

Yes.

Can you describe that? What exactly is nirguna bhakti?

Nirguna means 'no *guna'*. [The *gunas* are the three components of all manifestation. (See the Glossary.) If there are no *gunas*, there is no manifestation.] There is no image, and nothing else. It is said, 'There are many rivers, but they all discharge into the ocean'. In the ocean, the name and form of the river is no more.

Children can play. They can concentrate on their toy images. But finally the divine will, through its grace, informs the child, 'Now you have grown up. You don't need toys anymore.' Then It will appear in the Heart Itself and speak to you.

Mira, the great Krishna *bhakta*, started her *bhakti* with the aid of a statue of Krishna. She was only nine years old at the time. A marriage procession was passing her window, but she didn't know what it was. She asked her mother what was happening, and her mother told her that a wedding was about to take place. She didn't know what marriage was, so her mother had to explain the details to her.

'That man there,' she said, pointing to a man on a horse, 'he is the groom. He is going off to meet and collect his future wife.'

Then Mira asked, 'Where is *my* groom?' Her mother was a Krishna *bhakta*, so she took Mira to a Krishna temple, pointed out His statue, and said, 'He is your groom'.

She never knew the real meaning of marriage, but she had learned enough to know that the bride should love her husband. After that first introduction, she developed a great love for the image of Krishna which grew stronger and stronger as the years went by. Krishna would appear before her and she would speak and play with Him. She never knew He was God. She believed her mother's explanation that this was her groom, and she played with Him as she would with any of her friends.

Mira was a princess and eventually her father arranged for her to marry the king of a neighbouring state. This marriage did not affect her love and devotion for Krishna. He continued to appear before her, and she still used to play with Him.

Mira used to dance and sing in the king's palace because her love for Krishna made her ecstatic. She was always singing love songs to Krishna or dancing for Him.

The king's sister told her, 'This is not the way for a queen to live and behave. You are a member of the royal family, the wife of the king, so you should behave in a way that befits the queen of a country.' Mira paid no attention to her and carried on with her singing and dancing.

The king had a chess board on which Mira used to play chess with Krishna. Once, as they were playing behind locked doors, the king's sister heard two voices laughing inside. She called her brother the king and told him that Mira was locked inside the room with a man.

The King got very angry. He broke the door down and demanded to know where the man was. He couldn't see Krishna there. Only Mira could see Him.

Mira said, 'Krishna is here. I am playing chess with Him. She pointed at the empty chair, but the king could not see Him. The king looked at the board and saw that a game was in progress. He could see that she had been playing with someone. He accepted her explanation, even though he couldn't see Krishna. By way of an apology, he touched her feet and said, 'Now you can do whatever you like'.

Other saints have also had God appear before them. Saint Theresa of Avilla was devoted to a statue of Jesus. It is still there in her house. I have seen it there. One day Jesus appeared before her in that form and kissed her.

Feeling very happy, she went off to see Saint John of the Cross who lived nearby. I have seen his house also. On her arrival she told him that Jesus had appeared before her, and she added, 'He laughed and smiled and then he hugged me and kissed me'.

Saint John didn't believe her because he thought that Jesus didn't laugh or smile. Christianity has the idea that everyone, including Jesus, has to suffer.

When Saint Theresa said, 'He came to me smiling,' Saint John replied, 'No, it must have been a demon. Only demons smile. If he was happy, he must have been a demon. It was a demon who visited you.'

I have also read a similar story about Saint Francis and Saint Clare. Jesus appeared to her also.

Master, did not Mira later meet a Guru who initiated her into nirguna bhakti? *Was it Ramanand?*

Not Ramanand, it was Ravidas. But even this Ravidas eventually had to touch her feet.

Going back to *nirguna* and *saguna*, and the story of Mira, she eventually wrote a poem about her *nirguna bhakti*. The form of Krishna used to come and play with her, but eventually she wrote a poem which said: 'On the ninth story there is an empty chamber where there is a bed for the honeymoon, my honeymoon with *nirguna*. Krishna used to come and then run away from me, and this separation was very troublesome. But now I sleep with That. There will be no separation now.' You see, *nirguna* always stays.

You mentioned earlier this evening that a man who is on fire to become free should jump into a river and have his fire quenched. Then you said that the man should have gratitude to the river and not move from its banks. What about the devotional fire that the bhakta *has? When tremendous devotion to the Guru arises, along with a desire for his grace, what is the best way to work with this devotion to take one to freedom? When tremendous devotion to the Guru arises, do you permit the devotee to have devotion to your form?*

There have been such people, and there are some even now. But none of them belong to the West. Westerners have already sold their minds and their bodies to somebody else. In Hinduism, we only offer to God flowers which have never been smelt. Who has got a heart to offer to God which has not been smelt by somebody else? How can you offer such a flower or such a heart to God?

By the Guru's grace, cannot that smelt flower become pure again? What is the best way to work with devotion to the Guru, to utilise that devotion for freedom?

I don't think that love can be taught in any university. It is there naturally. It is just there. Do you have to ask your neighbours' or your father's permission to fall in love with someone? What would your father say? When you fall in love, you just fall in love. You don't need advice from anyone else on how to do it.

Master, what is surrender in the context of bhakti *and especially of Guru* bhakti? *What is surrender?*

Surrender means, 'Surrender your *ahankara*, your ego'. Surrender your separation and merge with the Guru, merge with devotion, merge with the Lord. Surrender until you can say, 'I am the Lord Himself'. Surrender and keep quiet.

Is that surrender gradual or immediate?

Immediate. Surrender is immediate, not gradual. What would you say if some woman came up to you and said to you, 'I want to marry this man. But after I marry, sometimes, maybe once a week, I will go back to my old boyfriends.'?

I actually encountered a situation like this when I was in Paris. I was visiting someone and he said, 'I allow my wife to go and visit her old boyfriend. We made this agreement before we married.' On that particular day his wife was with her old boyfriend.

I told him, 'What kind of wife do you have? Reject her. She has gone to that man to sleep with him. Bring the phone. I will speak to her. I will tell her that she must not come back here.'

'Oh, my hand is shaking,' he said, as I put the phone in his hand and tried to make him do it. 'This has been happening for seventeen years.'

I offered to speak on his behalf, but in the end he agreed to do it himself. I stood by the phone and made him do it.

Can there not be a growth in love? Does not love seem to become greater and greater? Can surrender not become more and more?

Love is fathomless. Love is fathomless. The more you dive into the love, the more you want to love again. The more you get into the depths of love, the more you want to stay there. You don't want to come to the surface again.

You sometimes say that devotion to God cannot lead one to freedom because God is a projection of the human mind. A projection of the mind cannot take one beyond the mind. Does this hold true

of devotion to the Guru? Can devotion to the Guru, Guru
bhakti, *take one to freedom?*

I will answer this question by telling you who the real
Guru is and what he does.

When you are a child, you go to primary school. Your
first teacher there is your first guru. Later in life, you go to
university and get a Ph.D. If you then go back to your primary school, your old teacher will be very happy because
one of his students has gone on to get a Ph.D.

Next, the same student becomes a high government
official. He becomes Governor of the state. The teachers at
both the primary school and the university are happy that
one of their students has gone on to achieve great things in
the world. Everybody is happy with his success.

A devotee may graduate from teacher to teacher and
eventually he may become the Lord Himself. If this happens, all his old teachers will be happy.

Different gurus teach different things: some give instruc-
tion for beginners, others have more advanced teachings.
Finally, though, the student will graduate to his final
teacher, who is the *Sadguru*. The *Sadguru* is one: there are
not many different *Sadgurus*. The *Sadguru* is the one who
enables you to recognise your own Self. All other teachers
will send you to someone else. The *Sadguru* will not send
you to someone else. He will give you perfect knowledge
and liberate you immediately from the cycle of rebirth. He
will give you the direct awareness of the highest truth:
'You are not born. The universe was never created.' This is
the ultimate *sat*, the ultimate truth, the ultimate reality.

*This is a very high teaching. Supposing the disciple in all sincerity
does not understand this teaching when he or she first hears it.
What then do you prescribe for such a person?*

Next life! What is *samsara*? The endless cycle of births leads to the moment when this truth is understood. A person will be reborn and reborn until he finally understands. Everyone has to return home. If not today, tomorrow, and if not tomorrow, next life. Finally one sees that there were never any incarnations at all. It will be discovered that 'I have never moved from body to body. This only was a concept. Time was a concept. Ignorance was only a concept.' Finally, this will be understood.

The Guru cannot make you 'understand' this. No one can make you 'understand' this. You have to 'not understand'. Then something will happen to you.

This does not seem to be a very compassionate approach. Is there not something a person can do in the way of spiritual practice in order to prepare himself or herself?

This is postponement, no? Postponement. One who says, 'I have to prepare myself,' is deceiving himself, fooling himself. Whatever can be done tomorrow can also be done today.

Is there not a place for sadhana *in your teaching?*

No.

No sadhana*? You give devotees, disciples, nothing to do?*

Nobody is doing anything here. The people who come here have already done many things with other teachers. I only tell them, 'No effort, no thinking, and keep quiet'.

Does not this in itself imply a practice?

Somehow, this is working. People from all over the world are coming here. All of their previous teachers have given them some teachings, but there have been no results.

There are many ashrams in the world, many centres. Many different things are going on in these places, but they are not producing results. No one is getting freedom in these places. People come and tell me things like, 'For the last thirty-four years I have been doing yoga, but I have not achieved any results. My mind is still not quiet.'

Any yoga or practice that one does is done with the mind and the body. Yoga is done with the body, meditation with the mind. Any understanding that you get from meditation must therefore be only mental.

Yes, indeed.

So mind cannot arrive there.

What then was the purpose of your many years of practice? You practised. You did sadhana *for many years, very hard* sadhana.

Not just many years, many lifetimes. I know, I have seen them all.

Was the result of all this zero?

I got fed up with them. Then I met my Master. He told me, only once, 'What appears and disappears is not real'.

And when you heard that you became free. But will you not admit that your practice prepared you so well that when you heard the Truth you became It and never left It? It was not just a glimpse for you, it was permanent. Did all this practice not make you a fit receptacle for this teaching?

225

It may have.

If you say no, what is your comment on the upanishadic story in which Sukadev goes to meet Janaka? Before Janaka will admit him into his palace for instructions, he asks Sukadev to walk all round the palace, carrying a jar of oil. He instructs him not to spill a single drop. This seems to indicate that one should demonstrate one-pointedness of mind before the Truth can be heard with lasting effect. Is it not better to help a disciple who does not initially understand the Truth? A bone with no meat on it may be better than nothing at all.

It was not me who told him to walk round the palace, it was Janaka. I would have told him, 'Throw away all your desires along with the vessel itself'. Why carry these burdens? If he throws away the pot, his hands will be empty. It will only be empty when he has thrown away the pot full of oil.

Many people come to you, receive this teaching, and get a glimpse of it through a direct experience. But the glimpse disappears, maybe because they are not fit to hold on to that teaching. These people then get disappointed. They feel....

Yes, yes. They get a glimpse of it here, and then they go away, fully satisfied, to the West. But they come back, saying that they have lost it on the way.

There was one girl from Vancouver who told me a story like this. There is also a boy here now who said the same thing. I told the girl, 'You lost it because you always tried to maintain it. You tried to keep it, therefore you lost it. It is not your father's property. It is not something that you can keep. Now you have come for a second time.

'You had a glimpse. Don't try to hold on to it. Don't try

to maintain it. It came. Now let it go. Don't care. Let it go. It's not your possession. It's not an object to be possessed. A glimpse is a glimpse.'

Would it not be more helpful to equip such a person with the means of holding onto the experience?

The best way of equipping oneself is to give up the intention of holding.

But that means to give up the search!

Yes, give up the search! Then what will happen?

I will ask you, 'What will happen?' How will a person who doesn't search ever change? He will just remain as he is.

That is what I say, he will become changeless. If not, he'll be changing all the time.

[Laughing] Now you're playing with words.

No I'm not. Do it and see. Why do you want to have a friendship with something that changes?

Perhaps one cannot help it. This is what I mean. If one doesn't understand the Truth at the first glimpse....

No one can understand Truth! No one can understand Truth! You are Truth Itself. How can you understand what you already are?

All right. If one does not become Truth Itself....

It is not becoming!

Recognise then, remove the illusion that one is not Truth.

Not even that. Not even recognising. To recognise 'something', you must be 'someone'.

You seem to make freedom depend solely on grace. Perhaps not even grace. You seem to make it dependent upon a roll of the dice. Either you get it or you don't. If you get it, fine!

You can't 'get' it....

And if you don't, tough luck. You have to wait till your next birth.

Who is this person who wants freedom? Freedom alone is. Consciousness alone is. There is nothing else. Emptiness alone is. There is nothing else.

But until one experiences that for oneself....

There's no one to experience.

That's just words, that's just words.

I repeat: 'There is no "one".' If you don't have the concept of 'one' for one second, there is no one. In the first second that you sleep, is there any 'one'? Is there oneness or twoness?

No.

No? Then what do you lose by giving up this 'one'? What is your loss?

This is a natural occurrence. The wave arises naturally in the ocean. When one wakes up, the wave of 'I' also arises naturally.

I say that it is not natural. It is your intention to wake up at 5.00 a.m. or some other time that causes you to wake. If you have no intention at all, you are not bound in time. If you are not in any way bound by time, you are free. This is freedom from time. This is freedom.

Indeed. But we are not free from time. Most of us are not.

Yes, yes. So freedom from time is freedom. Any attainment which you get through doing *sadhana* will occur within time, and time will later destroy it. What is gained in time will always be lost.

But what will be destroyed in this way? Maybe ignorance itself will be destroyed.

No, no. You have a concept of what freedom is. And you have other concepts: 'I will get freedom through spiritual practice, I will be benefited if I do this, I will get results if I do these practices.'

But Master, even the search itself is illusory. So, within this illusory search....

That's what I am telling you: 'Don't search. Give up your search.'

But you are asking the impossible.

No I'm not.

What then would be the meaning of the scriptures?

You will know the meaning. The scriptures only tell you this one thing: 'Keep quiet. Keep quiet.'

Indeed, that's true. But they also encourage sadhana.

They say this to dull-witted people. For these people, they prescribe *sadhana*. But they also say, *'sadhana na'*—'Don't practise'. This they also say.

Is it not possible that sadhana *could perform what Vidyaranya calls....*

We have seen many yogis who have done intense *sadhana*. But can you cite anyone who did all this *sadhana* and got liberation through it? What results are there?

Well, take your own case. Do you not think that the sadhana *you did fitted you to become what you are today? I agree that everything is* maya, illusion, *but Ramakrishna once said, 'Some* maya *can take you up and some* maya *can take you down'.*
    A seeker is like a man in a dark cave who wants to find his way to the entrance, to the light. Can sadhana *not be like a string he can follow, a string which will take him towards the light. Now I know that the string is not real, that it is also* maya, *but it can lead one to the real. Vidyaranya said, 'A man sees a light in a window, which is shining on a gem. The man who follows the light back to the lamp gets nothing. But the man who follows the light to the gem, he obtains the precious jewel.' The light in the jewel is an illusory light, but for the one who goes towards it, it is a fruitful illusion. Cannot* sadhana *be a fruitful illusion that can help to reduce karmas, reduce the weight of conditioning, reduce the weight of* samskaras? *Can it not fit the*

mind to hear the Truth from a teacher?

Whenever you are doing any practice, any *sadhana*, at that time ask the question, 'Who is doing *sadhana*? Who is doing *sadhana*?' What is *sadhana*? It is something done with the mind, yes?

With the mind, yes.

If you do something with your hand, some activity, the benefit can only be physical. The hand is not going to get freedom. What is it? It's just flesh, bone and blood.

OK. But some benefit can be there.

Any benefit from a physical activity has to be physical. Any benefit from a mental activity can only be mental.

Master, let me go back to that seeker in the cave.

Yes.

If you show that seeker light, he has a glimpse of light and is encouraged. Then you leave him with no sadhana, no string, no way out. The man is as he was before. You show him a glimpse and then you go away. That glimpse did not stay. What is he to do next? Is not a string leading to the entrance better than no string at all?

No, no. The string may be there. There may even be a light or a candle that can take him to the entrance of the cave. But the light through which you yourself see the candle is more important. That is your own light, and it is far more important.

Right. OK.

So find out who is seeing *this* light.

When I come to the entrance of the cave I can realise what this light is, but in order to get to the entrance of the cave I still need the string.

If you are doing any practice, where does the energy come from to do it? Where does the energy come from to lift your hand? Now you are speaking to me. Your tongue is moving. Where does the energy come from to speak? Where does the energy come from to ask me these questions?

Not from the tongue. From behind it.

So go behind. Where is the reservoir which contains all this energy?

Behind [gesturing behind his head].

Achcha. I am telling you to go behind. You are going forward.

And manas *[the thinking faculty]. It is behind* manas.

You are always going forward, but have you ever gone backwards? Now, or at any other time? Why don't you go back to that place where the energy is coming from? That place which gives you the energy to perform any *sadhana*, the energy to see, smell, taste, touch and speak.

One has and one does by your grace. But mind is very strong.

The conditioning of the past is very strong. Therefore, that glimpse does not remain.

There are people here who have lost that glimpse. I tell them, 'This glimpse has come from within you. So look within and see It right now! It has not come from Lucknow!'

I tell them, 'It has not come from me. Not from Poonjaji. Not from any person. Not from any thing. Not from any object.'

The number one thing to understand is that this glimpse has not come from any person. So, avoid all persons, including yourself. You are also a person. And avoid all things. All things. Don't think of things and don't have any objects in the mind. Give up all ideas including 'I have had a glimpse' or 'I have not had a glimpse'. No ideas, no things, no persons. Don't think of any of these three things. Then look. What do you see?

I can only repeat what I said before: 'This is a fallacy.' You are asking the person to be that which he already seeks.

I am asking you to avoid seeing and instead look from where you get the energy to see, to think, to speak, to touch and to taste. Why don't you go to the reservoir? [Points to a light switch on the wall.] Switch on, switch off. Where does this light come from? No one has gone there. Only the electrical engineer knows. He alone can take us there. And that electrical engineer is the Guru. He will take you there. He will call you, saying, 'My dear boy, please come'.

I say, 'Come. Let us go to the reservoir.' The reservoir for this electricity may be five kilometres away, but the reservoir I am speaking of is nearer than your own retina. It is behind the retina, from where you get the sight to see. It is behind the breath. It is so close. You do not have to make an effort to get there. Why can't you do this just for one second? Give me one second of your life. I am begging one second from you. Can you not give me one second of your life and then give me the result? Go to the reservoir. How to do it? Don't think of a person, a thing or an idea.

Master, your teaching is noble and pure. There is no doubt about this. It is your love for us all that makes you speak like this, as though it were so easy. And yet you yourself have said that in your life, out of a million people that you have met, perhaps only two or three have managed, like yourself, to achieve this. So this simplicity is paradoxically extraordinarily difficult. There are many of us who love freedom and want to be free, but who do not have the good fortune to become free at a stroke. For those of us in this situation, some sadhana *can be helpful. It can at least be helpful in removing the idea that one is a doer.*

I am very satisfied with what is happening in the satsang in Lucknow. I'm very satisfied. I have seen many ashrams in the last sixty years. I have been to ashrams all over India, right from Kanyakumari up to Srinagar, from Dwarka to Puri. I have seen many centres in Europe also. I am friendly with all the swamis in these places. But I don't see any results in these ashrams. No one in these places is getting freedom. When I go to these places, I find that the people there are spending their time on quarrels and litigation. I have seen what happens in these places, so I have not established any centre here. No ashram, just a rented house. When I pass away—finish.

Right now I'm living in the house of my daughter-in-law. I have had very good offers to live in other places, such as France, Spain, Venezuela. People have even offered whole islands for me to live on.

I tell such people, 'No thank you, I am not going to lay

a brick here in the transit lounge'.

If I ever felt, 'I am doing this work,' or if I ever got greedy, then I would not be an honest man. My word would not work. If a teacher is greedy for anything, he's not a true teacher at all. The word of such a man has no power. It will not work. There are so-called teachers like this all over the world. Either they don't have Knowledge or they are commercial, just making money.

I think that your word does work, Master. Perhaps it is we who are not working [laughter].

I am very satisfied with what is going on here. It is the grace of the Supreme. It is That which is doing all this. He is using Poonjaji, and I am happy that I am being used. I am very happy.

I haven't the heart to say anything further about sadhana. *For the two years or so that I've known you, I've never known another human being who has worked and served humanity as hard as you have. Day and night you do it. You keep nothing for yourself, you make no distinctions between the people who come to you, and you take nothing from anyone else. You just serve people with love and compassion, absolutely and completely... [Gets up and prostrates to Papaji].*

[Laughs] Beautiful, eh? What a satsang we have had! You played your part very well.

[I had asked Rama to do this interview to gather material for a film on Papaji called *Call Off The Search*. Just before the interview started I encouraged him to challenge Papaji as often as possible because I thought it would make the interview more lively and more telegenic. —David Godman]

With your grace only [laughing]. Really, there's not another person alive like you!

Thank you. Thank you very much.

Thank you so very much. I don't know how to express it [hugs Papaji and cries on his shoulder]. I don't know what karmas I did to have you in my life, Papa. I've been trying to figure you out for a long time. I just don't know how you do it! You don't depend on any human source. Nothing! You don't depend on any human source for love, affection or energy. It's uncanny. It's unreal. How you are, what you do, day and night. Unbelievable! I've never seen anything like it. It's the grace of my life to be up close, to be in the presence of such a being. I don't even know if you are human [laughs]! Honest to God, I mean it. You completely baffle me, totally baffle me. Now I'll just give all this up [gestures to the thousands of philosophical and spiritual books which line his study].

Summa Iru

by David Godman
Botanical Garden, Lucknow, 1993

P*apaji, we are trying to make a film about your teachings. How can we make a film when you say you have no teachings?* •

To have any teaching is preaching. A real teacher has no teaching, no method, no way. To know your own Self, you don't need any teaching. What you really are, always you are That Itself. No one is going to teach you. You have to realise who you are, here and now, in this moment.

Do you regard telling people in which direction they should look as teaching?

People should not look in any direction. [Laughter] Looking in a particular direction means abiding in an object, the object you are directing your attention towards. People get lost this way. But if they do away with all directions, if they have no concept of any direction in their mind, then they will know what they really are. They will know that they are That Itself: That which they always are and That which they always will be.

Do you regard yourself as a Guru, Papaji?

No, not at all! [Laughter] I never declare, 'I am a Guru'.

What about all these people who think they're your devotees and disciples? Are they your devotees?

When there is no Guru there is no question of any devotees. When they come to see me, I welcome them. Whosoever comes, I welcome them. If they don't come, I still wish them good luck. And when they leave me I say, 'Farewell. Be happy wherever you are.'

You are encouraging everyone who comes to you to look for their own Self. Why are you doing this? What motivates you to do this?

My own happiness. These people are sleeping. They are all suffering when the treasure is within them. Everybody, all the human beings of this world, are suffering because they are trying to find peace and happiness in objects. They are examining and experiencing objects one by one, but this is only resulting in pain and suffering. There is no object in the mind, no person, no thing, no concept that can return you to happiness and peace of mind. So I just tell them, I just give them this information: 'Don't look here, there, any-where. Peace is within you and within the Heart of all be-ings. So keep quiet, don't look anywhere, don't allow your mind to abide anywhere, and you will see that It is peace, happiness itself. That is the fundamental truth. Every being in the world is happiness itself.'

I think that most people who come to you think that you are giv-ing out something more than just information. I think they feel that in your presence there is some power, some grace which en-ables them to discover what you are pointing at. Do you have any comment on this?

Definitely. I am pointing at their own Self which is the fountain of grace, of beauty. In that place love and peace also arise. I just point this out by saying, 'Look within yourself for one second. You don't need to search, you don't need to find. Just look within yourself and you will see that you are peace itself.' I just point this out. People are asleep. It's better to wake them up because they are dreaming. These dreams are only mental projections, but because people take them to be real, they cause a lot of suffering. If you see a tiger in your dream, you get afraid. If you get attacked by a dream robber you get afraid.

Stop all the mental projections. See that the dream is only a dream. See that it is not real. Whatever you see, it's just a dream. Wherever there is an object, wherever there is a seer and the seen, there is a dream. If there are objects and a subject who sees them, there is a dream. But if you somehow get rid of subjects and objects and of the relationship between them, what's left?

When you look at people who come to you and tell you, 'Papaji, I suffer,' do you feel compassion for them, and when they wake up, do you rejoice?

I do feel compassion. What else is there for me? I have compassion for all beings who are suffering and who are dreaming. I just tell them, 'Wake up, my dear friends. My dear children, wake up. There is no suffering at all. It's only a projection of your mind. It's not real. You are dreaming. Wake up from the dream, and all the suffering will end.'

I would like you to tell the story of the Japanese professor with one lung who couldn't stop laughing. I think that it is a very good story about your teaching. Can you tell the whole story?

[Papaji laughs] When he arrived I was upstairs in my house, giving satsang to some people there. He asked the people downstairs if I would come down and see him because he had been told by his doctor that he should not climb stairs.

He was told, 'Papaji is very busy right now. He is giving satsang upstairs. If you cannot wait, you must go up and see him.'

This man had a great desire to see me, so he decided to climb the stairs, rather than wait for me to finish. The people downstairs helped him, but even so, he climbed very slowly, and with great difficulty.

When he arrived everyone in the room, including me, was laughing. For the whole time he was there, there were no verbal teachings given out. There was just continuous laughter. He also joined in, even though he didn't know why we were laughing. Then, as it was lunchtime, we all went downstairs to eat.

During lunch he remarked, 'I only have one lung. The other has been surgically removed. My doctor has told me not to climb stairs and not to laugh because these activities put too much strain on the lung. If I laugh or climb stairs, I am supposed to take some medicine to help my lung recover from the exertion. But here I don't feel any need to take the medicine. In fact, I feel as if my other lung has been replaced.'

And then he started laughing again. During all the time he was with me, he never asked any questions. He only laughed and laughed and laughed. It put no strain on him and he never needed to take his medicine.

Later, after he had returned to Japan, he sent one of his students to see me. This student told me that after his professor had arrived back in Japan he was asked, 'What have you brought from Lucknow? What is the teaching of Poonjaji?'

His only response was to start laughing. He laughed and laughed and laughed.

When the laughter finally subsided, he was asked again, 'What is the teaching of Poonjaji?' and he replied, 'Laughing. Laughing and dancing.'

When a person laughs he has no mind, no thought, no problem, no suffering.

So long as the laughter persists, there is no mind.

No mind. You try! [Laughter] Those who don't laugh, they have got minds. They look very serious and have many problems. They have minds because for any problem, for any suffering, you need to have a mind. It's the mind that suffers, you see. So laugh away your problems. If any problem comes, laugh it away! If you laugh, it will go away, it will run away, it will fly away.

So, laughter is a response to the absence of pain and suffering. Would you say that?

What do you say?

When all the mental problems go, then spontaneously laughter arises?

Of course, of course, yes, yes. Only the man who has got rid of all his problems, he alone laughs, he alone dances. As a solution to all his problems, he only has to dance, he only has to laugh.

There was once a saint who lived on the top of a mountain. At midnight, on a full moon night, he started laughing and laughing. All the people of the village woke up wondering, 'What has happened to this monk?'

They went to the top of the hill and asked him, 'Sir, what happened?'

The saint answered, laughing, 'Look! Look! Look! Look! There's a cloud! There's a cloud!'

Many people see clouds but who laughs at them? Only the one who has no mind. Anything he sees will give him occasion to laugh. Because, as he looks at it, he becomes that thing itself. The cloud is there, the moon is behind it. If you have no mind, this sight alone can make you laugh.

So, when you see the world, Papaji, you mostly laugh at it. You think it's all a big joke?

[Laughter] I only joke, what else is there to do? I don't study any *sutras*, I've never studied any *sutras*, nor do I refer to any *sutras*. I only make jokes. [More laughter]

Papaji, we are making this film for a foreign television audience which probably does not know much about either you or your teachings. Will you please tell them exactly what enlightenment is, in terms they can understand?

Enlightenment is for those people who have not found any satisfaction in sensory indulgence. It is for those people who are fed up with things, with objects, and the enjoyment of them. The desire for freedom, for enlightenment, arises when one begins to understand that permanent happiness cannot be found in sensory pleasures.

The objects which the five senses record cannot give you permanent happiness. If you have a desire for something, some object which the senses are recording, happiness will briefly arise at the moment when your desire is fulfilled. But it is not the object itself which gives you the happiness, it is the fulfilment of the desire for it. When the desire is there, while there is still a wanting to achieve or get something, there is no happiness. The desire drops only at the moment when it is fulfilled. At that moment there are no thoughts, no desires. If you look closely at your own experience you will discover that happiness arises spontaneously only when there are no thoughts and no desires, and that it disappears when thoughts and desires come back.

What can one deduce from this? The simple conclusion is that when you are empty of thoughts and desires, happiness arises, and when thoughts and desires are there, happiness is no longer experienced. Happiness therefore lies in the emptiness of no thought, not in the quest for more and more things.

Objects and the desire for them are transitory—they come and they go. Whatever comes and goes is not permanent. If you want permanent happiness you must understand that you can never get it through the pursuit of things that come and go.

The emptiness of no-thought, of no desires, is permanent. It is the source of true, permanent happiness. In fact it is happiness itself. When you understand and fully accept this, the mind no longer reaches out for external gratification because it understands that the very act of reaching out causes desire and suffering to arise. When you can abide in that emptiness, that permanent happiness, without feeling a need to search for happiness anywhere else, you are free from desires and suffering. That freedom is enlightenment.

Once you have established yourself in that state, you no longer need to worry about or pursue anything in this world. The people and things of this world will still be there, but they will not cause you any trouble or suffering because the desire to get pleasure and happiness through them will never arise. The emptiness, the happiness, will never be diminished even if you lead an active, worldly life because the thoughts and desires which formerly resulted in misery, suffering and frustration will simply not arise.

When you have a desire for freedom, when you begin to understand that permanent happiness cannot be gained through the pursuit of worldly pleasures, you should look for a perfect being. Someone who has permanently established himself in the state of true and permanent happiness. Such a being, whose Heart is perfection itself, can make you aware of the happiness and the emptiness that lie within you. He may do it by the power of his thought, by looking at you, by touching you or simply by being quiet. Anyone who comes into contact with such a being will be benefited by his presence. Such a perfect being has no sense of self, no sense of being an individual person. Though everyone who comes to him is benefited by being in his presence, that perfect being never thinks that he is helping anyone because he knows that there is no one who is separate or apart from him.

You all make the mistake of believing that you are separate people, with separate minds and bodies. This idea is just a thought. In the presence of a fully-enlightened being, this thought can disappear, leaving behind it an awareness of who you really are. The emptiness of no-self, of pure happiness that you experience in the presence of an enlightened being is the direct knowledge of Reality Itself.

I never advise anyone to renounce the world. This is not the way to get enlightenment. It has been tried both in the West and the East for thousands of years, but it has not given any good results. My advice is different. I simply say, 'Keep quiet. Stay wherever you are. Don't reject your worldly activities. Simply keep quiet for a single second and see what happens.'

This is a very new idea. I don't think that it has been given out by anyone before. Formerly, people used to do *tapas* for years and years in remote places in an attempt to win enlightenment. Even kings would give up their kingdoms, go to the forest and devote all their energies to gaining enlightenment. But it didn't work. Why? Because freedom, enlightenment, is not something that can be 'won' or 'gained'. It is already here and now, within you as your own Self. You don't have to go looking for it anywhere else. It is concealed by the wrong ideas you have about yourself. You think, 'This is my body, this is my mind'. These ideas are the hindrances which stop you being aware of your real nature. If you can remove them, you are free. You can give up these ideas anywhere. You don't need to go to a forest to discard them.

People in the West are always being given advice from spiritual teachers. Everybody is telling them, 'You join our group and you will be happy. You follow our advice and you will be happy.' What is different about your message, and why should people believe it?

They advise the people in order to destroy them. I tell them to reject those teachers and preachers and come to me. I will give you good advice. Don't listen to anybody's advice, not even mine. Peep within yourself and listen to your own voice. What do you hear? Don't listen to any advice, because all advice belongs to the past. If someone gives you some advice, that advice has come from something the adviser has heard, read or experienced. So all this advice comes from the past. You don't need any advice to know your own Self. So, don't listen to anybody's advice. Just keep quiet. This is the best advice. I tell people, 'Keep quiet. Don't think and don't make any effort just for a single second.' This is my advice. And if you follow it, you have done very well, not only for yourself, but for everybody, for all the beings of the world.

So following any advice except the advice 'Be quiet' takes one away from the Self, not towards it?

Of course, of course, it has to because it takes you to the past. I repeat: any advice that you can mention has come from someone who has heard it or read it. It is all from the past. It cannot show you what you are right now, this moment. Don't believe any of the messages that come to you. Don't even believe the information that your senses are sending to you. Ignore all advice, transcend the senses and all the information they are giving you. Then and only then will you know what you are. You have tasted sensual pleasures for millions of years. Now, for the first time you are wearing a human form. Make the best of it.

Don't listen to any advice. Advisers have not shown good results. Advisers only teach you to fight, to quarrel with your neighbours and all the other people who don't belong to your church. And if you follow their advice, some other teachers will then tell you, 'No, don't follow their advice, follow my advice'. Once this happens, quarrels are inevitable.

You say, Papaji, that a strong desire for freedom is required. Are any other qualifications needed?

I don't think that this can be called a qualification. It rises spontaneously from within. In a few rare ones it rises from within and dances on the bosom.

When a desire arises for a sense object, you are happy to go out and meet that object. But freedom is neither an object nor a subject. The desire for freedom rises from the source, plays on the source and settles down in the same source. When it is there, It plays with Itself, enjoys for some time, and then settles down. The rising and falling is never a problem, because It is always the same, whether It rises or not.

When people say, 'The desire for freedom rises and subsides,' what they are saying is that for the rest of the time other desires rise and fall. Also, when you say, 'The desire for freedom has arisen in me,' you are implying that there was a time when the desire was not there. I myself never felt the desire for freedom rise because it was always there. Right from childhood it was there.

Do we need to have faith in anything Papaji? Do we need to believe in the teacher's words? Do we need to believe we can get freedom? Do we have to have faith in something?

Yes, of course you need faith. Faith in your own Self. Faith that 'I am free'. If you want to have faith in something, this is the best faith you can have. 'I am already free.' You are now believing, 'I am suffering, I am bound.' Why not instead change it to the best faith, that 'I am free'? What difference does it make?

If one has the absolute conviction 'I am free,' then the conviction becomes experience. Is that what you are saying?

No, not 'experience'. Freedom is not an experience. Experiences are always with something else. The desire for freedom will finally vanish, leaving freedom Itself. When freedom knows Itself, It alone will remain. Right now, you are busy with other desires. When they have all left you, It, freedom, will remain and reveal Itself to you.

Papaji, you say that enlightenment is a very easy thing to discover and yet I have heard you say many times that the number of people who have fully woken up to their own Self can be counted on one's fingers. If it is so easy, why do so few succeed?

It is so easy because you don't have to work for it. It is so easy because you don't have to go anywhere to get it. All you have to do is keep quiet. Attaining freedom is therefore a very easy thing. People say that it is difficult only because their minds are always engaged with something else. Freedom Itself is not difficult. It is giving up the attachment to other things that is difficult. Disengaging yourself from attachments may be difficult. You have to make a decision to do it. You can decide now or put it off till your next life.

Is it necessary to have a Master who is himself realised to succeed?

Absolutely! Absolutely! Otherwise how can you know whether you are on the right track?

Many people in the West, Papaji, have spent a lot of time looking for a realised Master. How can they find one? What advice would you give them on how to find one?

They cannot find. They cannot find. A true Master cannot be seen with the eyes. If people try to find out through their senses, they will not make a correct judgement because the Master is beyond the senses and beyond any judgement.

When you want to be free, freedom Itself is already there. But you have not acquired the habit of depending on freedom; you don't know the language of freedom, the language of emptiness, the language of love. You don't understand these things because you have sold yourself to other's objects.

So, you don't understand what this freedom really is, but still you have an intense desire for It. When this happens, freedom, out of compassion, takes a physical form to speak to you in your own tongue so that you can understand what freedom really is.

Then it teaches you, 'I am your own Self'. It enters your own Self and becomes one with It. This is the role of the teacher, to point out to you, 'I am your own Self. I am That Itself.' This is the role of the teacher. For sometime It becomes a teacher just to apprise you of the fact that you are That. You don't listen to the impersonal That which is always within you. Therefore He becomes a teacher. That becomes a teacher in order to tell you, 'You are That Itself'. When you understand this you see that you and the teacher are one.

Papaji, Ramana Maharshi also said that one cannot see who is and who is not a true Master, but he did say that there were two signs that one should look for. One should check whether or not one feels peace in his presence, and one should look to see whether he deals equally with all the beings around him. Do you agree that these are useful indications?

Of course I agree. You can easily be misled by the talks that a teacher gives, by the statements that he makes. But if you feel your mind is quiet near him, and if you feel some kind of happiness and peace around him—these can be the outer symptoms of a teacher. Not everyone can feel this peace. Only those people who are intensely devoted to freedom, they alone can sense it, not others.

So, when you go to a teacher, just keep quiet. You need not give any question. Don't expect any answers from him.

Sit quietly, and feel if your mind is quiet or not. If it is quiet, then you can conclude that this is the man who can teach you, that this is the man who is worth staying near.

Papaji, you are advising people to sit in satsang with a realised Master and to keep quiet. When the Master dies and physical satsang is no longer possible, what should the disciple do next?

If he's a true disciple, he will not agree that the Master ever dies. The body dies, but the Master is not the body. All bodies will die, but the Master was never a body. So the death of the body doesn't matter for the disciple because he knows that the Master is something else. The Master is always seated within the Heart of a disciple. The disciple who knows this doesn't need anything else. He knows perfectly well, 'I don't miss my Master. My Master is here and now, always within me.' This is the relationship between the Master and the disciple.

If the disciple has that attitude, then realisation is possible after the Master's death?

If the disciple...?

If the disciple has this attitude, 'My Guru was not the body which died, he is my own Self,' then with that attitude he can still realise the Self. He need not look for any other physical teacher.

The teacher is the one who takes away the body and mind of the disciple. If he has not done or cannot do this, he cannot be accepted as a real teacher. In order to look for another teacher, you need a mind and a body, don't you? If you haven't got a mind or a body any more, where will you look? How will you look?

Papaji, can you please describe your own enlightenment and in particular the role which your own Master, Ramana Maharshi, played in it?

It's a long story.

Will you tell a short version?

It' s a long story. To tell it all I would have to begin from childhood. However, I can start at the point where I went to see Ramana Maharshi. I entered his ashram and all was quiet, all was quiet. This man was quietness itself, an incarnation of silence. He was not speaking to anyone. There was a tremendous silence there. I never saw anybody so silent. The people who went to see him, their minds didn't enter the hall where he lived. He just sat quietly and silence was there.

He would tell people, 'Keep quiet, keep quiet,' but most people didn't understand the import of what he was trying to say. Even today people still don't understand what he was trying to say.

He would talk about many things: how to be free, how to get enlightened, and sometimes he would say things like, 'You need grace'. But most of the time he said in Tamil, '*Summa iru*,' which means, 'Keep quiet'. Most people did not understand the true meaning of this, but I grasped it immediately. Nowadays I use this phrase a lot because I agree with my Master that the best teaching is, 'Keep quiet'.

If a man who is quietness itself tells you to keep quiet, then that phrase comes from authority and has authority. It works immediately. If an ordinary man tells you to keep quiet, it will not work, but if a man who is silence itself tells you, then, automatically, you become quiet.

Can you describe what happened on the day you finally got it? How did it happen?

I had been a devotee of Krishna from childhood. So much so that Krishna even would manifest in front of me in a physical form. I could register him with all my senses in the same way that I could see ordinary things.

I had been spending about four days in Adi-annamalai on the other side of the mountain. On my return the Maharshi asked me, 'Where you have been?'

I replied, 'On the other side of the mountain, staying by myself and playing with Krishna'.

'Oh, very good, you have been playing with Krishna!' he exclaimed.

'Yes sir, I have been playing with Krishna. He is my friend.'

'Do you see him now?'

'No sir, I don't.'

Then he said, 'What appears and disappears is not real. The seer remained. You saw him, he disappeared. He remained, the same seer. Now you are here also, the seer remained. Now, find out who the seer is.'

This 'seer' was just a word, but it struck me with such an impact that I became the seer. I became the seer.

Nowadays when I give satsangs, I tell people, 'Don't hold on to the word. Go to the root of the word. Go to that which the word is describing or indicating. If you do this, instantly you will get true understanding.'

When you say the word 'freedom', for example, go immediately to freedom and stay there. When someone says, 'Let us go to lunch,' food is being spoken about, and you suddenly become one with the food. Why can't you do this when I say the word 'freedom'?

When we speak of freedom, we must be one with the freedom, we must smell freedom, enjoy freedom. But this doesn't happen. With other things the word takes you to the right place, but when I say the word 'freedom', you don't go to the right place to understand it. For the word 'freedom' we need so many satsangs, so many teachers, but still we don't catch the real meaning. What's wrong? We are tied to somewhere else.

Papaji, many people in the West have experimented with different meditation techniques. Some of them have meditated very intensively for many years. I have heard you say several times that practising like this will not bring about enlightenment. Could you please explain why you think this is so?

First of all, meditation is just to fatigue your body and your mind so that you will get fed up with it. Then the idea can occur to you: 'Maybe there is something else.' With this thought you may go off in search of a real teacher. If you find one, he will not tell you to meditate, he will not give you some method. He will simply say, 'Keep quiet'. He will not tell you to do anything or to stop doing anything. Lectures on what you should do or not do come from preachers, not from teachers. The true teacher has no teaching, no do's and no don'ts. He simply tells you, 'Keep quiet'. There can be nothing else that a teacher can say.

This is going to work. This is the best teaching that a teacher can give. As I was telling you before, if he says, 'Keep quiet', you not merely hear the words, you actually become quietness. What is the trouble? Why does everyone find this so difficult?

It is the same in satsang. I tell people, 'Enquire, investigate, ask yourself "Who am I?"', and they reply, 'We can't do it, we can't do it. We have tried, but it gives us trouble. We get a lot of tension and headaches when we do it.' Only some rare ones get it. The others fail because their minds are otherwise engaged. I do not know why this is so. I cannot give you any explanation as to why it suddenly works with some people and not with others.

If you keep quiet, you will fall in love with It, that silence and peace. Everybody needs happiness and peace, whatever they are doing. And there can be no happiness, no peace, no love, no beauty in anything except this silence, which is always here and now within you. Therefore I always say that you don't need any meditation. You need a mind to meditate, and whenever you use your mind, the result has to be mental. You also need your body. You are told to sit in a particular position, with hands and feet positioned in a particular way. Physical activities give you physical results, mental activities, mental results. But what I speak of is beyond the body, beyond the mind. It cannot be approached through mental and physical means.

If some spiritual idea sounds good to you, and you follow it, the result has to be intellectual. So, shun all ideas. Don't try to approach this silence through physical, mental or intellectual routes. Just give up all notions, all ideas, everything you have heard and read, and you will discover that you are emptiness Itself.

Many people have tried to be quiet, to be still, but they haven't succeeded. What are they doing wrong?

They should give up the intention to keep quiet. If they can't keep quiet, I would tell them, 'Give up the intention to keep quiet'. If they do, what will happen?

You frequently tell people, Papaji, to ask themselves 'Who am I?'
Why does this work when every other method fails?

Because this is not a method. Other methods are just clip-ping the branches, but enquiry strikes at the root, the root of the mind. If you cut a branch, after some time it will grow again. But if you go to the root of the mind and pull out the root, it can never come back. Inquiry uproots the mind. When you inquire 'Who am I?', you strike at the root of the mind and destroy it permanently. In fact, it would be more accurate to say that through enquiry you discover that there is no mind at all.

'I' is the mind. When you ask yourself 'Who am I?', 'I' is interrogating itself to find out what is the real nature of mind. No one has ever asked 'Who am I?' No one. People are always asking, 'Who are you? Who is he? Who is she?' But no one ever asks 'Who am I?' When you question yourself like this for the first time, you are not merely strik-ing at the root of the mind, you are striking at the root of all creation because the 'I', the mind, is the source of all cre-ation. When you make the enquiry, it is not just the 'I' that disappears, creation itself also vanishes. You discover that there is no Creator, no creation and no beings created. This 'Who am I?' is such a powerful tool. It takes you to the depths of the Self, that place where you discover that neither you nor creation ever existed.

Many people have asked themselves 'Who am I?' without getting the right answer. Mind still remained. Should they keep on ask-ing till they get the right answer?

No, only once. If you do it properly, you only need to ask once. If you do it properly, it will strike at the right place. When you ask 'Who am I?', don't expect any answer. You must get rid of the expectation that you will get an answer. You must not do the enquiry with the intention of getting somewhere, of getting an answer. The purpose of this question is not to get an answer. Rather it is to merge, in the same way that a river merges into the ocean. It doesn't go to the ocean to remain a river, it goes there to lose itself. In the enquiry 'Who am I?', there is a merging into the divinity, into the Self, emptiness Itself. Just keep quiet and see what happens.

While doing this enquiry, one must not wait for an answer. When the question is finished, the 'I' is also finished. 'Who am I?' What can come after this 'I'? You become That into which the 'I' has discharged. That place has to be emptiness.

Papaji, you frequently say, 'Truth exalts a holy person'. You also say that a holy person is one whose mind is spotless, pure, immaculate. And yet at the same time you never ask anyone to make their minds spotless, pure or immaculate. How can Truth exalt us if we don't do anything to make our minds pure, spotless, immaculate?

You cannot make the mind pure. Mind itself is dust. You cannot clean dust with dust. Imagine that you have a dusty mirror that you want to clean. You bring more dust and add it to the original layer. This is cleaning the mind—adding dust to the dust. All your attempts to clean the mind through meditation or yoga will fail because they will just add dust to the dust that is already there. So what I say is, 'Keep quiet'. If you keep quiet you are removing the mirror itself so that no dust can alight anywhere. This is what I mean by holiness. Truth exalts holiness, and you become holy by removing the mirror of the mind.

If you have a mirror in front of you, your face will be

reflected in it. This reflection is a spot, an impurity. While that spot is there you are not holy. How to remove the reflection? Simple. You throw away the mirror. What will then happen to the reflection? It will go back to your face. If you throw away the mind for one second, just one second, holiness will reveal Itself and you will merge back into that holiness.

Therefore I say, 'Truth exalts a holy person'. All the objects you see around you are reflections in the mirror of your mind. All objects are dust. Throw away the mirror and there will be no mind, no objects and no dust.

Most people, Papaji, think that enlightenment is something which can be achieved after a long period of arduous preparation. What is wrong with this belief?

This is wrong from start to finish. Any belief is wrong. Why should you believe in anything? Do you need to believe that you are David Godman? You are very sure about it, no? Do you need to ask someone? Do you go to Madhukar and say, 'Please tell me where David Godman is. He was living in this house.'?

He will tell you, 'You are David Godman and this is your house'. How did you lose the certain knowledge and conviction of who you really are? You don't embark on arduous preparation to find out who you are if you already know who you are. You get attached to wrong ideas. Because you believe them, you end up thinking that you have to do something to be what you already are. You get stuck with these things and forget where your real home is.

I think this is a major problem in the West, Papaji. People will not be convinced that they are ready for realisation right now. They all think they have to do something.

Of course. That's what I hear. That is why all the yoga teachers are very successful in the West. I have seen yoga centres even in small villages. There are about five thousand yoga teachers in Europe. I have talked to some of them and they're all doing very well.

I asked one of them, 'What you are teaching?' And he answered, 'How to keep young and fit up to ninety years of age'. This is what most of them are aiming at, and if this is what you want from yoga, it can help you to achieve it.

Many books on yoga are sold in the West—I have even seen them on stands by the side of the road. *Yoga for Sex* was one—you must have seen it.

So, the yoga that is taught in the West is to maintain the health and vitality of the body. I remember one girl in Dusseldorf. She was in her twenties and she looked very good and very happy. I saw her meditating so I asked her, 'When you meditate, what do you meditate upon?'

She replied, 'I want to keep young for a long time. I am twenty-seven now and I want to be healthy till I'm eighty-five.'

I gave her the name Ratna, which means 'diamond'. I met her boyfriend and called him Ratnasagar, which means 'ocean of diamonds'. They were both very good people, but they were not getting any results from their meditation. No one gets real results from meditation.

I want to ask you some questions about happiness, Papaji. I have heard you say that nobody in the whole world is happy, they only think they are. How can you justify this?

Because no one *is* happy in this world. This is a true statement. I have not seen any such person. I have travelled all over the world, and in each country I visited everyone I saw was suffering. Everyone is suffering, even the richest people.

I once met a very rich man in Switzerland. I went to see him because I had looked after his son in India. This boy had had some mental problems, so someone suggested to him, 'Go to Poonjaji in Rishikesh. You will get better if you stay with him.' This boy stayed with me for about a year. He was a little paranoid or schizophrenic, but he became well again after staying with me. He travelled all round India with me—Lucknow, Haridwar, Rishikesh, Delhi and Bombay—before going back to Switzerland.

On my next trip to Europe his father invited me to stay. He put me in a revolving flat on top of an apartment block. This man was clearly very rich, but he could not sleep at night. First he would have a few drinks and then three or four sleeping tablets. Even then he couldn't sleep.

I asked him, 'Why can't you sleep? I'll make you sleep. You decide when you want to sleep and I will see that you get some.'

His trouble was that he had a car factory—5,000 assembly-line workers plus all the administrative staff. It was a very big complex. Throughout the night the telephones were ringing—dispatching, selling, booking. This was the way he was. He was so busy, he couldn't sleep.

I told him, 'Come with me tomorrow in your car and don't ask me where we are going'.

The next day he said, 'I cannot go with you because some people here have come with some orders'.

When you always have some business in your mind—something to be done today, tomorrow or the next day—these thoughts will be continuously revolving in your mind. If you don't reject them, how can you sleep? People in the West are always working. They don't have time to sleep. Have you been born only to work, or are you born to be peaceful? What is happening in the West? Work, work and more work. It costs people their health, but still they will not rest. That is why they are not happy; that is why they are in trouble.

They think, 'We have got a fat balance in the bank, a good apartment and the latest model car'. But this doesn't help a man to be happy. To be happy the best prescription is contentment. Whatever you have, be contented with it. If you want to compare your wealth with other people's, look at the people who have less than you and be happy. Don't look at some billionaire sheikh and feel jealous that he has more than you. Look at people who are worse off than you. 'Look at that man. He is begging. Thank God I am better off than him. I have food and I don't need to have a begging bowl in my hand.' If you have this attitude, you will sleep very well.

Henry Ford, the man who started and owned Ford Motors, was once the richest man in the world. But he couldn't eat properly. He once said, 'I look at my workers when they are eating lunch. I see how much they're eating. I feel that I could never eat that amount of food because my doctors have advised me to eat very little. I am only allowed to eat two ounces of food at each meal.'

Have you come here not to eat, not to sleep? Are you here only to earn money, money that you will leave behind you when you die? I am not saying, 'Don't earn money at all'. I am simply saying, 'Earn, work and live well, but don't get lost with these things'. Don't forget that you have come here to have peace, not to earn money.

Many people experience happiness as a result of indulging in physical pleasures. Is that happiness which they experience the same happiness which you know to be your own Self, or is it a different kind of happiness?

No, no. To be your own Self is the only real happiness. If

you pursue happiness anywhere else, you just fatigue yourself, only to find out that the happiness you are striving for is not the real happiness. If you need to repeat the process again and again to get happiness, then what you get is not true happiness. You want to repeat the process again and again because the experience of happiness you got each time did not fully satisfy you. That is why you repeat it.

I am not talking about processes, Papaji, I'm talking about the result. If I am suddenly very, very happy as the result of doing something, is my happiness the same as your happiness, or is it different?

Happiness is one. Happiness is one. But when you attribute it to something which is not abiding, then it is different. You say 'your happiness'. When you say 'my' happiness or 'your' happiness, then it is not that happiness which I point at. I point to unattributed and unearned happiness, not 'my' happiness or 'your' happiness. This is the only difference. You are using 'my' and 'you'. If you remove 'you' and 'me', there is no difference.

What about states such as ecstasy and bliss? Are they mind experiences or are they from the Self?

Ecstasy is a state of mind. For some time it will stay and then it will again dwindle and disappear. Many people get into ecstatic states just by listening to a poem or by singing a song, or by some other means. One can get into ecstatic states, but they go away because they are dependent on transient circumstances.

Bliss is different. It can be compared to the dawn before sunrise. When dawn comes, you know that the sun will soon follow. The sun is not there, but some sign of it is showing above the horizon. So, when you feel some bliss, and you are not attributing it to some external object, you are focusing on the dawn of the Self. To see the sun rise, you must look to the east, not to the west, to the point where the rays of the sun are coming from. When the bliss comes, focus on the bliss. Become one with the bliss. When you experience That from which the bliss is emanating, the bliss will be rejected. Bliss is also a mental state. In the end it will be rejected.

Do we have to reject it consciously or will it happen automatically?

It will happen automatically.

Some people say that bliss is an obstacle to realisation and that the final experience is peace and stillness.

This is an idea that comes from yoga. The *anandamaya kosha*, the sheath of bliss, is one of the five sheaths that limit the 'I'. First there is the *annamaya kosha*, the physical sheath, then the *pranamaya kosha*, the sensory or 'vital' sheath, then the *manomaya kosha*, the mental sheath, then *vijnanamaya kosha*, the intellectual sheath, and finally the *anandamaya kosha*, the sheath of bliss. In the yoga system, you have to reject all these five sheaths one by one, including the bliss. You have to remove your attachment to these things one by one. When you have removed your attachment to the physical body, the senses, the mind and the intellect, bliss will come. Bliss will be there when the intellect goes. But one should not get attached to it. Most yogis get attached to blissful states and don't go beyond them. This is a consequence of the yogic system which aims at getting blissful states.

Don't get attached to this final *kosha* [sheath]. Don't be satisfied with bliss. Stay quiet and let the bliss become That. As the mind absorbs the bliss more and more, it becomes the bliss. After some time there will be no question of rejecting the bliss, because, from the other side, from beyond the mind, from no-mind, freedom Itself will come to receive you and embrace you. At that stage no one can reject the bliss.

If you can feel the bliss, you have done very well. The bliss of the Self, the *atman*, is called *atmananda*. It will take the form of *atman* Itself. Though everything has gone when you reach this state, it is still not the final state. 'No-mind', which is related to mind, is still alive.

If you can reach this state of no-mind, you have done very well. When you reach this stage your work is over, because from then on, it is the task of the beyond. This beyond is fathomless. It will take hold of you and work on you in a very beautiful way. It will reveal Itself more and more with each passing moment. It will show you a different beauty, a different love and a different form that are so entrancing, you will always be engaged with It. It will be engaged with It. Even if the body leaves, you cannot get rid of It. This can be described as the Ultimate, as 'Ultimateness'.

Papaji, no-mind, dead mind and silent mind, what are the differences?

Silent mind means to keep quiet temporarily. It is simply a suppression of the objects in the mind. It can happen many times, but it will not last. Still mind is also temporary. Meditation or concentration can result in still mind. It is like the flame of a candle. When there is no breeze, the flame will be still. When a wind comes, the candle will flicker and go out. Still mind will be blown away as soon as it encounters the wind of a new thought.

As for no-mind, I am hearing this question for the first time. No person from India or the West has ever asked me about this before. I am very happy to deal with this question for the first time.

Before we speak about no-mind, we have to see what mind is. Let us start from consciousness. Sometimes you want to look in a mirror to see what you look like. In the same way, consciousness sometimes wants to look at Itself to see what It is. A wave will arise in consciousness. It will ask Itself, 'Who am I?' This wave that arises in consciousness imagines Itself to separate from the ocean. This wave becomes 'I', the individual self. Once it has become separate, this 'I' degenerates further and starts to create. First there will be space, the vast, frontierless emptiness of infinite space. And along with space, time will be created, because wherever there is space, there must be time. This time becomes past, present and future, and from these three attachments arise. All creation rises within the past, the present and the future. This is called *samsara*. *Samsara* means time. *Samsara* is endless past, present and future. Anything which is born in time, which stays in time, will be finished in time. And all this is mind. The 'I' arose and created space, then time, then *samsara*. This 'I' has now become mind, and this mind is 'I'.

Then at some point, an intense desire for freedom will arise. This desire will arise from consciousness Itself. Originally there was a descent from consciousness—from the 'I' to space to time to *samsara*. Now there will be an ascent. As you ascend, attachment to physical objects will go, then vital, then mental, then intellectual. Finally, you return to 'I' alone. This 'I' is still mind.

This 'I' has rejected everything. It exists alone with no

attachments. It cannot go back to the world of attachments, to *samsara*. It has a desire for freedom; it wants to return to its original place. This 'I' which rose from consciousness is now returning to consciousness. It takes the decision, 'Become no-mind now,' and with that decision the 'I' is gone, mind is gone. The 'I', which is the mind, has been rejected, but there is still something there which is between the 'I' and consciousness. This in-between thing is called no-mind. This in-between entity will merge into consciousness, and then it will become consciousness Itself.

Look at this cup [pointing at a tumbler on the table]. There is space, emptiness, both inside and outside the cup. The space inside we call 'inside space' and the space outside is called 'outside space'. Why? Because the name and form of the cup divides the inside from the outside. When the name and form are removed, the space inside and the *mahat*, the greater space, become one. In fact they were always one. From the point of view of the space itself, there never was an inside or an outside. Name and form made it appear that there was an inside and an outside, but the space was never affected by these artificial divisions. Likewise, freedom is always there, always unaffected by names and forms. Name-and-form is 'I'. When the 'I' goes, the walls which appear to divide consciousness are removed. This becomes This.

When you go from mind back to consciousness, you go through this stage of no-mind. In that state there will be the feeling, the recollection, 'Now I have no-mind'. Gradually, slowly, this no-mind will merge back into the beyond. But how it happens, I do not know.

Can no-mind become mind again? Can it come out? Can it become manifest?

A process has taken place. Now there is consciousness It-self. Why to speak of mind and no-mind?

In ancient times, when a king died without leaving an heir, a royal elephant was sent out to select the new king. There was a tradition that whoever the elephant picked up and put on his back became the new king. One time when this happened, the elephant picked up a beggar, and this beggar became king. Everyone was happy. The ministers saluted him, gave him golden robes, and put him on the throne. This man who used to be a beggar didn't have to do anything any more. Everything was done for him. Everything came to him without his asking. All the court-iers and ministers knew how to attend on him. He didn't need to beg anymore. At the appropriate time during the day, food would be brought to him, and during the night all the queens took care of him. Once a beggar has had a taste of being the king, will he want to go back to his vil-lage and be a beggar again?

This is what happens when you become aware that you are consciousness. The person is still there, the body is still there, but there is no one who thinks, 'I have to do this or that'. There is instead a knowledge that consciousness takes care of everything. If you are consciousness, the king, the five senses become the ministers who serve you. The sense activities will go on automatically, you will not have to think about them. If it is time for the king to have a *pan* [laughter], *pan* will come. If it is time for coffee, coffee will come.

When you are consciousness, the brain will become the prime minister, the sense organs will become ministers, and they will all serve you. You will not have to think at all.

If you want this to work, you must have the authority and power of a real king. If you behave like a king, without having the authority, no one will listen to you. Authority must be there, and this authority can only come by being consciousness Itself.

I will tell you a good story about another king. This king wanted to see his prime minister urgently. Since the prime minister was not in the palace at the time, the king went to see him in his home.

On his arrival the king was told by the prime minister's wife, 'He is in the *puja* room'.

'Then call him,' said the king.

'I can't call him,' replied the wife. 'I am not allowed to disturb him while he is in his *puja* room.'

The prime minister, though, had heard the king arrive. He came out of his *puja* room in his *puja* dress, so the king asked him, 'What are you doing?'

The prime minister didn't give any reply. This made the king very angry because he saw it as a gross act of insubordination. The king called one of his police officers and ordered him to arrest the prime minister. The police officer stepped forward, but before he could make the arrest, the prime minister said, 'Wait, wait'. The king signalled the policeman to stop and then waited for the prime minister to give an explanation. Instead, much to everyone's surprise, the prime minister pointed at the king and ordered the policeman to arrest him. The policeman, of course, didn't move, because he had no authority to arrest the king.

Then the prime minister explained his actions to the king. 'When you said "Arrest him," the policeman carried out your order because you have the authority to give such an order. But when I said, "Arrest him," the policeman didn't obey because I have no authority over you. The order was the same in each case, but the authority was different. You had the authority. I did not.

'I didn't reply to you when you came in because I was doing the *gayatri* mantra. I could not tell you about this mantra because you have not been initiated into it. I myself do not have the authority to tell you about this mantra, so I kept quiet.'

So, if you want to have the authority of the king, you must be consciousness Itself. Then the senses will obey you. Everything will be beautiful because all commands will come from consciousness. Kings can make mistakes, but consciousness always makes the right decision at the right time. When you have no-mind, you cannot do any work of your own accord. You are simply being graced. And you are obeying. You yourself are not doing anything because doership has gone. Mind is no more there. All the various functions of the mind are no longer there. You will stay with the body for a stipulated period that has already been decided, and during that time you will be an instrument of consciousness.

Some people cannot stand the shock of freedom for more than twenty-one days. That has been stated in the books. Imagine a man who unexpectedly wins a billion dollars in a lottery. The shock of so much wealth suddenly coming might kill him. He could get a heart attack and die.

It is sometimes the same with enlightenment. So much happiness coming suddenly and unexpectedly can take away the body. But the enlightenment will not be affected.

Some people live on after enlightenment only to benefit other people. This benefit is not coming from some 'person', it is coming directly from consciousness. The teacher, who is consciousness, knows that it is not 'I' who is working. His attitude is: 'I have been picked out to speak, but it is not 'I' who speak.' If the teacher thinks that 'he' is speaking, this is only arrogance. His words will not work.

When you have that direct experience, it's of no concern

to you what you say. It's not your problem if someone is benefited or not benefited, nor if people come or don't come. It's all the same to you.

So consciousness has ordered you to teach. Is that what you are saying?

Consciousness...?

Has ordered you to teach. Is that what you are saying? You are just carrying out the order.

[Long pause] Consciousness and me—we have become so much one, I cannot say if 'It' can order 'me'.

But some power is compelling you to give satsang, yes?

Yes, 'some power' is like this: [stretches out his hand in front of him] if I want to drink water do I say, 'Poonjaji, pick up the glass'? Before I put it in the mouth, do I say to my hand, 'Put it in the mouth'? And before I drink, do I give the order, 'Drink'? [Papaji laughs, picks up the tumbler and drinks.] Now, I have not commanded the hand. It's all me, you see. People who are benefited are not 'others'. The hand is my own, the stomach is my own and the requirement for water is my own. Who are the others? Who is other than me?

Who, first of all, is ignorant? If people say so, I don't believe them. Who wants to be free? If someone tells me this, I don't believe him. Who is not already free?

So, when people come to me and say, 'I am in trouble, I am bound,' I think they are joking, so I joke back, 'You are not bound, you are free'.

'Does it take a long time?' they ask.

'No, no,' I say. 'You can get it now itself.'

All this is a joke, so I take it as a joke. The statement, 'I am a bound,' is it not a joke? The people who speak like this don't show me the chains, nor the fetters, nor the prison. What kind of jail is this? So it's all a big joke to me, and I enjoy the joke.

So when you look at people in satsang, Papaji, you only see enlightened people who are pretending not to be enlightened?

[Long pause] Oh, it's a difficult question, but I have to answer it because I answer all questions. First of all, I absorb them all and give them a seat in my Heart, in my Heart. As the lover gives a seat to the beloved in his Heart, you are always seated in my Heart. So I open here and say, 'You and I, we will speak together. Yes. You are not apart from me, you are within the Heart. You are in my Heart. Let us speak.'

Grace is working in satsang, Papaji. Does it come from you, through you, or is it simply just there?

From grace only. Grace has to come from grace, no? A wave has to come from the ocean. Grace has to come from grace, the ocean of grace.

It seems to flow very strongly in your proximity, though.

I don't know.

Papaji, I've heard you say several times, 'I know many tricks to wake people up. If one doesn't work, I use another.' What are these tricks, and how do you use them?

One trick is, 'Keep quiet! Keep quiet!' The second trick is, 'Don't think at all'. The third trick is, 'Don't activate your mind'. If these don't work I have a fourth trick. I say, 'Come to me and I will teach you yoga. I will teach you how to do *shirshasana* [a yogic position with the head on the floor and the feet in the air]'.

I make them stand in front of me and then I say, 'Now, head down, feet up in the air, this is *shirshasana*'. I know how to do it myself, so I can easily show them.

Then, while they are standing on their heads, they will say, 'But I want freedom'.

While they are still in that posture I will tell them how to gain freedom. I will say, 'Keep quiet, keep quiet'. At that time they will listen because by then they will be suffering a little. When people start to have trouble through over-indulgence in sensory pleasures, they come to me, and they listen. If anyone is upside down for long enough, they begin to suffer, and once they begin to be aware of their suffering, they come to me. So, I know many tricks and I have often used them in the West.

Mostly good people are coming to see me in Lucknow. I have no problem with them. People from all over the world are coming to India and Lucknow for the first time, and I am very happy with them. When I speak to them, they listen to me. They listen to me as they would to their father, or to any other respected person who gives good advice. They want to end their suffering, their mental pain. So I give them this trick: I tell them to be quiet. Most people like this advice very much because I am not asking them to do anything. They get happiness and peace by doing nothing, by simply being quiet.

Who doesn't want happiness? Who doesn't want peace? Who doesn't want beauty? Everyone is interested. So they listen to me and I am happy. Everyone is benefited.

They all return to their respective countries as ambassadors from this city of Lucknow. And then they send their friends. Thousands of people have come here simply because they have heard good reports from other people.

No one complains about what is going on here. There are no charges, there is no ashram, there are no big appeals for funds. I live in my own house and I belong to this place. For fifty years I have been living here. I have also spent a few years living abroad. I like travelling but now my old age has compelled me to stay here. That's why you are here. Until recently I used to visit people in their own houses. I didn't like to trouble anyone, you see.

So now many people are here and I am very happy that some message of peace is being spread. We need it very badly.

Two thousand six hundred years ago it was India which sent messengers of peace all over the world in the persons of Mahendra and Mitra. The Emperor Ashoka's own son and daughter were sent out as emissaries. Other people went to China, Japan and Korea on the same mission. There was tremendous peace in the world at that time. So let us resolve again to send out this message of peace, and let us send it from the same place. The Buddha belongs to this state. I am very happy that the message of peace is being sent out once again from the place where the Buddha lived. Many tourists now come to this state to visit the holy places which are associated with the Buddha's life. They visit places like Kushinagar, Siddharthanagar and Lumbini. All of these places have become holy because of one man who spread a message of peace from here.

You can have peace in the world by enlightening yourself. This enlightenment Itself is a message. When you go back to your own country you may speak, or you may keep quiet. It will work, you will see. When your friends ask you, 'What happened?' you can keep quiet. Again they will ask you. Just keep quiet, that's all you need to do.

Papaji, many people have heard you say, 'I have not given my final teachings to anyone'. What are these final teachings, and why you are not giving them out?

They are not worthy of them. Nobody is worthy to receive them. Because it has been my experience that everybody has proved arrogant and egotistic. This has resulted in suffering. Many people are suffering. Nowadays, I am making another trial. I will see what happens.

I don't think that anyone is worthy to receive them. You have to prove holiness to be worthy. Why should you trouble people instead of helping them? This is arrogance, you see.

If a king sends a messenger to another country, his only job is to deliver the message. I sent a messenger to the West, but he tried to become a king. Many people have been troubled by this. I have seen it in many cases. What to do? This kind of behaviour demonstrates unworthiness.

Perhaps I am too generous, perhaps I do not read people properly. Maybe it is my mistake because I think that everyone is good. Though I speak the Truth to everyone, the Truth will reject those who are not worthy of It. Only a holy person can receive this teaching. Such a person will be worthy of It.

If the worthiness is not there, the Truth will enter their head and become intellectual knowledge. Westerners want intellectual understanding. They are very happy when they understand. That's all the West wants: knowledge through the intellect. Everyone knows that there is something 'beyond'. But when I talk about it the Westerners say, 'I don't understand, I don't understand'. So I say to them,

'You don't need to understand at all'.

I had a friend who lived in Paris. He had been a follower of J. Krishnamurti for thirty-five years. He used to travel around the world, following Krishnamurti wherever he went: Australia, New Zealand, Switzerland, England. He had read and studied all the books.

He came to me in Saanen and I talked to him for some time. After he had listened he said, 'I don't understand, I don't understand'.

I told him, 'You are not to understand this. This is not something to be understood. You have to be it.'

He disagreed. 'No, no. I have to understand. I don't understand you and I don't understand Krishnamurti either.'

I told him, 'You don't need to understand either Krishnamurti or me'.

Then he explained to me why he was having so much trouble with Krishnamurti. 'I am at point A and Krishnamurti is at point B. But when I shift my perspective from A to B, he moves to point C. So, I don't even understand Krishnaji.'

Krishnamurti was also in Saanen at that time, so a lot of his followers used to come and see me. One day a man came and started talking: 'Poonjaji and Krishnaji are saying the same thing. Krishnaji says, "Remove all concepts from the mind," and Poonjaji is saying the same. They are both saying, "Unless you empty the pot of the mind, you cannot be enlightened."'

One man who was listening, he was a follower of Krishnamurti, disputed this statement. He said, 'No, no, there is a big difference between Poonjaji's and Krishnaji's teachings. Krishnaji teaches us to empty the pot, Poonjaji teaches us to break to pot.'

That is the difference, and this is something that cannot

be understood with the mind. You can understand when the cup is full, or when the cup is empty, but when the cup does not exist, who are you and what are you going to understand? So what I say is, 'Mind itself does not exist, so you don't need to understand'. You have to see It and feel It when I speak. Thinking will not help you.

Mind itself is only a notion. Get rid of this notion. And mind is past, so get rid of the past also. Come to the present and then I will tell you what to do next. Come to at least the present and you will see.

Papaji, many people come to satsang and they have waking-up experiences. Some of them come back weeks or months later and say, 'I lost it'. What is happening there?

Again, this is unworthiness.

Most of the time you blame these people for losing it. You tell them, 'It's your fault'.

Yes, yes. They lost it because they did not take good care of it. I tell these people, 'If I give you a big diamond, you can live off it for the rest of your life. You can sell it and get millions of dollars for it. If, instead, you don't recognise its worth and you give it away, whose fault is it? If you give it to a fisherwoman who uses it to balance her scales, because she doesn't know what it's worth, whose fault is it?'

This enlightenment is a diamond. It should not be passed on to unworthy people who will misuse it. And they do misuse it. I don't differentiate between all the people who come to me. I tell them all the same truth. Some get it and then they throw it away by misusing it.

They come back and say things like, 'My girl friend left me. I phoned her and she came back. Now I am happy again.' Is this freedom? Next time they will tell me, 'I went back, but she left me again. Now I am in trouble again.' Every day I hear stories like this.

Papaji, when people leave you, you never tell them, 'Take care of this diamond I've given you. Look after it.' You only blame them for having lost it when they come back.

Not all of them lose it. Some of them are very beautiful people. They write to me and say, 'I am keeping it. I am still keeping this precious gift. Not only am I keeping it, I am distributing it to others. Even after distributing it, I see that the same amount is still with me. It doesn't decrease. What a gift you have given me!' Not all of them lose it. Although I want everyone to be benefited by this thing, I also know that not everyone can get it. Even so, the results here are very good. I look at other ashrams and see what is going on there. Compared to them, the results we are getting here are quite satisfactory. I am very satisfied.

One final question, Papaji. All your life you have been trying to express your own inner experience. Will you please make one more attempt for us. Who are you? What are you? What is your own experience of your Self?

A very easy reply is: 'I am your own Self. I am your own Self, and this is Truth. How can it be that I am myself only? I am your own Self and the Self of all the beings that exist and that have to exist.

<u>Note</u>

This interview and the one by Rama Crowell *(No Teaching, No Teacher, No Student)* were filmed in Lucknow. Extracts from both interviews appear in a documentary film on Papaji entitled *Call Off The Search*. These published interviews are edited versions of the original conversations. Video tapes of both interviews can be obtained from Satsang Bhavan, Lucknow, and from other distributors. For more information see page 305.

Glossary

Words are spelled here without their standard diacritical markings. Common alternative forms and plurals are within parentheses. Words are defined primarily for the meanings that are relevant to the contexts of this book, or they are the generally accepted standard meanings as used in classical Hindu religious and philosophical literature.

Abbreviations used:

c.	*circa*, around
e.g.	for example
esp.	especially
H.	Hindi
Lit.	Literally
P.	Pali
q.v.	*quod vide*, see entry under that title
S. or Skt.	Sanskrit
T.	Tamil
U.	Urdu

achcha (H.) - Good, all right; well; OK.

advaita (S.) - Lit. 'not-two'. Non-duality or absolute unity; pure monism. A school of *Vedanta* (*q.v.*), one of the six orthodox schools of Indian philosophy; specifically the non-dualistic, non-theistic interpretation of the *Upanishads* and *Brahma Sutras* given by Adi Shankaracharya (788-820 A.D.). Its central teaching is the identity of the individual soul with

Brahman (*q.v.*). It affirms that what is, is only *Brahman*, the Ultimate Reality. It also affirms the unreality of the world and the empirical self.

ahankara (S.) - Lit. 'I-maker'. That faculty of mind which stamps the contents of consciousness as being 'me or mine'; the individuating, self-conscious principle, or ego, responsible for the limitations, divisions and variety of the manifest world as it appears to consciousness.

Ananda Moyi Ma - Lit. 'bliss-permeated mother'; a celebrated 20th century Bengali saint (1896-1982).

anandamaya kosha (S.) - Lit. 'the bliss-composed sheath'; the subtlest and most refined of the five 'envelopes' covering the human soul or *jiva* (*q.v.*). Locus of non-dual consciousness, it is the source of all happiness experienced by the *jiva* and is the constituent of the causal body which, with the *vijnanamaya kosha* (*q.v.*), reincarnates with the *jiva* until final liberation is attained.

annamaya kosha (S.) - Lit. 'the food-composed sheath'; the gross sheath encasing the physical body, produced by food and consisting of five elements: earth, water, fire, air, and space or ether (*akasha*).

Arunachala (S.) - Lit. 'red mountain'; a sacred mountain in Tamil Nadu, South India; considered to be the manifestation of Lord Shiva as the formless Absolute; at its foot lies Tiruvannamalai, site of the ashram founded by Sri Ramana Maharshi.

Arya Samaj (S). - Lit. 'Society of Nobles'; a Hindu social and religious reform movement started by Swami Dayananda (1824-1883) chiefly in North India as a reaction to western influences upon Hinduism. It held the cow to be sacred, attacked polytheism and idolatry, and held the *Vedas* to be infallibly, literally true.

Ashoka (The Great) - King of the Mauryas in North India, he reigned from 272-236 B.C. After extensive military campaigns of conquest, he became disgusted by war and converted to Buddhism, using his power and influence to spread the Buddha's message of peace and deliverance throughout his empire.

ashram(a) (S). - A forest retreat, dwelling place of sages, yogis, and their monastic students.

atman (S.) - Lit. 'eater of thoughts'; in *Vedanta*, the immortal real Self of human beings, identical with *Brahman* (*q.v.*), but used to refer to *Brahman* as individuated within the person.

aum (S.) - See *om*.

Aurobindo - Sri Aurobindo Ghose (Ghosh) (1872-1950). Indian saint and patriot who taught a system called 'Integral Yoga'. His ashram is in Pondicherry, South India.

avatar(a) (S.) - Lit. 'descender'; an incarnation or 'descent' of a deity, esp. one of the ten incarnations of Vishnu (the *dasa avatara*) which include Rama and Krishna.

avidya (S.) - Ignorance, esp. ignorance of one's true nature.

Ayodhya - A town in present-day Uttar Pradesh, North India, held to be the birthplace of Lord Rama, the seventh *avatar* of Vishnu.

Babaji (H.) - Lit. 'revered father'; respectful term of address for a *sadhu* or holy man; also applied in families for father, grandfather and child.

Bhagavan (S.) - The Lord, God. 1) An epithet of Vishnu and Shiva; 2) One of the titles by which Sri Ramana Maharshi is known.

bhajan (S.) - From the Skt. root *bhaj*, 'to love, adore, worship'; a devotional song or hymn.

bhakta (S.) - A lover of God, a devotee; one who follows or practises the path of *bhakti*, the *bhakti marga* (*q.v.*).

bhakti (S.) - 'Loving devotion to God'; the ideal religious attitude according to theistic Hinduism. It leads to the *prasada* (grace or favour) of God which enables the devotee to attain liberation.

bhakti marga (S.) - Lit. 'path of loving devotion'; the way of salvation through loving faith in and surrender to a personal God, as distinguished from the way of mystical knowledge (*jnana marga*) which is directed towards union or identity with God, and from the way of dutiful action (*karma marga*) which has a better rebirth as its primary goal.

bhava (S.) - Lit. 'attitude', 'mood', 'disposition', one's psychoemotional 'mode of being'; in *bhakti marga* (*q.v.*) used to designate one of the five classical modes of relationship to the Lord: peace (*shanta-bhava*); loving service (*dasya-bhava*); loving parent toward a child (*vatsalya-bhava*); friend (*sakhya-bhava*); or lover (*madhurya-bhava*).

Bodhisattva (S.) - In Mahayana Buddhism, a *Bodhisattva* is a highly-evolved being who postpones his own entry into *nirvana* in order to help others to attain enlightenment.

Bodhidharma - Indian Buddhist monk who travelled to China, where his famous interview with the Emperor in 520 A.D. resulted in the introduction of Buddhism to China. He was the first Chinese Zen Patriarch and the father of Zen Buddhism in Japan.

brahmachari (S.) - 1) One who practises *brahmacharya* (*q.v.*), the first of the four stages of life; 2) The period of student discipleship; 3) A young celibate student, usually living in the house of his guru.

brahmacharya (S.) - Lit. 'dwelling, abiding in *Brahman*' (*q.v.*); the first stage of life in orthodox Hinduism, that of a chaste student; often it simply means celibacy.

Brahma (S.) - In Hindu cosmology, God as creator, the first conscious mind in the universe and the first created being.

Brahman (S.) - The designation in Hinduism for the impersonal Absolute Reality, ultimate Truth, existence-knowledge-bliss; the one, formless, non-dual Absolute, substratum of all that exists; identical with *atman* (*q.v.*).

brahmin (S.) - The priestly class or a member of the priestly class, having the duties of learning, teaching, and performing rites (*pujas*) and sacrifices (*yajnas*).

buddhi (S.) - That faculty of the human mind which determines and knows Truth; the highest, most subtle part of the mind, the intellect, the judging faculty, conscience.

Chadwick, Major - A British devotee of Sri Ramana Maharshi who lived at Sri Ramanasramam 1935-62.

chapati (H.) - Round, flat, unleavened bread, a ubiquitous presence in all North Indian meals.

chitta (S.) - In Indian philosophy, esp. Yoga and *Advaita Vedanta*, the human mind considered as the seat of all memory and experience, matrix of self-identity, and the actual locus of thoughts.

darshan(a) (S.) - From the Sanskrit root, *drs*, meaning 'to see'; sight of a holy person, esp. when the eyes meet; to be in, or be received into, the presence of a saint.

Dayananda, Swami (1824-1883) - Crusading reformer-swami who started the Arya Samaj (*q.v.*) in 1875 in North India as a conservative bulwark against modernising tendencies affecting Hinduism. He started the Cow Protection League to keep cows away from the British slaughterhouses.

Devaraja Mudaliar - One of the principal devotees of Sri Ramana Maharshi; author of *Day by Day with Bhagavan*, a diary of Sri Ramana's life and conversations in the 1940's.

Dhammapada (P.) - Lit. 'path of *dhamma*'; the most famous scripture of the Pali (Theravadin) Canon, in which the Buddha teaches the Liberating Law of *Dhamma* (Skt. *Dharma*) or Noble Action, based on the Four Noble Truths; said to be the actual words of the Buddha.

dharma (S.) - Lit. 'that which bears, supports'; 1) The eternal principle of Right Action; 2) Moral duty; 3) Virtue; 4) Divine Law; 5) Religious tradition.

dhobi (H.) - Washerman, launderer.

dosa (T.) - A South Indian sourdough pancake, commonly eaten for breakfast or supper.

Ganga (S.) - The Ganges River.

garuda - In Hindu mythology, a demi-god in the form of an eagle, king of birds and destroyer of serpents; the sacred mount of Lord Vishnu and his consort, Lakshmi.

gayatri mantra - The most famous and sacred mantra of Hinduism (*Rig Veda* III.62.10) which orthodox Hindus of the upper three castes are enjoined to chant several times a day. It is a prayer to Savitri, the sun, for divine inspiration.

Gita (S.) - Lit. 'song'; the *Bhagavad Gita* or *'Celestial Song'*; the most famous sacred text of Hinduism, found in the sixth chapter of the *Mahabharata*, composed about 500 B.C. It consists of the soteriological teachings given to the Aryan prince Arjuna by Lord Krishna (*q.v.*), on the battlefield at Kurukshetra.

gopi(s) (S.) - Shepherdess(es) of Vrindavan (*q.v.*) who left their chores and homes to play and dance with Sri Krishna; they are held to be paradigms of loving devotion. The chief *gopi* was Radha.

guna (S.) - Lit. 'quality'; many Hindu sects maintain that nature consists of three 'qualities' or 'strands', never at rest, called *sattva* (brightness), *rajas* (activity) and *tamas* (inertia), one of which is always predominant. The mutual interaction of the *gunas* accounts for the quality of all change in both manifestation and consciousness.

guru (S.) - Lit. 'remover of darkness', or 'heavy one'; a spiritual teacher or preceptor, qualified to initiate disciples into a spiritual tradition or lineage of teachers. As capitalised in this book, it refers to the *Sadguru* or true Guru, the Self.

Hanuman - The monkey-god, renowned as the devoted servant of Rama. Helped Rama retrieve Sita from captivity in Lanka. The story is recounted in Valmiki's *Ramayana* and its medieval *bhakti*-cult version, the *Ramacharitamanasa* in Hindi by Tulasidas (1532-1623); today worshipped in his own right.

Heart - A term frequently used by Sri Ramana Maharshi, it is a translation of the Skt. word *hridayam*, which literally translates, according to Sri Ramana, as 'this is the centre'. When capitalised in this book it is synonymous with 'the Self'. It denotes the spiritual centre of one's being.

iddly (T.) - A South Indian sourdough steamed cake of rice and black gram commonly eaten for breakfast or supper.

Janaka - King of Videha, the father of Sita. He is the ideal of the sage who lives serenely in the world after liberation.

japa (S.) - Lit. 'uttering'; the scientific repetition, usually after initiation, of a word or words (mantra), or a name of God; repeated as a means of invoking grace, a vision of a deity, or Self-knowledge.

-ji - A Hindi and Sanskrit honorific suffix, added to a name to denote respect; a respectful term of address, short for *jiva* (*q.v.*).

jiva (S.) - Philosophical term denoting the individual embodied human soul, esp. when unenlightened. Indian schools of thought differ on what degree of reality it has. In *advaita*, it has a formal, relative reality only until one is enlightened, after which it is seen to be not-separate or one with all that is.

jivatma(n) (S.) - In Indian philosophy, the one Self considered as embodied in human form; the human soul, esp. in its natural, enlightened state.

jnana (S. cognate to Greek *gnosis*) - Knowledge, wisdom, esp. knowledge which is incontrovertible and unsublatable, knowledge absolute; the equivalent of *prajna* in Mahayana Buddhism.

jnani (S.) - Lit. 'one who knows'; person who has *jnana*; a liberated or enlightened one. It is not an experience of True Knowledge, it is Knowledge Itself. 'There are no *jnanis*, there is only *jnana*.' – Sri Ramana Maharshi.

John of the Cross, Saint - Spanish mystical Carmelite saint and poet (1542-1591) born near Avila. Associated with Saint Theresa of Avila, his senior contemporary; author of the mystical poem, *The Dark Night of the Soul*.

Kabir - Celebrated medieval saint, poet and mystic of Benares (*c.* 1440-1518). An illiterate weaver by trade, his poetry and mystic teachings still form the focus of a popular sect in modern India. Kabir was above caste and class distinctions, against ritualism and idolatry, and equally disposed to Hindus and Muslims. He espoused a form of *nirguna bhakti* to a non-dual reality he called Ram.

karma (S.) - Lit. 'action', 'rite', 'work'; the law of retributive action, the retributive moral force generated and accompanying all performance of action, held to bring back upon the doer good or evil according to the doer's motive, in this or a future life.

kosha (S.) - Lit. 'sheath'; the ancient doctrine first found in *Taittireya Upanishad* (II.7) that the human soul is encased in five increasingly subtle sheaths of matter: the *anna, prana, mana, vijnana* and *ananda maya koshas* (*q.v.*).

Krishna - The ancient cowherd-god whose charming flute-songs and sportive ways enchanted the *gopis*; His instructions to Arjuna on the battlefield during the great *Mahabharata* war form the text of the *Bhagavad Gita*. The eighth *avatar* of Vishnu, He is considered to be an incarnation of love and is worshipped in His own right.

kriya yoga (S.) - Lit. 'yoga of action'; *kriya* denotes all forms of human action and endeavor, esp. an act performed to attain higher knowledge; 1) In Patanjali's *Yogasutra* (II.1) defined as the triple *sadhana* of austerity, self-study and surrender to God; 2) An esoteric technique made famous by Paramahamsa Yogananda in his book, *Autobiography of a Yogi*; 3) In Hathayoga, certain physical exercises, such as *Basti, Neti, Nauli*, which cleanse and tone the body.

kumbha mela (S.) - A great Hindu religious fair held once every twelve years at Allahabad where the two holy rivers Ganga and Yamuna meet.

Kushinagar - The township in northern India where the Buddha passed into *parinirvana*. One of the four holy places of Buddhism.

Lakshman(a) - Faithful brother of Rama who accompanied Rama and Sita into exile in the forest; the Hindu ideal of the devoted brother.

leela (lila) (S.) - Lit. 'sport', 'play'; held by the Vaishnavas to be the divine purpose behind the creation of the manifest universe.

Lumbini - Small town in modern Nepal, birthplace of the Buddha.

mahatma (S.) - Lit. 'great soul'; a fully-realised saint; a title given to Mohandas Gandhi (1869-1948), leader of India's independence movement.

mahavakya (S.) - Lit. 'great saying'; used to refer to one of the four great sayings of the *Upanishads*, one from each *Veda*, which express in different ways the fundamental Truth— the equation of *Atman* with *Brahman*.

Mahayana (S.) - Lit. 'great vehicle'; one of the two great divisions of Buddhism, the other being the Hinayana (Lesser Vehicle) or Theravada (Doctrine of the Elders).

Mahendra (Mahindra) - Son of Ashoka (*q.v.*), Emperor of the Mauryas. He led Buddhist missionary activity in Sri Lanka, helping Buddhism to become established there in the 3rd century B.C.

mala (S.) - In Hinduism, a rosary of 108 beads used in the practice of *japa* (*q.v.*).

manas (S.) - From the Skt. root *man*, 'to think'; in Indian philosophy, that faculty which receives, compares and organises sense-data; the 'lower' mind, it operates in association with *chitta*, *buddhi* and *ahankara* (*q.v.*).

manomaya kosha (S.) - Lit. 'thought-composed sheath'; the mental sheath, one of five 'envelopes' covering the empirical self; its attributes are thinking, doubting, anger, lust, exhiliration, depression, delusion, etc.

marg(a) (H., S.) - Path, way, road, street.

Mira(bai) - Celebrated medieval North Indian princess, saint and poet (1498-1546) whose lyrical verses on passionate surrender and devotion to Krishna are still sung today in India. Her love of Krishna is a prime example of the *madhurya-bhava* (*bhava q.v.*).

Mitra (Sanghamitra) - The sister of Mahendra, daughter of Ashoka the Great, and ally of her brother in the introduction of Buddhism to Sri Lanka; a legendary figure according to modern scholars.

moksha (S.) - In Indian philosophy, the emancipated state of the *jiva* (*q.v.*) or individual soul; freedom from the round of rebirths (*samsara q.v.*); Self-realisation.

mulla(h) (H.) - In Islamic India, a learned man, a teacher, a doctor of Islamic Law; also, commonly, a schoolmaster.

mumukshutva (S.) - The intense, burning desire to be free; one of the four essential qualifications of the true disciple according to Shankara (*advaita vedanta q.v.*).

neti-neti (S.) - Lit. 'not this, not this'; the famous dictum, in *Brihad-Aranyaka Upanishad*, that *Brahman* (*q.v.*) cannot be described in words or encompassed by thought, being beyond all subject-object, subject-predicate distinctions; refers to the *jnana marga* teaching of negation (*nirvritti marg*) which proceeds to discover the Absolute by progressively negating everything It is not.

nirguna bhakti (S.) - Love of the Absolute *Brahman* in its formless aspect. Beloved of *jnanis*, said in the *Bhagavad Gita* to be 'difficult of attainment for embodied beings'.

nirvikalpa samadhi (S.) - The *samadhi* (*q.v.*) in which no differences arise or are perceived; the supreme superconscious state; the formless, intensely blissful *samadhi* of non-dual union with *Brahman*, the highest state of consciousness according to *Vedanta* and Yoga.

Nisargadatta Maharaj - Renowned *jnani* of modern India (1897-1981) who lived in Bombay and taught a type of *advaita* similar to that of Sri Ramana Maharshi and H.W.L. Poonja. It was brilliantly presented by his disciple, Maurice Frydman, in his edition of Maharaj's conversations entitled *I Am That*.

Nischal(a)das(a) - An obscure but esteemed scholar-saint of early 19th century North India whose learned and original works on *Advaita Vedanta* elicited the admiration of Swami Vivekananda, Swami Ram Tirtha (*q.v.*) and Sri Ramana Maharshi.

Om (S.) - According to Hinduism it is the primordial sound from which all creation springs. It is the most important element in most mantras.

Om shanti, shanti, shanti (S.) - '*Om* (*q.v.*) peace, peace, peace'; ancient vedic benediction concluding the 'peace mantras' which introduce many of the classical *Upanishads*; a common form of benediction after the recital of a mantra or at the conclusion of ritual worship (*puja*). Papaji begins all his satsangs with this benediction.

padmasana (S.) - 'Lotus-posture'; in Hatha and classical Yoga, the full-lotus posture in which the body is seated with the legs folded over the thighs, left ankle over right, spine and neck straight. Properly mastered, it allows the body to remain for long periods in trance (or *samadhi q.v.*) without falling.

paisa (paise) (H.) - A unit of currency now equal to 1/100th of a rupee.

pakora (H.) - A preparation of chopped vegetables coated with batter or stuffed into pastry and deep-fried.

pan (paan) (H.) - The betel leaf; a preparation of chopped Arecanut, lime and other ingredients wrapped in a betel leaf and chewed. It colours the teeth a characteristic red. The red juice, later spat out, can be seen on walls and roads all over India.

pir (H.) - A Muslim saint or holy man.

Pondicherry - The town in South India where Sri Aurobindo lived and established his ashram.

prajna (S.) - Lit. 'knowledge beyond'; transcendental wisdom, the knowledge inherent in Freedom; equivalent to *jnana* (*q.v.*).

prajna paramita (S.) - 1) Lit. 'the perfection of wisdom'; one of the six *paramis* (perfections) to be practised on the path to Buddhahood; 2) A class of Buddhist Mahayana scriptures in which the Buddha's teaching on emptiness (*shunyata*) is featured. The *Diamond* and the *Heart Sutras* are the most famous *prajna paramita* texts.

prana (S.) - Vital energy; life-breath; life-force; common basis of breath and mind.

pranamaya kosha (S.) - Lit. '*prana*-composed sheath'; the second grossest sheath in which human consciousness is enveloped; the 'case' of subtle energy, the departure of which leads to death.

puja (pooja) (S.) - Ritualistic worship; adoration and decoration of a deity or saint with mantras, *yantras*, *mudras*, hymns and offerings of light, water, flowers, sandalpaste, food, gifts, etc., in a prescribed manner as laid down by *Tantra Shastra* (*q.v.*).

Radha - Chief of the *gopis*, the shepherdess cow-girls of Vrindavan who were favourite lovers and playmates of Sri Krishna; in some schools Radha is elevated to a status equal to, or even surpassing, that of Krishna, being worshipped in her own right as His *shakti* (divine power) or *hladini* (blissful energy).

raja yoga (S.) - Lit. 'kingly yoga'; in Indian philosophy, usually taken to mean the yoga of meditation (*dhyana* or *samadhi* yoga) associated with the yoga school of Patanjali (*c.* 500 B.C.) and expounded in his *Yogasutras* and allied texts. It has non-dual *nirvikalpa samadhi* as its highest goal.

Ram Tirtha, Swami (1873-1906) - Famous North Indian saint and mystical poet whose lyrical celebrations of the pristine advaitic state in Hindi, English, Persian and Urdu rank among the best of their genre. A contemporary of

Vivekananda, whose talks he arranged at Lahore, he also travelled to the United States (1902-04), meeting President Theodore Roosevelt, before returning to India where he retreated to the high Himalayas. He roamed among the snows in perfect bliss, before being swept away by the Ganga at Tehri, Garhwal, in 1906. He was the maternal uncle of Sri H.W.L. Poonja.

Rama - The seventh *avatar* of Vishnu, said to be the incarnation of *Dharma* (*q.v.*); he is the eponymous hero of India's second great national epic, the *Ramayana*, which recounts the story of his rescue of Sita, his queen, from her capture by Ravanna, the demon-king of Lanka. The *Ramayana* is said by scholars to be the single most popular religious text in the world.

Ramakrishna (1836-1886) - The great Bengali saint and visionary mystic, who realised the truth of the world's great religions by direct experience. Guru of Swami Vivekananda, he had a great harmonising and revivifying influence on modern Hinduism. Despite his attainment of *jnana*, he remained a life-long devotee of the Divine Mother whom he identified with Kali.

Ramakrishna Mission(s) - Any branch of the Ramakrishna Order; a monastic order established by Swami Vivekananda and his fellow disciples after the passing away of their Master, Sri Ramakrishna Paramahamsa, in 1886.

Ramalingar Swami (1824-1874) - A great South Indian saint and *siddha* (adept), born in Chidambaram in Tamil Nadu, who is said to have died by transforming his body into light and disappearing from a locked room.

Ramana Maharshi, Sri (1879-1950) - South Indian saint and sage who lived in Tiruvannamalai in Tamil Nadu. He taught primarily through silence and encouraged most seekers to undertake self-enquiry. He is the Guru of Papaji.

Ramayana - The second of India's great national epics, it recounts the story of the Solar God Ram (*q.v.*). The original version was composed in Sanskrit by Valmiki Rishi *c.* 500-300 B.C.; the *bhakti*-cult version was composed in Hindi by Tulasidas (1532-1623) and is called the *Ramacharitamanasa*. It is the most popular scripture in modern India.

Ramdas, Swami (1884-1963) - A revered South Indian saint and Rama *bhakta* who advocated devotion to Lord Rama through *japa* and *bhajans*. He lived in an ashram in Kerala with his disciple and longtime companion, Mother Krishnabai.

Ravidas - A low-caste cobbler from Benares (1450-1520). He was a contemporary of Kabir and was famous for his *nirguna bhakti* Hindi poetry. Tradition makes him the *advaita bhakti* guru of Mirabai (*q.v.*).

Sadguru (S.) - Lit. 'Truth-teacher'; the Self or *atman* (*q.v.*) manifesting and teaching through a human form.

sadhak (S.) - One who practises spiritual exercises or *sadhana* (*q.v.*).

sadhana (S.) - From the Skt. root *sadh*. 'To go straight to the goal, be successful'; conscious spiritual exercise; that which produces success (*siddhi*) or the result sought; spiritual practice.

sadhu (S.) - An ascetic, holy man; one who does *sadhana*, esp. as a way of life.

saguna bhakti (S.) - Loving adoration and worship of the Absolute (*Brahman*), conceived of as having form and qualities; esp. as Shiva, Rama, Krishna, or as Devi, the Divine Mother.

sakshi (S.) - The 'witness' consciousness, uninvolved 'onlooker' of the three states of the embodied soul or *jiva*, namely waking, dreaming and deep sleep; also present in non-dual awareness, the 'fourth' or transcendental state (*turiya*).

samadhi (S.) - Lit. 'to bear or support together'; 1) An intensely blissful superconscious state or 'trance'; the highest condition of human consciousness, in which the seer-seen, subject-object distinction is transcended. 2) The tomb of a saint.

samsara (S.) - The empirical world of names and forms, esp. as it appears to the unenlightened mind and senses; the continuous round of death and rebirth, to which the *jiva* is subject until liberated.

samskara (S.) - Latent impression, more pronounced than a *vasana* (*q.v.*), esp. a previous-life tendency or pre-disposition.

sannyasa (S.) - Renunciation; specifically, the monastic rite enacting the vow to renounce; the last and highest stage of Hindu life when one leaves worldly cares and family for the wandering life of a monk, living on alms, having freedom (*moksha*) as the sole aim of life.

sannyasin (S.) - One who has taken *sannyasa vrata*, the vow of renunciation; a renouncer.

sari (H.) - Traditional form of dress for Hindu women in which five or six metres of cloth are draped gracefully about the body.

satsang(a) (S.) - Lit. 'fellowship or company with Truth'; the conversation and/or company of a realised saint; the group of seekers and disciples who form such company; conversation which leads one towards Truth; a sacred and essential component of spiritual life for all traditions in orthodox Hinduism.

Self - The term adopted in English, when capitalised, for the Skt. *atman* (*q.v.*).

Shankara (Adi Shankaracharya) - The great Hindu scholar-saint and reformer (788-820 A.D.), whose commentaries on the classical *Upanishads*, *Bhagavadgita* and *Brahmasutra* revived orthodox Hinduism which was stagnating under pharisaical brahminism. He established *Advaita Vedanta* on an impregnable popular footing, rendering it proof against the onslaught of Mahayana Buddhism (esp. the Madhyamika School of Nagarjuna), which gradually died out in India.

Shankaracharyas - Honorific title given to the heads or pontifs of the five principal monastic institutions established by Adi Shankara at the cardinal compass points in India—North (Joshimath, at Badrinath), South (at Kanchi), East (at Puri), West (at Dwarka), and centre (in Sringeri). Each of these monasteries (*maths*) traces its lineage back to one of Shankara's four direct disciples. Their heads therefore customarily adopt this title and are collectively known by it.

Shastras (S.) - From the root *sas*, to enjoin, teach, instruct; strictly, a manual or compendium of rules or instructions containing the authoritative teaching on a subject or tradition, esp. a religious treatise, sacred text, or scripture of divine authority; sometimes applied collectively to whole departments of knowledge, *e.g.*, the *Dharma-Shastras*, or Law Texts, or to refer to the whole corpus of Indian orthodox religious philosophical literature.

sheath - *q.v. kosha*.

shirshasana (S.) - Lit. 'head-posture'; the headstand, a prescribed exercise in Hatha Yoga for toning and vitalising the physical vehicle so that it poses no obstacle in meditation.

siddhi(s) (S.) - From the Skt. root *sidh*, to be accomplished, succeed; the major and minor supranormal powers which are manifested by highly-advanced *mahatmas* or yogis. The eight major *siddhis* (*ashtama siddhi*) are enumerated in Patanjali's *Yogasutras* (III.16-48).

Sita - Daughter of Janaka, King of Videha, wife and consort of Rama, Solar King of the Raghus and seventh incarnation of Vishnu; their story is told in the *Ramayana* (*q.v.*).

Siva (Shiva) - Lit. 'the auspicious one'; in the Hindu trinity, the Hindu god of destruction; the God of the *Shaivas*, Absolute Good, dear to *jnanis* as the destroyer of ego or ignorance.

Sivananda, Swami (1887-1963) - A popular North Indian swami who founded the Divine Life Society in Rishikesh. His world tours and his more than 300 books did much to popularise Hatha Yoga and meditation in the 1960's and 1970's in India and the West.

sloka (S.) - A type of Sanskrit verse, esp. from a sacred text, of four half-lines containing, usually, praise or precept; a literary term in modern Hindi applied to many types of verses.

Sri (Shri) (S.) - Lit. 'the auspicious one'; a name for Devi, the Divine Mother, or for Lakshmi, the consort of Vishnu; often used as an honorific prefix.

Sri Ramanasramam (T.) - The ashram of Sri Ramana Maharshi in Tiruvannamalai. Founded in 1922, Sri Ramana spent the last twenty-eight years of his life there.

Sukadev - The son of the great Vyasa, traditional 'composer' of the *Mahabharata* and *Brahmasutra*, and 'arranger' of the *Upanishads*.

summa iru (T.) - Lit. 'be quiet'. '*Iru*' is the imperative form of the verb 'to be' and the verb 'to stay', so it can mean 'be still', 'stay still', 'keep quiet', etc.

sutra (S.) - Lit. 'a thread, suture'; a short, pithy, aphoristic statement in Skt. religious or philosophical literature. Because they are often meant to function as a mnemonic device, they often need further explanation or commentary.

swami (S.) - Lit. 'one's own'; strictly, 'one's own Master', a person who has realised the Self; a spiritual preceptor, guru; often used as a respectful term of address for senior monks, approximately equivalent to 'sir'.

Tamil - The Dravidian language spoken mainly in Tamil Nadu, South India; the native tongue of Sri Ramana Maharshi.

tantra (S.) - An esoteric religious movement and literature, of obscure origin, which arose in India after the Gupta period (3rd to 4th centuries A.D.) as a successor to vedic brahminism. It identified *nirguna Brahman* with Shiva and exalted the worship of Devi or the Divine Mother, which was identified with *saguna Brahman*, as the active feminine principle of cosmic power or divine energy responsible for all change.

tapas (S.) - Lit. 'heat'; asceticism or ascetic practice; one of the adjuncts to *sadhana* (q.v.) for the Yoga School; *Vedanta* too has its counterpart. It is a deep-rooted notion in Hinduism that some form of restraint or discipline (psychological 'heat') is needed for transformation.

Tapovan Swami (1889-1957) - Revered sage, famous for his travels in the high Himalayas and journeys to Mt. Kailash about which he wrote with entertaining erudition. Renowned for spending his life in the high mountains and never descending lower, it is said, than 12,000 feet. He was the guru of Chinmayananda Swami of Bombay.

tathata (S.) - Lit. 'suchness'; one of the central notions of Mahayana Buddhism, referring to the indescribable true nature of all things, beyond all concepts and dualities.

Theresa of Avila, Saint - Medieval Spanish Christian Carmelite mystic (1515-1582). She experienced a 'spiritual marriage' with Christ and helped Saint John of the Cross to found a monastic order.

Tiruvannamalai (T.) - A small town in Tamil Nadu about five hours by bus from Madras. The place where Sri Ramana Maharshi lived and had his ashram.

Upanishads (S.) - Lit. 'sitting close to'; the later, *Jnana Khanda* or knowledge portion of the *Vedas* which incorporates the profound speculations and teachings, originally secret, of the ancient Aryan seers of Hindustan. Since these teachings came later, after the *Karma Khanda* or ritualistic portion of the *Veda*, as a group they are called the *Vedanta*, or 'end of the *Veda*'.

Urdu - The Hindustani language, produced by the confluence of Hindi and Persian during Mughal rule. Similar to Hindi in grammar, it is written in a Persian-Arabic script and contains numerous Persian, Arabic and Turkish words. It is the national language of Pakistan.

Vaishnavism - One of the three great divisions of modern theistic Hinduism (the other two being Shaivism and Shaktism) which identifies Vishnu—or one of his incarnations, Rama or Krishna—with *Brahman*, the Supreme Being.

vasana (S.) - Subtle desire; a tendency created in a person by the performance of an action or the enjoyment of it; the subtle impression of an action which remains unconsciously in the mind and which is capable of developing itself again into action.

Vedanta (S.) - Lit. 'end of the *Veda*'; the system of Hindu thought based on the *Upanishads, Bhagavad Gita* and *Brahma Sutras,* and holding primarily the doctrines of pure non-dualism (*advaita*) and qualified non-dualism (*visistadvaita*).

Vedas (S.) - Lit. 'knowledge, wisdom'; the highest, oldest, and most sacred scriptures of the Hindus and the oldest written religious texts in the world.

vibhuti (S.) - Ash from a sacred fire used for worship. It is applied to the body and sometimes swallowed as *prasada* (object consecrated by the deity).

vidya (S.) - Knowledge. It includes both higher Absolute Knowledge and lower relative knowledge.

Vidyaranya - Celebrated 14th century saint and scholar, the pontif of Sringeri Monastery, a renowned seat of *advaita* learning. He wrote several important works in Sanskrit on the *advaita* system including *Panchadasi* and *Jivanmukti Viveka*. He taught a version of the *advaita* reflection theory called *ahasavada*.

vijnanamaya kosha (S.) - Lit. 'sheath of intellect'; one of the five subtle sheaths of matter encasing the soul or *jiva*; the intellectual sheath, whose attributes are discrimination and decision; it is a component of the *sukshma sarira* or astral body which is dissolved only at final liberation.

vipassana (P.) - Lit. 'insight' or 'intuitive cognition'; one of the main forms of meditation in Theravada Buddhism. Called 'Insight Meditation', it is said to be the practice by which Buddha himself attained enlightenment. It analyses sensations in the body-mind field, leading to insight into the true nature of things as being empty and void of all self-content (*swabhava*).

Vishnu - 'The strider', 'the pervader'; in the Hindu trinity, the Lord of preservation and appearance. He is the ruler of *maya* and the guardian of *dharma*. As his *avatars* (*q.v.*) Rama and Krishna, He 'descended' from His celestial abode in order to defeat various demons plaguing humanity and to uphold the eternal human aims of *dharma* and *moksha*.

viveka (S.) - Lit. 'to see or know apart'; the faculty of discrimination, esp. between the real (*sat*) and the unreal (*asat*). It is held by Shankara to be one of the four requisites of a disciple which qualify him to hear the *advaita* teachings from a preceptor.

Vrindavan (Brindavan) - The temple-town on the banks of the Yamuna outside Mathura. The town where Sri Krishna grew up. He enacted His divine *leelas* there with Sri Radha and the *gopis* (*q.v.*). A holy place of pilgramage for devout Radha-Krishna *bhaktas*, to whom its very dust is sacred.

Yajur Veda - One of the four principal revealed or 'heard' scriptures of orthodox Hinduism (*shruti*). They have the highest authority and antiquity, and consist of sacrificial formulas to be chanted along with sacred rites.

Yoga Vasishta - A Sanskrit work of 32,000 lines, it is classified as an epic (*Itihasa*). It contains the teachings on liberation given to Lord Rama by his Guru, the great Vasistha. Advocating a radical form of *advaita* called *ajativada* which denies causation as an explanation for the appearance of the empirical world, it holds that change, the soul, the self, freedom and bondage do not really exist. In *ajativada*, *Brahman* alone exists.

yoga (S.) - Lit. 'to yoke, harness, unite'; the orthodox system of Indian philosophy associated with the *Yogasutras* of Patanjali (*c.* 500 B.C.). It comprises the 'Eight-limbed path' set out in the *Yogasutras* comprising physical exercises (*asanas*), breath control (*pranayama*) and meditational stages (*dhyana-samadhi*), leading to *asamprajnata samadhi* or 'superconscious ecstasy', the *nirvikalpa samadhi* of *Vedanta*.

yogi (S.) - One who practises Yoga; one who strives earnestly for union with God, particularly by the path of *Raja* Yoga (*q.v.*); one who has achieved *siddhi* (success) in Yoga; one who has become 'harmonised' or 'yoked' in *Brahman*; a spiritually advanced or freed soul.

Are you interested in finding out more about Papaji?

Papaji holds public satsangs in Lucknow, India, five days a week. Video and audio tapes of these satsangs can be obtained from the addresses given below. There is also a 102 minute documentary on his teachings entitled *Call Off The Search*. For further information on any of these items, call or fax one of the numbers listed below.

Information

Satsang Bhavan
A-306 Indira Nagar
Lucknow 226016, U.P.
India
Tel.: 0091-522-381189
FAX: 0091-522-381553

Poonjaji Tapes
2888 Bluff St., Suite 390
Boulder, CO 80301-9002
U.S.A.
Tel.: 001-303-440-9670
FAX: 001-303-443-0232
Attention: Kamal

There are two other books in print on his teachings: *Wake Up and Roar, Volume One* and *Wake Up and Roar, Volume Two*. Both of these books contain edited highlights of conversations which seekers have had with Papaji over the last few years. They are available from:

Pacific Center Press
P.O. Box 818
Kula, HI 96790
U.S.A.
Tel.: 001-808-878-3000 & 808-878-3833
FAX: 001-808-878-2733
